AWAKENING
THE HEROES
WITHIN

Also by Carol S. Pearson

The Hero Within: Six Archetypes We Live By

The Female Hero in American and British Literature
(with Katherine Pope)

Who Am I This Time? Female Portraits in American and British Literature
(with Katherine Pope)

Educating the Majority: Women Challenge Tradition in Higher Education
(with Donna Shavlik and Judith Touchton)

AWAKENING THE HEROES WITHIN

Twelve Archetypes to Help Us Find Ourselves and Transform Our World

Carol S. Pearson

HarperSanFrancisco
A Division of HarperCollinsPublishers

The book *Awakening the Heroes Within* by Carol S. Pearson is available on tape from Harper Audio, a Division of HarperCollins Publishers.

For more information about the programs, services, and publications offered by Carol Pearson's organization, contact Meristem, 4321 Hartwick Rd., Suite 416, College Park, MD 20740, (301) 277-8042.

FIRST EDITION

Library of Congress Catalog Card Number: 90-5529
ISBN 0–06–250678–1

91 92 93 94 95 VICKS 10 9 8 7 6 5 4 3 2 1

This edition is printed on acid-free paper that meets the American National Standards Institute Z39.48 Standard.

To David

"The hunt isn't over until both your heart and your belly are full."

Sun Bear, *Walk in Balance*

Contents

Acknowledgments

Awakening the Heroes Within is the product of a twenty-year study that began in graduate school when I became captivated with the subject of the hero's journey, an enthusiasm that gave rise to my dissertation on fools and heroes in contemporary literature (1970).

As with any work that is the culmination of twenty years of study, it is impossible to acknowledge all the books, theories, and individuals who have influenced or supported its work. However, some stand out so that they cannot be forgotten. While I was in graduate school, Joseph Campbell's *The Hero with a Thousand Faces* served as a "call to the quest" to undertake this work. As I wrote this book, I felt very grateful to my professors in graduate school in the English Department at Rice University, especially Monroe Spears, William Piper, and David Minter, for teaching me so much not only about literature but about soul. I am also grateful for my involvement with the women's studies programs at the University of Colorado and the University of Maryland, my work on staff with Anne Wilson Schaef's Intensives for Professional Women, and my collaboration with Donna Shavlik and Judy Touchton at the Office on Women at the American Council on Education, and with Katherine Pope in the editing of *Who Am I This Time? Female Portraits in American and British Literature* and the writing of *The Female Hero in British and American Literature*.

While conceptualizing and writing this book, I also benefited greatly from my affiliation with the Midway Center for Creative Imagination at the Psychiatric Institute Foundation of Washington, D.C. and with the Professional Enrichment Program in Depth Psychology at the Wainwright House in Rye, New York.

Through the Midway Center, I took David Oldfield's one-year training course in Creative Mythology Methods to learn strategies for working with archetypal and mythic material in experiential ways. Not only did I learn to do so, I also benefited greatly from the theories about soul and soul development presented there.

Later I had the opportunity to teach the training course for the Midway Center, which gave me the chance to work with professionals in a variety of fields using the theories and exercises presented in this book. I am grateful to the Midway Center and to David Oldfield for the opportunity to pilot these ideas to such an exceptional group of participants. The impact of this group of people on me and this work cannot be overstated. They encouraged me about the work's significance, experimented with applying the theories in their work and their own lives, read draft chapters, and generously shared their own insights and processes.

I participated for two years in the Wainwright House's enrichment program, where I had the opportunity to deepen my knowledge of Jungian psychology. I particularly want to thank Franklin Valas, director of the Wainwright House, and Don Kalshed and Sidney McKinsey, director and coordinator, respectively, of the Professional Enrichment Program in Depth Psychology, for creating such a rich educational experience and making it available just at the time I needed it.

I most want to thank my colleagues at Meristem, especially Sharon V. Seivert, who has collaborated with me in designing our "Heroes at Work" project, which explores many of the same archetypes as those described in this book and applies them to organizational settings. Hence, there has been great cross-fertilization of ideas between the two projects; our work together has so influenced my thinking that the effect of our collaboration appears throughout this book, particularly in Parts II through IV, where the individual archetypes are described.

Similarly, the team that worked with me to design the Heroic Myth Index (HMI) in several of its forms greatly added to my understanding of the archetypes. The team that developed Form D (with ten archetypes) included Sharon Seivert and Mary Leonard, with technical assistance from Beth O'Brien and Barbara Murry and expert input from Francis Parks, Polly Armstrong, David Oldfield, and John Johnson. The group that developed Form E (with twelve archetypes) included Hugh Marr, Mary Leonard, and Sharon Seivert. I particularly want to thank Hugh Marr, who conducted the validity and test-retest reliability study on the instrument and spearheaded development and refinement of new questions.

A special thank-you to Sharon V. Seivert, coordinator of the "Heroes at Work" project at Meristem and coauthor of *Heroes at Work: Workbook*, and to the Heroic Myth Index team for helping to develop and crystallize some of the ideas that are basic to this book. Ten of the archetypes discussed here were previously included in the *Heroes at Work: Workbook* and in Form D of the Heroic Myth Index (privately published by Meristem in 1988).

I also wish to thank members of Mary Leonard's graduate seminar in the Counseling Department of the University of Maryland who gave me feedback and advice on the design of the instrument; the Sandy Spring Friends School for providing a test-retest site for Form D; and the Mt. Vernon Center for providing a test-retest site for Form E. I would also like to note the importance of Hugh Marr's dissertation in progress, which will provide further study and development of the HMI.

During the writing of this book, I collaborated with Laurie Lippin in the design of workshops on "Type and Archetype," which brought together Myers-Briggs Type theory with the system developed in this book, a collaboration that increased the clarity of my thinking about archetypes and helped me understand how type and archetype complement each other in our understanding of any individual's psychology.

I am extremely fortunate to have Thomas Grady as my editor at Harper San Francisco. I appreciate his encouragement and direction during the writing of this book, his thoughtful consideration of the book's format and design, and his deft editorial hand. I appreciate Naomi Luck's assistance in cutting what was an unmanageably long work to readable proportions. A special thanks to Sandra Letellier for typing numerous drafts with the same careful professionalism she brings to all her work. I'm also grateful to the following people, who read and commented on the manuscript: David Merkowitz, Joan Herren, and Alice Abrash.

I want to thank my husband, David Merkowitz, and my children, Jeff, Steve, and Shanna, for their love, support, and encouragement of this project. Thanks also to Cozi, the support group that has immeasurably influenced my emotional and spiritual growth over many years; to my colleagues at Meristem; to my analyst, Dr. Francis Parks; and to my parents, John and Thelma Pearson, whose love and faith have provided a firm foundation for my life.

Finally, I want to thank readers of *The Hero Within: Six Archetypes We Live By*. I have been immensely gratified by the public response to the book and inspired by stories readers have told me about its impact on their lives. In it I requested readers not to ask me several years hence to defend what I had written, but rather to ask me what I had learned since writing it. Many have done just that, and I have clarified my thinking by responding one-on-one or with groups as I have spoken and conducted workshops throughout the country on the hero's journey. This book provides a more expansive answer to that question.

Introduction

Some people, we say, have "soul." They have loved, they have suffered, they have a deep sense of life's meaning. Perhaps most important, they know who they are.

Other people seem to have lost their souls. They may have material possessions—the right house, the right car, the right job, the right clothes; they may even have a stable family life and be religious. But inside themselves, they feel empty. Even when they go through the right motions, it is movement without meaning.

Still other people love and suffer and feel life intensely; but they never really get their lives together. They cannot seem to find work or personal relationships that truly satisfy them, and so they feel constantly constrained. Although they may be connected to their souls, they feel cut off from the world.

Saddest of all are people who never learn how to make their way in the world or how to be true to their own souls. Their lives are empty and unrewarding—yet unnecessarily so: virtually all of us are capable of finding meaning and purpose in our lives and in the life of the human community.

We find a model for learning how to live in stories about heroism. The heroic quest is about saying yes to yourself and, in so doing, becoming more fully alive and more effective in the world. For the hero's journey is first about taking a journey to find the treasure of your true self, and then about returning home to give your gift to help transform the kingdom—and, in the process, your own life. The quest itself is replete with dangers and pitfalls, but it offers great rewards: the capacity to be successful in the world, knowledge of the mysteries of the human soul, the opportunity to find and express your unique gifts in the world, and to live in loving community with other people.

Awakening the Heroes Within is for people at all stages of life's journey: it is a call to the quest for those just considering or beginning the journey; it provides

The hero's journey is first about taking a journey to find the treasure of your true self.

reinforcement for longtime journeyers; and it is a tool for people already far along on their journeys who are looking for ways to share and pass on what they have learned. Each journey is unique, and each seeker charts a new path. But it is infinitely easier to do so having at least some knowledge about the experiences of those who have gone before. When we learn about the many different heroic paths available to us, we understand that there is room for all of us to be heroic in our own unique ways.

●

Stories about heroes are deep and eternal. They link our own longing and pain and passion with those who have come before in such a way that we learn something about the essence of what it means to be human, and they also teach us how we are connected to the great cycles of the natural and spiritual worlds. The myths that can give our lives significance are deeply primal and archetypal and can strike terror into our hearts, but they can also free us from unauthentic lives and make us real. If we avoid what T. S. Eliot called this "primitive terror" at the heart of life, we miss our connection to life's intensity and mystery. Finding our own connection with such eternal patterns provides a sense of meaning and significance in even the most painful or alienated moments, and in this way restores nobility to life.

The paradox of modern life is that at the same time that we are living in ways never done before and therefore daily recreating our world, our actions often feel rootless and empty. To transcend this state, we need to feel rooted simultaneously in history and eternity.

We had the experience but missed the meaning. —T. S. Eliot

This is why the myth of the hero is so important in the contemporary world. It is a timeless myth that links us to peoples of all times and places. It is about fearlessly leaping off the edge of the known to confront the unknown, and trusting that when the time comes, we will have what we need to face our dragons, discover our treasures, and return to transform the kingdom. It is also about learning to be true to ourselves and live in responsible community with one another.

In classical myth, the health of the kingdom reflected the health of the King or Queen. When the Ruler was wounded, the kingdom became a wasteland. To heal the kingdom, it was necessary for a hero to undertake a quest, find a sacred object, and return to heal or replace the Ruler. Our world reflects many of the classic symptoms of the wasteland kingdom: famine, environmental damage to the natural world, economic uncertainty, rampant injustice, personal despair and alienation, and the threat of war and annihilation. Our "kingdoms" reflect the state of our collective souls, not just those of our leaders. This is a time in human history when heroism is greatly needed. Like heroes of old, we aid in restoring life, health, and fecundity to the kingdom as a side benefit of taking our own journeys, finding our own destinies, and giving our unique gifts. It is as if the world were a giant puzzle and each of us who takes a journey returns with one piece. Collectively, as we contribute our part, the kingdom is transformed.

The transformation of the kingdom depends upon all of us. Understanding this helps us move beyond a competitive stance into a concern with empowering ourselves and others. If some people "lose" and do not make their potential contribution, we all lose. If we lack the courage to take our journeys, we create a void where our piece of the puzzle could have been, to the collective, as well as our personal, detriment.

The Journey

Heroism is also not just about finding a new truth, but about having the courage to act on that vision. That is, in a very practical way, why heroes need to have the courage and care associated with strong ego development and the vision and clarity of mind and spirit that come from having taken their souls' journeys and gained the treasure of their true selves.

Most people know that heroes slay dragons, rescue damsels (or other victims) in distress, and find and bring back treasures. At the close of the journey, they often marry. They have reached a "happy ending" to their journey in which their "new renewing truth" becomes manifested in the life they now live – in community with their new family and with other people. This new truth they bring back renews their own lives and also the lives of their kingdoms, and thereby affects everyone they touch.

This mythic pattern is true for our personal journeys, although the happy ending is usually short lived. As soon as we return from one journey and enter a new phase of our lives, we are immediately propelled into a new sort of journey; the pattern is not linear or circular but spiral. We never really stop journeying, but we do have marker events when things come together as a result of the new reality we have encountered. And each time we begin our journeys, we do so at a new level and return with a new treasure and newfound transformative abilities.

What the Journey Requires

When we believe that our journeys are not important and fail to confront our dragons and seek our treasures, we feel empty inside and leave a void that hurts us all. Psychologists in the leveling modern world have a name for the rare case of someone with "delusions of grandeur," but do not even have a category for the most pervasive sickness, the delusion that we do not matter. While it is true that no one of us is more important than anyone else, we each have an important gift to give—a gift we are incapable of giving if we fail to take our journeys.

Taking your journey requires you to leave behind the illusion of your insignificance.

This book is designed to help you and others understand your significance and potential heroism. Perhaps most of all, it offers the potential to leave behind a shrunken sense of possibilities and choose to live a big life. Many of us try to achieve a big life by amassing material possessions, or achievements, or property, or experiences, but this never works. We can have big lives only if we are willing to become big ourselves and, in the process, give up the illusion of powerlessness and take responsibility for our lives.

There is a profound disrespect for human beings in modern life. Business encourages us to think of ourselves as human capital. Advertising appeals to our fears and insecurities to try to get us to buy products we do not need. Too many religious institutions teach people to be good but do not help them know who they are. Too many psychologists see their job as helping people learn to accommodate to what is, not to take their journeys and find out what could be. Too many educational institutions train people to be cogs in the economic machine, rather than educating them about how to be fully human.

Basically, we are viewed as products or commodities, to be either sold to the highest bidder or improved so that eventually we will be more valuable. Neither view respects the human soul or the human mind except as used as an acquisitive tool. As a consequence, people increasingly are disrespectful of themselves. Too many of us seek to fill our emptiness with food, or drink, or drugs, or obsessive and frantic activity. The much-lamented pace of modern life is not inevitable—it is a cover for its emptiness. If we keep in motion, we create the illusion of meaning.

We are subtly and not so subtly discouraged from seeking our own grails and finding our own uniqueness by an ongoing pressure to "measure up" to preexisting standards. And, of course, when we try to measure up rather than find ourselves, it is unlikely that we will ever discover and share our unique gifts. Instead of finding out who we are, we worry about whether we are good-looking enough, smart enough, personable enough, moral enough, healthy enough, working hard enough, or successful enough.

We look outside ourselves for others to tell us if we have lived up to some version of perfection. How many of us aspire to the perfect movie star face and body, the Nobel Prize–winning mind, the goodness or mental clarity of a great enlightened being (Christ, for instance), the financial success of a billionaire? It is no surprise that so many of us spend our lives alternately striving and flailing ourselves for our inability to measure up.

As long as this is our process, we will never find ourselves. Instead we will become compliant consumers, paying all the people who claim that they can help us overcome our ugliness, sinfulness, sickness, and poverty. And, in the process, we will keep them as stuck as we are—striving for something above us, rather than searching to know what is genuinely in us and ours.

Initially, we may be called to the quest by a desire to achieve some image of perfection. Ultimately, however, we need to let go of whatever predetermined ideal holds us captive and just allow ourselves to take our own unique journeys. The hero's journey is not another self-improvement project. It is an aid in finding and honoring what is really true about you.

Knowing that you are a hero means that you are not wrong. You have the right mind. You have the right body. You have the right instincts. The issue is not to become someone else, but to find out what you are for. It means asking yourself some questions: What do I want to do? What does my mind want to learn? How does my body want to move? What does my heart love? Even problems and pathologies can be responded to as "calls from the gods" to a previously denied or avoided stage in your journey. So you might also ask yourself, "What does this problem or illness help me learn that can aid my journey?"[1]

The rewards of self-discovery are great. When we find ourselves, everything seems to fall into place. We are able to see our beauty, intelligence, and goodness. We are able to use them productively, so we are successful. We are less caught up in proving ourselves, so we can relax and love and be loved. We have everything we need to claim our full humanity, our full heroism.

Everyone who takes a journey is already a hero.

Archetypes: Our Inner Guides

We are aided on our journey by inner guides, or archetypes, each of which exemplifies a way of being on the journey. *Awakening the Heroes Within* explores twelve such inner guides: the Innocent, the Orphan, the Warrior, the Caregiver, the Seeker, the Destroyer, the Lover, the Creator, the Ruler, the Magician, the Sage, and the Fool. Each has a lesson to teach us, and each presides over a stage of the journey.

The inner guides are archetypes that have been with us since the dawn of time. We see them reflected in recurring images in art, literature, myth, and religion; and we know they are archetypal because they are found everywhere, in all times and places.

Because the guides are truly archetypal, and hence reside as energy within the unconscious psychological life of all people everywhere, they exist both inside and outside the individual human soul. They live in us, but even more importantly, we live in them. We can, therefore, find them by going inward (to our own dreams, fantasies, and often actions as well) or by going outward (to myth, legend, art, literature, and religion, and, as pagan cultures often did, to the constellations of the sky and the birds and animals of the earth). Thus, they provide images of the hero within and beyond ourselves.

We each experience the archetypes according to our own perspective. I have found at least five different ways to explain what an archetype is:

1. Spiritual seekers may conceive of archetypes as gods and goddesses, encoded in the collective unconscious, whom we scorn at our own risk.

2. Academics or other rationalists, who typically are suspicious of anything that sounds mystic, may conceive of archetypes as controlling paradigms or metaphors, the invisible patterns in the mind that control how we experience the world.

3. Scientists may see archetypes as being similar to holograms and the process of identifying them as similar to other scientific processes. As archetypes are both within and beyond us (and hence are the heroes within and beyond), an entire hologram is contained in any of its parts. Modern science has in fact verified the ancient spiritual parallel of macrocosm and microcosm by determining how a holograph really works. So, too, the science of psychology often determines what is true of the individual human mind by looking at the creations of the species.

Physicists learn about the smallest subatomic particles by studying the traces they leave; psychologists and other scholars study archetypes by examining their presence in art, literature, myth, and dream. Carl Jung recognized that the archetypal images that recurred in his patients' dreams also could be found in the myths, legends, and art of ancient peoples, as well as in contemporary literature, religion, and art. We know they are archetypal because they leave the same or similar traces over time and space.

4. People who are committed to religious positions that emphasize one God (and who worry about the polytheism inherent in any consideration of gods and goddesses) can distinguish the spiritual truth of monotheism from the pluralistic psychological truth of archetypes. The God we mean when we speak of one God is beyond the human capacity to envision and name. The archetypes are like differ-

ent facets of that God, accessible to the psyche's capacity to imagine numinous reality. Some people, however, have become so committed to a monotheistic vision that they have shrunk their conception of God to be consistent with a single archetypal image. For example, they might envision God as an old man with a flowing white beard. Such people inadvertently have closed themselves off to a sense of numinous mystery that is deeper than any one image can convey.

Even in early monotheistic Christianity, it was necessary to conceptualize a Trinity to find an adequate way of expressing truth about God, and many modern theologians are adding images of the feminine side of God to the more traditional patriarchal pantheon of God the Father, God the Son, and God the Holy Spirit. Buddhism posits one God, divisible into the 40, the 400, and the 4,000 facets or aspects of that single deity, each of which has its own name and story. Thus the archetypes help us connect with the eternal; they make the great mysteries more accessible by providing multiple images for our minds to ponder.

5. Finally, people who are interested in human growth and development may understand the archetypes as guides on our journeys. Each archetype that comes into our lives brings with it a task, a lesson, and ultimately a gift. The archetypes together teach us how to live. And the best part about it is that all the archetypes reside in each of us. That means we all have this full human potential within ourselves.

The Guides and the Hero's Journey

Although we are heroes at every stage of the journey, how we define and experience heroism is affected by which guide is most active in our lives, culturally and individually. For example, in our culture, when we think of the hero, we usually think of a warrior, slaying dragons and rescuing damsels in distress. Because the Warrior archetype is also associated in our cultural mind with masculinity, we are likely to think of the hero as male—and often (in Western culture) as a white male at that. Women, and men who are not white, are seen as supporting characters on the journey: sidekicks, villains, victims to be rescued, servants, and so on.

The Warrior archetype is an important aspect of heroism—for all people, whatever their age or gender—but it is not the only or even the most essential one. All twelve archetypes are important to the heroic journey, and to the individuation process.

How we view the world is defined by what archetype currently dominates our thinking and acting. If the Warrior is dominant, we see challenges to be overcome. When the Caregiver is dominant, we see people in need of our care. When the Sage is dominant, we see illusion and complexity and strive to find truth. When the Fool is dominant, we see ways to have a good time.

Each of the twelve archetypes, then, is both a guide on the hero's journey and a stage within it—offering a lesson to be learned and a gift or treasure to enrich our lives. The chart on page 10 summarizes the approach of each archetype.

Once we have opened to learning from all twelve archetypes, we might experience all twelve in a single day, or hour. Suppose, for instance, something goes wrong—you become ill or your job or primary relationship is in jeopardy. For the first few minutes, you do not want to look at the problem (shadow Innocent), but then your optimism returns (Innocent), and you plunge into investigating the situation. Your next experience is to feel powerlessness and pain, but then you ask others for support (Orphan). You marshall your resources and develop a plan to deal with the problem (Warrior). As you implement it, you also pay attention to what you and others need in the way of emotional support (Caregiver).

You gather more information (Seeker), let go of the illusions and false hopes (Destroyer), and make new commitments to change (Lover) in order to come up with a solution (Creator). That is, you respond to the crisis as a way of growing and becoming more than you were. Once the crisis is handled, you also look to see how you might have contributed to creating the problem (Ruler)—if you did— and act to heal that part of yourself (Magician) so that you will not create such a difficulty again. Or you may simply heal the part of you in pain over a situation you had no part in creating. This allows you to see what can be learned from the situation (Sage). Learning it frees you up to go back to enjoying your life (Fool) and trusting life's processes (Innocent).

When one or more archetypes are not activated in our lives, we skip steps. For example, if we have no Warrior, we will fail to develop a plan for dealing with the problem. If we have no Sage, we may neglect to gain the lesson the situation could teach us. Or we might express the archetype in its shadow forms: Instead of making a plan, we indulge in blaming others. Instead of gaining the lesson of the situation, we judge ourselves or others.

The movement through the twelve archetypal stages is an archetypal process that helps us develop invaluable skills for day-to-day living.

Stages of the Journey

The hero's journey includes three major stages: preparation, the journey, and the return.[2] During the *preparation* stage, we are challenged to prove our competence, our courage, our humanity, and our fidelity to high ideals. On the *journey,* we leave the safety of the family or tribe and embark on a quest where we encounter death, suffering, and love. But most important, our selves are transformed. In myth, that transformation is often symbolized by the finding of a treasure or sacred object. On our *return* from the quest, we become Rulers of our kingdoms, which are transformed because we are changed. But we must also continually be reborn and renewed, or we become ogre tyrants, clinging dogmatically to our old truths to the detriment of our kingdoms. Whenever we lose our sense of integrity and wholeness or begin to feel inadequate to current life challenges, we must embark on the quest again.

Preparation

The first four archetypes help us prepare for the journey. We begin in innocence, and from the Innocent we learn optimism and trust. When we experience "the fall," we become Orphans, disappointed, abandoned, betrayed by life – and especially by the people who were supposed to care for us. The Orphan teaches us that we need to provide for ourselves and stop relying on others to take care of us, but the Orphan feels so powerless and helpless that its best strategy for survival is to band together with others for mutual aid.

When the Warrior comes into our lives, we learn to set goals and develop strategies for achieving them, strategies that almost always require the development of discipline and courage. When the Caregiver becomes active, we learn to take care of others, and eventually to care for ourselves as well.

The first four archetypes help us prepare for the journey.

These four attributes – basic optimism, the capacity to band together for support, the courage to fight for yourself and others, and compassion and care for yourself and others – together provide the basic skills for living in society. But almost always, we still feel unsatisfied if this is all we can do, even though we have learned what is necessary to be both moral and successful in the world.

The Journey

We begin to yearn for something beyond ourselves, and become Seekers, searching for that ineffable something that will satisfy. Answering the call and embarking on the journey, we find that soon we are experiencing privation and suffering, as the Destroyer takes away much that had seemed essential to our lives. Initiation through suffering, however, is complemented by an initiation into Eros, the Lover, as we find ourselves in love with people, causes, places, work. This love is so strong it requires commitment – and we are no longer free. The treasure that emerges out of this encounter with death and love is the birth of the true self. The Creator helps us begin to express this self in the world and prepares us to return to the kingdom. These four abilities – to strive, to let go, to

The Twelve Archetypes

ARCHETYPE	GOAL	FEAR
Innocent	Remain in safety	Abandonment
Orphan	Regain safety	Exploitation
Warrior	Win	Weakness
Caregiver	Help others	Selfishness
Seeker	Search for better life	Conformity
Lover	Bliss	Loss of love
Destroyer	Metamorphosis	Annihilation
Creator	Identity	Inauthenticity
Ruler	Order	Chaos
Magician	Transformation	Evil sorcery
Sage	Truth	Deception
Fool	Enjoyment	Nonaliveness

DRAGON/PROBLEM	RESPONSE TO TASK	GIFT/VIRTUE
Deny it or seek rescue	Fidelity, discernment	Trust, optimism
Is victimized by it	Process and feel pain fully	Interdependence, realism
Slay/confront it	Fight only for what really matters	Courage, discipline
Take care of it or those it harms	Give without maiming self or others	Compassion, generosity
Flee from it	Be true to deeper self	Autonomy, ambition
Love it	Follow your bliss	Passion, commitment
Allow dragon to slay it	Let go	Humility
Claim it as part of the self	Self-creation, self-acceptance	Individuality, vocation
Find its constructive uses	Take full responsibility for your life	Responsibility, control
Transform it	Align self with cosmos	Personal power
Transcend it	Attain enlightenment	Wisdom, nonattachment
Play tricks on it	Trust in the process	Joy, freedom

love, and to create—teach us the basic process of dying to the old self and giving birth to the new. The process prepares us to return to the kingdom and change our lives.

The Return

The journey is fundamentally about metamorphosis.

When we return, we realize we are the Rulers of our kingdoms. At first we may be disappointed at the state of this realm. But as we act on our new wisdom and are more fully true to our deeper sense of identity, the wasteland begins to bloom. As the Magician is activated in our lives, we become adept at healing and transforming ourselves and others so that the kingdom can continually be renewed.

However, we are not completely fulfilled or happy until we face our own subjectivity, and so the Sage helps us know what truth really is. As we learn to both accept our subjectivity and let go of imprisonment to illusions and petty desires, we are able to reach a state of nonattachment in which we can be free. We are then ready to open to the Fool and learn to live joyously in the moment without worrying about tomorrow.

This final set of attainments—taking total responsibility for our lives, transforming and healing ourselves and others, nonattachment and a commitment to truth, and a capacity for joy and spontaneity—is itself the reward for our journey.

The Spiral Nature of the Journey

Thinking of the hero moving through stages of preparation, journey, and return, and being aided by twelve archetypes in order, is useful as a teaching device, but in most cases, of course, growth really does not happen in such a defined, linear way. Our guides come to us when they—and at some level we—choose.

The pattern is more like a spiral: the final stage of the journey, epitomized by the archetype of the Fool, folds back into the first archetype, the Innocent, but at a higher level than before. This time the Innocent is wiser about life. On the spiral journey, we may encounter each archetype many times, and in the process gain new gifts at higher or deeper levels of development. Each encounter leaves a psychic imprint, which operates like netting or webbing. When we experience reality—and we have the webbing or netting appropriate to hold that reality—we can take in that experience and make meaning of it. The archetypes we have not yet experienced are like holes in the net; experiences that we have little or no way of understanding simply pass through.[3]

How to Use This Book

Awakening the Heroes Within is organized in five parts. Part I introduces the heroic quest as a journey of consciousness. It traces ways the archetypes aid in constructing and balancing the psyche itself, as they help us form our Egos, connect with our Souls, and then both develop a sense of our true Selves and express these Selves in the world. The first five chapters provide a basic understanding of the process of individuation and consciousness expansion, which forms the basis for learning to realize fully your human potential.

Parts II, III, and IV explore, in detail, the archetypal guides that help us on our journeys. Part II describes the archetypes that help us prepare for the journey: the Innocent, the Orphan, the Warrior, and the Caregiver. Part III considers the archetypes that aid us in the journey itself: the Seeker, the Destroyer, the Lover, and the Creator. Part IV focuses on the archetypes that facilitate a successful and transformative return to the kingdom: the Ruler, the Magician, the Sage, and the Fool.

Each chapter discusses how one archetype expresses itself in our individual and cultural lives: the skills it teaches us, its negative or shadow forms, and the gifts and lessons it offers. Since each archetype can manifest itself in relatively primitive or more sophisticated forms, each chapter also explores stages of development of the archetypes.

Part V looks at how our journeys are affected by age, gender, culture, and our own uniqueness—factors that serve as a prism that diffuses this monomyth into thousands of unique patterns and forms, providing adequate room for individual variation and creativity.

Uses of This Book

I have written this book for the general reader. It can also be used in schools, colleges, and universities; drug and alcohol prevention and recovery programs; psychological, spiritual, and marriage and family counseling; employee assistance programs; *Awakening the Heroes Within* support groups—and by those who want to awaken the hero within themselves and others. These theories are designed to be applied in the following ways:

1.   As a developmental transpersonal psychology

2.   As a description of twelve key stages in human development, each with its own lesson, task, and gift

3.   As a way of understanding and appreciating human diversity by dominant archetype, gender, age, psychological type, and cultural background

4.   As a nonpathology-based diagnostic and intervention model to be used by educators and therapists for determining an individual's current developmental challenge

5.   As an aid in educating individuals for success, citizenship, and leadership in a democratic society

6.   As an investigation of archetypal, timeless spiritual truths found in religion, myth, literature, and psychology, and, hence, as a psychologically rather than theologically based guide to spiritual development

7.   As a tool for self-understanding and personal growth

Individual readers may use these theories to recognize where they may be possessed by shadow forms of the archetypes to the detriment of their lives and how they might analyze the heroic "guides" within them. Most of all, they can use the theories to recognize the stages of their journeys, so they can gain the lessons of each archetype.

Recognizing the Shadow Forms of the Guides

For some people, the whole area of the inner life is an undiscovered country. They may feel real fear about taking any kind of psychological journey. This is partly because they fear what they do not know, and partly because the more unknown this territory is to them, the more likely it is that they are pushing down archetypes that would like to be expressed in their lives. If so, these people will feel them initially in their negative forms; of course, this just makes them intensify further their efforts to repress the archetypes because otherwise they might be opening the door to monsters.

Indeed, if this is the case for you, just read this book without any intention of applying it to your own psyche. Reading it will educate your Ego and in due time allow some orderly integration of the more positive sides of the archetypes into your psyche. It will also allow you to recognize the archetypes that already are expressed in your life, and to see the richness you have gained from them. Very likely, you are still reaping their benefits. When you are ready to incorporate some new lessons into your life, it will not be difficult to do so.

Heroes confront dragons, and these dragons can be of many kinds. Indeed, for those who have not allowed many, if any, of the archetypes from the collective unconscious into their lives, both the inner and outer worlds seem populated with dragons—and the world seems a very frightening place to be.

The twelve heads of the dragon are the shadow sides of each archetype (see the accompanying chart); they can be as lethal as the seven deadly sins if we do not find the treasure they are hiding from us. Many times when we feel awful, we are stuck expressing an archetype in its negative guise. To feel empowered once again, we need simply to examine what archetype has possessed us, and then refuse to be possessed by it. However, usually we can do that only if we honor the archetype by expressing it in some way. In this case, what we want to do is move to expressing its more positive side.

To the degree that you have not allowed a particular archetype into your life as a guide, it is likely to trip you up as a dragon.

The Shadow Sides of the Archetypes

ARCHETYPE	SHADOW
Innocent	Evidenced in a capacity for denial so that you do not let yourself know what is really going on. You may be hurting yourself and others, but you will not acknowledge it. You may also be hurt, but you will repress that knowledge as well. Or, you believe what others say even when their perspective is directly counter to your own inner knowing.
Orphan	The victim, who blames his or her incompetence, irresponsibility, or even predatory behavior on others and expects special treatment and exemption from life because he or she has been so victimized or is so fragile. When this Shadow of the positive Orphan is in control of our lives, we will attack even people who are trying to help us, harming them and ourselves

simultaneously. Or, we may collapse and become dysfunctional (i.e., "You can't expect anything from me. I'm so
wounded/hurt/incompetent").

Warrior	The villain, who uses Warrior skills for personal gain without thought of morality, ethics, or the good of the whole group. It is also active in our lives *any time* we feel compelled to compromise our principles in order to compete, win, or get our own way. (The shadow Warrior is rampant in the business world today.) It is also seen in a tendency to be continually embattled, so that one perceives virtually everything that happens as a slight, a threat, or a challenge to be confronted.
Caregiver	The suffering martyr, who controls others by making them feel guilty: "Look at all I've sacrificed for you!" It evidences itself in all manipulative or devouring behaviors, in which the individual uses caretaking to control or smother others. (It is also found in codependence, a compulsive need to take care of or rescue others.)
Seeker	The perfectionist, always striving to measure up to an impossible goal or to find the "right" solution. We see this in people whose main life activity is self-improvement, going from the health club to yet another self-improvement course, etc., yet who never feel ready to commit to accomplishing anything. (This is the pathological underside of the human potential movement.)
Destroyer	Includes all self-destructive behaviors—addictions, compulsions, or activities that undermine intimacy, career success, or self-esteem—and all behaviors—such as emotional or physical abuse, murder, rape—that have destructive effects on others.
Lover	Includes the sirens (luring others from their quests), seducers (using love for conquest), sex or relationship addicts (feeling addicted to love), and anyone who is unable to say no when passion descends, or is totally destroyed when a lover leaves.
Creator	Shows itself as obsessive, creating so that so many possibilities are being imagined that none can be acted upon fully. (You might remember a film called *The Pumpkin Eater,* in which a woman got pregnant every time she was face-to-face with the vacuousness of her life. So, too, we can fill our

emptiness with yet another inessential project, challenge, or new thing to do, as she filled herself with another baby.) One variety of this is workaholism, in which we can always think of just one more thing to do.

Ruler	The ogre tyrant, insisting on his or her own way and banishing creative elements of the kingdom (or the psyche) to gain control at any price. This is the King or Queen who indulges in self-righteous rages and yells, "Off with his head." Often people act this way when they are in positions of authority (like parenting) but do not yet know how to handle the attendant responsibility. This also includes people who are motivated by a strong need to control.
Magician	The evil sorcerer, transforming better into lesser options. We engage in such evil sorcery anytime we belittle ourselves or another, or lessen options and possibilities, resulting in diminished self-esteem. The shadow Magician is also the part of us capable of making ourselves and others ill through negative thoughts and actions.
Sage	The unfeeling judge—cold, rational, heartless, dogmatic, often pompous—evaluating us or others and saying we (or they) are not good enough or are not doing it right.
Fool	A glutton, sloth, or lecher wholly defined by the lusts and urges of the body without any sense of dignity or self-control.

Any of us at any time can have a whole slew of inner dragons telling us we are not good enough (shadow Sage), we cannot live without that lover (shadow Lover), we are imagining all our problems and everything is fine (shadow Innocent), and so on. And we will identify as dragons whomever or whatever we meet in the outside world that triggers those inner voices.

In the early journey, we may try to slay these dragons, seeing them as entirely outside ourselves; as the journey progresses, we come to understand that they are inside us as well. When we learn to integrate the positive side of the archetype within ourselves, the dragons within (sometimes also without) become transformed into allies. For example, when people who judge us trigger our inner shadow Sage, we can learn to respond with our positive Sage and explain that we are living up to our own standards, if not theirs. At the end of the journey, then, there is no dragon. We feel authentic and free.

Shadow possession is not always related to the negative Shadow. We can also be possessed by the positive form of the archetype. For instance, you could be a very high-level Caregiver: you love to give. You have no hidden agendas, and you get joy from helping others. You still can be possessed by the archetype if you are *always* a Caregiver, and never battle, or seek your own bliss, or just have fun. Until we have given birth to a sense of authentic Self, the archetypes are likely to possess us. Ideally, we want not only to express the archetypes in their more positive forms, but not to be possessed by any of them. We need to develop a genuine sense of ourselves so we can express many different archetypes in our lives without being possessed by any. Freeing ourselves from possession by our Shadows allows us to live freer lives.

Addictions, Compulsions, and Shadow Possession

Anne Wilson Schaef has argued in *When Society Becomes an Addict* that we can become addicted to behaviors and thought patterns as well as to substances. Any time an archetype possesses us, addictive or compulsive tendencies may result, whether or not chemical addiction is involved.

What behavior a person is addicted to depends on which archetype is dominant, but all of them limit our lives. The following chart lists behaviors and attitudes that we can become addicted or attached to when we are possessed by the corresponding archetype. The fewer archetypes active in their positive form in our lives, the more prone we may be to addictiveness.

It is important that people with chemical addictions seek treatment in Twelve-Step or other programs. Recognizing the archetypal nature of the pathology is most effective as a means of preventing addictions and of second-stage recovery, when an awareness of the positive desire beneath the negative addiction is most liberating. Recognizing the archetypal root of these difficulties moves us out of our pathology into the journey, for there is always a "god" (or archetype) calling. Knowing which "god" calls can open us to receive its gift.

Awakening the Heroes Within

The way to free ourselves of shadow possession is to awaken our heroic potential. Each of us has a hero within, but we are not always aware of that reality. The hero within is, essentially, sleeping. Our task is to awaken that hero. The most natural way to arise in the morning is to wake up when the sun shines in

Archetypes and Addictions

ARCHETYPE	ADDICTIVE QUALITY	ADDICTION
Innocent	Denial	Consumerism/sugar/cheerfulness
Orphan	Cynicism	Powerlessness/worrying
Warrior	Stoicism	Achievement/success
Caregiver	Rescuing	Caretaking/codependence
Seeker	Self-centeredness	Independence/perfection
Destroyer	Self-destructiveness	Suicide/self-destructive habits
Lover	Intimacy problems	Relationships/sex
Creator	Obsessiveness	Work/creativity
Ruler	High control needs	Control/codependence
Magician	Dishonesty (image)	Power/hallucinogenic drugs/marijuana
Sage	Judgmentalism	Being right/tranquilizers
Fool	Inebriation	Excitement/cocaine/alcohol

the room. The natural way to activate inner potential is to shine the light of consciousness upon it. When we begin to see that we have a hero within, the hero, quite naturally, wakes up.

So, too, with the archetypes. As we shine the light of consciousness upon them, recognizing that they are within us, they awaken to enrich our lives. If they are already active but in shadow form, consciousness can turn the beastly side of the archetype into the royal, prospering prince or princess it could be.

Some of us, as a result of a fast-paced contemporary life-style, do not awaken when the sun shines in our window. We are too exhausted or simply too out of touch with natural processes, and we need an alarm clock. Our psyche also provides alarm clocks—usually called symptoms—to wake us up and tell us that something is wrong. If we are willing to pay attention to these symptoms, we can move ourselves out of our somnambulism into wakefulness.

The archetypes in their roles as pagan gods and goddesses historically were invoked through ritual, prayer, and meditation, and by creating temples to them. Even today we erect places where the archetypes will feel at home. For example, competitive activities and organizations—from athletic events, to political debates, to the armed forces—are located in stadiums, capitols, and the Pentagon, which serve as auspicious "temples" to the Warrior. Churches, which teach primarily the virtues of compassion and giving, are temples to the Caregiver. Colleges and universities are temples to the Sage. To contact different archetypes, it is useful to go to their modern-day temples.

You can literally ask the archetype to come into your life. Or, you may prefer to act out its rites and rituals. For example, to invoke the Warrior, you can engage in confrontation, competition, or struggle. To awaken the Caregiver, give to others without thought of return. To activate the Sage, study, work to improve your thinking skills, and become aware of your own subjective biases. At first, you may feel that you are just going through the motions of some activity that does not really fit you. But then, one day, the inner Warrior, Caregiver, or Sage graces your activities with its presence, and what has felt forced and awkward feels like an organic expression of who you are.

Whether an archetype is active or in the process of being awakened, it is important to recognize the unique form of its expression in your life. Not all Warriors, for example, are alike. Some are primitive and ruthless, driven by a desire for conquest. Some are competitive game players. Some engage in crusades for the good of humanity. And so on. One purpose of shining the light of consciousness on the archetype is to see the specific form it takes in *your* life.

Finally, while awakening all twelve archetypes fosters a whole and rich life, it is not realistic to think they all will be equally active. As the ancients often honored all the gods and goddesses but had a special relationship with one or two, we may awaken all twelve archetypes in this pantheon but find a sense of the uniqueness of our own journeys through the specific mix of the two or three that are most dominant in our lives.

Some readers may want to take the time to do the exercises provided in this book to focus on awakening the archetypes within; some may not. Either way, simply reading about an archetype serves to awaken it because doing so moves it into your consciousness. You may do best simply to pay attention to the archetypes currently active in your life, opening to gaining their gifts without trying to awaken others. If you do so consciously, so that the organic emergence of a different archetype is nourished and supported rather than weeded out, the effect can enrich your life.

Tips on Reading This Book

You may wish to read the book straight through—and doing so, as with most books, is desirable. However, different parts of the book are designed with different readers in mind. Part I, for instance, is of interest primarily to those concerned with the workings of the human psyche, and how the hero's journey fosters its development. Parts II, III, and IV provide detail about each archetype and how it is evidenced in our lives as we move through the three major phases of the journey. Readers who have read *The Hero Within* might find Part II somewhat repetitive and choose to skip (or scan) it and move immediately from Part I to Part III.

Take the Heroic Myth Index (HMI)

Before you begin, I advise you to fill out the Heroic Myth Index (found in the Appendix), an instrument designed to measure archetypes active in people's lives. Also fill out the pie chart on page 23. By doing so, you can inform your reading about the archetypes with both the instrument's and your own appraisal of which ones are active in your life. Record your scores in the boxes provided for that purpose. Some readers may want to concentrate their energy on the parts of the book most relevant to their own lives right now.

Those motivated by a desire for personal understanding and growth undoubtedly will want to avail themselves of the exercises provided throughout to apply these understandings directly to their own life experiences. For such readers, working alone or in groups, this book can be read over a period of weeks or months to greatly increase self-awareness and effectiveness in the world. Some parts may be important to your life right now; others might be more relevant in a few weeks or months or years. Work with the book at your own pace and in your own way.

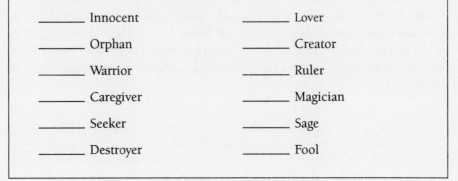

Charting Your HMI Scores

Turn to the Appendix, take the Heroic Myth Index, and follow the self-scoring instructions. Write your score for each archetype below:

_____ Innocent		_____ Lover
_____ Orphan		_____ Creator
_____ Warrior		_____ Ruler
_____ Caregiver		_____ Magician
_____ Seeker		_____ Sage
_____ Destroyer		_____ Fool

Ethics

The main rule to follow in applying these theories and models is never to use them to manipulate, label, judge, or put down yourself or another. All parts of this model should be used only to honor yourself and respect others, for implicit in the metaphor of the quest is the awareness that we all matter—and matter profoundly. Knowledge implies responsibility. The responsibility that comes with this model is to commit yourself to claiming your own power and, in so doing, to refrain from actions that make you or others feel demeaned or belittled. Instead, use your power and your wisdom to ennoble yourself and exert a transformative influence on those around you.

HMI Pie Chart

Mark on each axis your degree of identification with that archetype. Then shade in toward the center of the circle.

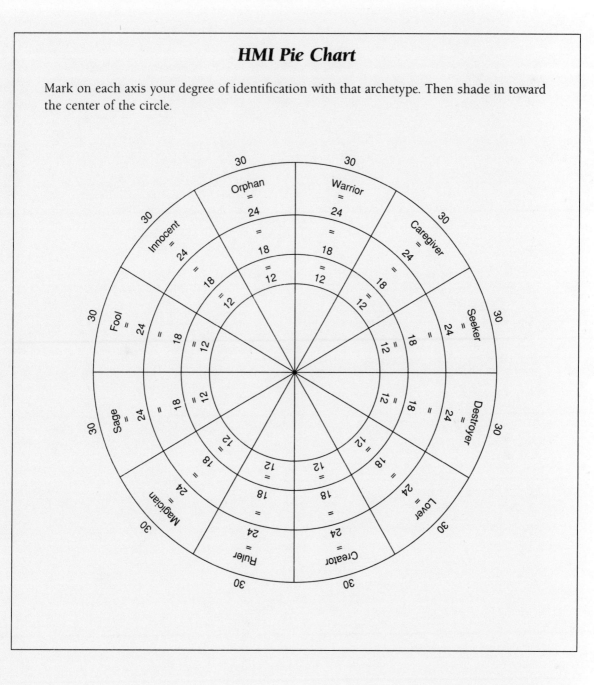

Part I

The Dance of Ego, Self, and Soul

1

The Stages of the Journey

The messages our culture gives us about the relative roles of Ego, Self, and Soul can be confusing and contradictory. Most management literature focuses on a healthy Ego, to the exclusion of both Self and Soul. Political theory tends to focus on such Ego concerns as equal access to jobs, pay, education, and status. Psychology generally emphasizes healthy Ego development, and many psychologies do nothing else.

Transpersonal psychology, as well as the better part of contemporary religion (whether Eastern or Western), develops the Soul and Spirit, but many times to the detriment of the Ego. Often this takes the form of a conscious and explicit desire to get rid of the Ego so that the individual can bow completely to God's will. Only archetypal psychology honors all three, and sometimes even in it practical Ego concerns don't get their proper emphasis.

There is a crying need in the contemporary world to honor Ego, Self, and Soul and to recognize the ways that the Ego should be reeducated (not eliminated) when higher order transcendent functions are developed. Indeed, it is the union of Ego and Soul that makes possible the birth of the Self. As I have studied contemporary psychology, theology, politics, management, and self-help literature, I have become more convinced that it is possible for each of us to be happy, successful, "self-actualized," and spiritual. It is also possible to "follow our bliss" and still be a responsible citizen, parent, and friend and to live in responsible and loving community with others. The secret is to take the journey and find yourself.

The twelve heroic archetypes described in *Awakening the Heroes Within* help our psyches develop. The three stages of the hero's journey—preparation, journey, return—parallel exactly the stages of human psychological development: we first develop the Ego, then encounter the Soul, and finally give birth to a unique sense of Self. The journey of the Ego teaches us how to be safe and

---

Mandalas of Ego, Soul, and Self

The illustrations that follow place each set of four archetypes in a mandala. According to Jung, the number 4 and the shape of the mandala are associated both with wholeness and with the discovery of the Self.

1. Place your score for each archetype in the box provided below it.

2. Add together your Innocent, Orphan, Warrior, and Caregiver scores to reach your aggregate Ego score. Place that number in the box provided for the heading "Ego."

3. Add together your Seeker, Destroyer, Lover, and Creator scores to reach your aggregate Soul score. Place that number in the box provided for the heading "Soul."

4. Add together your Ruler, Magician, Sage, and Fool scores to reach your aggregate Self score. Place that number in the box provided for the heading "Self."

The three stages of the hero's journey—preparation, journey, return—parallel exactly the stages of human psychological development.

successful in the world; the journey of the Soul helps us to become real and authentic as we encounter the deepest mysteries of life; and the journey of the Self shows us the way to find and express our authenticity, power, and freedom.

The *Ego* is the "container" for our life. The Ego creates a boundary between us and everything else and mediates our relationship with the world. It also helps us learn to fit into the world as we know it and to act to change that world to better meet our needs.

The *Soul,* which Jungians equate with the unconscious or the psyche itself, connects us with the transpersonal. The Soul is also the repository of all the potential of the human species, potential that lies within each one of us, like seeds germinating and ready to sprout if external conditions are propitious (analogous to enough sun, water, and fertile soil). For people who believe in an afterlife, the Soul is the part of us that lives on after the body dies. But it is not necessary to believe in an afterlife to connect with Soul or to use the concepts in this book.

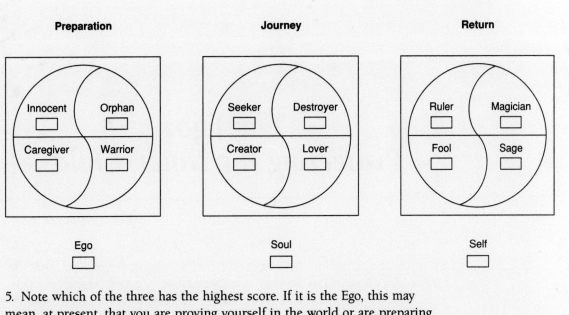

5. Note which of the three has the highest score. If it is the Ego, this may mean, at present, that you are proving yourself in the world or are preparing for the journey (or the next stage in it). If it is the Soul, it may indicate a time of great transition—that you are in the process of deepening and becoming more authentic and real. If it is Self, this may be a time of expressing yourself in the world, of being aware of your power and experiencing wholeness.

The *Self* signifies the achievement of a sense of genuine identity. When the Self is born, we know who we are, the disjointed parts of our psyche come together, and we experience wholeness and integrity. Our task then becomes to find adequate ways to express ourselves in the world, and in so doing make the contributions we alone can make to bring joy to our own lives and help the wasteland bloom.

The first four archetypes—the Innocent, the Orphan, the Warrior, and the Caregiver—help us prepare for the journey. From these four guides, we learn to survive in the world as it is, to develop Ego strength and, beyond that, to be productive citizens and good people, with high moral character.

The second four archetypes—the Seeker, the Destroyer, the Lover, and the Creator—help us on the journey itself, as we encounter our souls and become "real." The final four archetypes—the Ruler, the Magician, the Sage, and the Fool— mediate the return to the kingdom. In the process, they help us learn to express our true selves and transform our lives. They take us beyond heroism into freedom and joy.

2

The Ego:
Protecting the Inner Child

The hero is often said to be the archetype of the Ego, but this is only a partial truth. The heroic journey of individuation encompasses Ego, Soul, *and* Self. Establishing a healthy Ego, however, is the *prerequisite* for taking the journey safely.

The Ego is the seat of consciousness, the recognition that there is an "I" separate from the mother and the rest of the world, an "I" that can affect that world. The mature adult Ego develops its capabilities in order to fulfill *all* our needs, not just the need for safety. The developed Ego helps us meet our needs not only for survival, satisfaction, safety, love, and belongingness, but also for self-esteem, self-actualization, and even transcendence. It also balances our individual needs with the needs of others, and in that way contributes to the survival and development of the individual, the family, the community, the nation, and the species.

The Ego is the seat of consciousness, the recognition that there is an "I" separate from the mother and the rest of the world, an "I" that can affect that world.

In the beginning of life, however, the Ego is unformed. We come into this world small, fragile, and helpless. We have little or no control over our environment, only the ability to cry in pain or to inspire love and care by looking cute, vulnerable, and innocent. We are left in the care of parents or other adults who, however hard they may try, do not always guess right about what we need. As we gain some control over our movements, sounds, and actions, we begin to learn that what we do can affect what happens to us. With this awareness, Ego is born.

No matter how old, wise, or mature we become, each of us has within us a vulnerable little child who still bears the scars—whether great or few—of our formative years. The Ego's first task is to protect that inner child. At some point during childhood, the Ego begins to take on some of the protective function from the parents, and gradually, with maturation, assumes that task completely.

The Ego's next task, and its basic function, is to mediate our relationship with the outside world. It begins by ensuring our survival, and then concentrates on acquiring worldly success. In healthy situations, children can trust parents and other adults to look after their safety. Then they can focus on exploring the world and learning to interact effectively with it. In dysfunctional families, however, children's Ego development may be hampered if they have to take over responsibility for survival and safety needs too early. Nonetheless, the experience of some hardship or difficulty is critical to the development of Ego strength. Whether or not the externals of our lives are difficult, the period of preparation for the journey often seems very hard—if only because we do not yet possess the skills that can make life easier.

The Ego and the Hero's Journey

Because the challenge of the past few centuries has been the development of the Ego, the stories we identify most readily with the hero are those about Ego development. The classic hero on a white horse, the knight slaying the dragon and rescuing the damsel in distress, and the damsel in distress defending herself against the onslaughts of the would-be rapist or seducer are all versions of this classic story.

Whether the hero is a knight, cowboy, explorer, saint, or political activist, the story is essentially the same. The hero and the kingdom are in danger from some hostile force. The victim to be rescued may be inside oneself (one's inner child or inner damsel, one's virginity or liberty) or in the world beyond, but the key is having the courage and ability to defend the gates. The hero protects and defends the boundaries of the kingdom so that life within can flourish and grow.

The hero is often also the conqueror, the man or woman who goes after what he or she wants—new land, fame, fortune, love, liberty—and gets it. But the capacity to get what we want and protect our boundaries does not, in itself, make us heroes. Indeed, we share these qualities with great villains. What makes a hero a hero is a nobility of spirit manifested as concern and compassion for others. That is what causes heroes to rescue victims.

In the modern world, we act out this plot daily. Few of us literally slay dragons or even villains. The swords we use are less often literal weapons and more often money, status, image, power, influence, and highly developed communication skills. But the pattern remains the same.

Preparation for the journey requires each of us to be socialized adequately to be effective in the society in which we live, and then to separate from the collective view of the world enough to assert independent values, opinions, and desires. Finally, it demands that we use this capacity for autonomy and independence, not simply for selfish ends—although we do want to seek our own good—but for the good of the whole as well.

Archetypal Influences on Ego Development

The archetypes associated with Ego development—the Innocent, Orphan, Warrior, and Caregiver—help us learn to take responsibility for our lives, even when we do not yet know how to do so. Together they teach us the components of character: the trust required to learn the basic skills of living; a sense of the interdependence of human life and the ability to do our parts; the courage to fight for ourselves and others; and an identification with the greater good, which allows us to give to, and even sacrifice for, others.

These archetypes also help us establish the fundamental components of Ego consciousness. The Innocent helps us develop the persona, the mask we wear to establish our social role. The Orphan presides over the parts of our psyches we repress, deny, or simply hide so that we can establish a persona acceptable to ourselves and to others. The Warrior establishes the Ego per se, with its focus on protecting the boundaries and getting our needs met. It also acts in the service of the Superego, or Ego ideal,[1] to squelch or punish tendencies it sees as unethical, self-destructive, or harmful to others. The Caregiver presides over the opening of the heart so that our goodness is motivated by genuine compassion for self or others. Together, these four archetypes help establish a container—for brevity we can call it the Ego—that can allow the Soul to flow through.

The Innocent

The Innocent helps establish the persona—the mask we wear in the world, our personality, our social role. Although this external image lacks depth and complexity, it provides us and others with a sense of who we are and what can be expected of us.

The pressure to have a persona starts early with the question, "What are you going to be when you grow up?" Adolescents may seek a primary sense of identity in popular music, current fashions, and enjoyable activities. As adults, we identify ourselves by the jobs we do and perhaps also by our life-styles. The fact is, as every Innocent knows, we must have a persona to fit into the society.

The Innocent within wants to be loved and be a part of things.

Early in life, the Innocent in each of us looks around at available options and chooses a persona. The Innocent within wants to be loved and be a part of things. It wants us to be socially acceptable, to fit in, to make others love and be proud of us. Like a child, it is not particularly critical of the group it wants to join. At best, it will choose a persona that is positive and socially adaptive. At worst, it may choose a criminal persona to fit into an environment that perceives honesty as a sign of naïveté. Whatever the choice, the reason for having a persona is always to help us have a social place or place in the family—and ideally to be admired and well liked. Unless we do, we cannot engage in the world around us.

The Orphan

Once the Innocent chooses the persona, the Orphan within, who is a survivor and a bit of a cynic, sizes up the situation and sees which of our qualities will have to be sacrificed or go underground to fulfill that new image. For example, a child who chooses a conservative life-style will have to sacrifice his flamboyancy, while one who chooses a criminal persona will have to repress her concern for others. The third child in a family might think, "My big sister is the smart one and my brother is the talented one; I'll be the personable one"—thus repressing intelligence and talent in the interest of being fun or charming.

The Orphan tries to protect us from being abandoned, hurt, or victimized.

The Orphan is also the part of us that learns to recognize and thus avoid situations that are likely to hurt us—from the potential kidnapper, to the bully down the street, to the emotionally abusive relative. It tries to protect us from being abandoned, hurt, or victimized. To do this, it may act on knowledge the persona cannot even acknowledge having, thus becoming a secret and valuable, but hidden, sidekick.

We all have a collection of orphaned or banished selves living in the personal or collective unconscious. Many of these can be brought back into consciousness through analysis and other forms of therapy, greatly enriching the psyche. Others may remain unconscious. And some occupy a border zone. We know about them but because (perhaps rightly) we disapprove of them, we do not allow them freedom of action. Or because of our culture's values, we rarely allow them to be viewed by others.

The Warrior

The Id is the part of the psyche characterized by undifferentiated instinctual life. In it reside our primal passions and urges, and from it comes all desire. The Ego splits off from the Id and works to control it. Actually, its goals are not so different. The Ego wants to get its needs met, too, but also cares how they are met. It mediates between the Id and the outer world, providing some rational restraint to focus and harness the Id's desires. The Warrior helps with this task.

The Warrior brandishes the sword to cut off anything that seems to threaten survival of the body, the budding Ego, our integrity, and eventually a true sense of Self.

When the Warrior is acting strictly in terms of our self-interest, it is helping develop our Ego strength; when it is urging us to act morally or to assist others, it is helping develop the Superego. At the lower levels, the Superego is determined by the values of parents and the community, and their notions about what might be good for others. Their opinions form an Ego ideal. This ideal may be oppressive to us, because we tend to repress or deny elements of our own natures that do not fit it. As we take those attitudes into ourselves, the Superego may punish us when we violate them. For example, if we are in a relationship of which the Superego does not approve, we may get sick or even unconsciously sabotage the relationship to punish the deviation from the Ego ideal. At a higher level, the Superego reflects our own values, not just our parents' or the culture's, and is essentially very like the conscience.

The Caregiver

The Caregiver is associated with more kindly aspects of the Superego and helps us develop a sense of morality and care for others. It is concerned about the good of others as well as ourselves. It may well be a form of Ego that looks out for the survival, not just of the individual, but of the family, tribe, community, or species. The Superego will push us to sacrifice our own good for others so that ultimately the group may survive. As we mature and grow and become less dualistic, we also learn to balance our own good with that of others, so there is less and less conflict between the Ego and the Superego.

The Caregiver is asked to sacrifice many of his or her wishes, desires, and priorities, not only for the good of other people, but to find the Soul.

The Caregiver is concerned not only with our own children and the people with whom we work, but with the good of humanity. It feels compassion for the planet and concern over the harm humankind has done to it and is willing to sacrifice to heal wounds. It aches when it learns that people in other parts of the world are starving, or people in our own cities are homeless, and urges us to do something about it. The ability of the Caregiver to sacrifice the lesser for the greater good and the capacity to comfort and educate others are critical to developing a psyche with room for both Ego and Soul.

Readiness for the Journey

The Innocent and the Orphan prepare us for the journey by teaching us discernment and helping us differentiate helpers from tempters. The Warrior trains for battle and develops courage, and the Caregiver teaches humanity and compassion. While we are building these attributes, we often experience the "road of trials." Ordinarily, we do not sense its role as a heroic initiation: we just feel that life is very hard!

When we hear the "call to the quest" and begin our journeys as Seekers, we usually are tested to see if we are adequately prepared. For example, we find out whether we have learned the lessons of the Innocent and the Orphan by whether we can tell tempters from guides—knowing whom to flee and whom to follow.

We almost always need to prove our courage by facing a dragon (some thing, person, or situation that greatly frightens us). And, almost always, we are put in a position to demonstrate our compassion. For example, in many fairy tales, the hero meets an old beggar and shares his or her last bit of food with that person. The beggar, of course, ends up giving the hero some magical tool that helps the journey come to a good end. In ordinary life, this translates into passing up competitive advantage or following a heartfelt response to help someone, even when it requires considerable sacrifice, or simply practicing daily kindnesses to those we meet.

Generally, our journeys do not progress further until, through the way we handle these trials, we demonstrate successful preparation. When we have passed all these tests, we are ready to experience metamorphosis, to die to what we have been and be reborn into a new level of experience.

The Ego: Container for the Soul

Although the Ego has often been thought to be the enemy of the Soul, it actually helps us create and maintain our boundaries—our sense of where we end and others begin. This strength allows us to open to spiritual vision. Properly developed, the Ego grows but then empties itself, becoming the container that can house the Soul without threatening mental, emotional, or physical collapse. Without the well-built container, there can be no real psychological or spiritual development, because there is no safe place to put it. A confrontation with the unconscious or with the transpersonal can crack an inadequately developed Ego and result in psychosis.

Why, then, has so much negative been said about the Ego? Why is it often linked with egotism? Why have so many wise men and women argued that we must renounce Ego to find our true selves or to find spiritual enlightenment?

The answer is that we have misunderstood the nature of the Ego. First, most Egos we encounter are not very developed. They are threatened by the process of individuation, by the attendant exploration of previously repressed material, and by any sense of union with another. The primitive Ego is simply afraid in the first instance that the emerging qualities will get us in trouble in the external world, and in the second and third cases that they will swallow us up. The primitive Ego is also egotistical. It wants to take credit for all the achievements of our deeper sense of Self or, conversely, to deny the existence of anything beyond itself. Then the Ego can turn on the psyche. Because the Ego's job is to defend and to protect the psyche, it knows its every vulnerable place. Therefore, if it wants to stop action, it knows just which button to push.

The simplest way to deal with the underdeveloped Ego's terror at change is to observe it with detachment. The most effective way, however, is to remember that the Ego is our ally and needs to be brought on board to work for and not against the new need. The Ego may also need to be inspired to work at strengthening the container by developing a clearer structure and sense of who we are so that it is strong enough to allow for genuine intimacy, spiritual insight, and greater authenticity and wholeness. This usually is a matter of strengthening our boundaries by increasing our awareness of where we end and someone else begins, or where our conscious mind has lost control and our unconscious has driven our life.

The second reason the Ego has been misunderstood is that a mature Ego threatens many of our social institutions. Most people move from unquestioning dependency on parents or other adults to dependence on schools and colleges, health care, the media, government, religious organizations, or charismatic leaders. Many times and places in history put no value or emphasis on developing the Ego as an individualized container. Institutions served this purpose for most people. Soul and spirit were channeled through the container of a religious institution, "truth" through schools, universities, religious or political bodies, and so on.

The idea of individuals taking responsibility for making their own decisions is historically new—a part of the political rise of democracy, the philosophical rise of individualism, and the relatively new psychological emphasis on the development of individuality. Today, just as maturity demands that we withdraw our dependency from our parents so that we grow up and depend upon ourselves, eventually we must become capable of exercising judgment independent of our major social institutions.

This does not mean, of course, that we flout legitimate authority, break laws, burn books, behave unethically, or abuse our health. Maturity requires the ability to balance independence with continuing care and concern for one's parents—a recognition of human interdependence; it also demands care and concern for the social institutions designed to ensure our safety, educate and inform us, or help us live virtuous lives. What it does not require of us, however, is unthinking compliance.

As important as these institutions have been in developing the capacity to respond to the heroic call, the heroic life requires going beyond dependency. For some, this may mean leaving those institutions. But for most, it simply means changing one's relationship to them, moving from childlike dependency to adult responsibility and interdependence.

The next chapter provides an introduction to the world of Soul and an invitation to enter its mysteries. Before you embark on this journey, however, it is wise to remember the importance of the Ego. The most apparent cultural crisis of our time is that people whose Egos have not developed sufficiently are expected or even compelled to be autonomous and independent. In the absence of institutional support to contain this development, they flail about ineffectually, fall prey to charismatic leaders, or succumb to addiction.

The demands on the individual in our time are great.[2] This book is one support for your journey; undertaking that journey with the help of a group can be another. Before you can take the hero's journey, your rational Ego needs to say yes. The Soul does not need this book; it knows the way. But the Soul needs the Ego to come along, because it is the practical, down-to-earth Ego that will see to it that our Soul journeys do not unduly ravage our lives.

3

The Soul:
Entering the Mysteries

Soul is the part of the psyche that connects us with the eternal and provides a sense of meaning and value in our lives. In Jungian psychology, Soul is often used as a synonym for the psyche itself, or, variably, for the collective unconscious from which the archetypes emerge. In religious thought, the Soul is the part of each person that is immortal and that is capable of spiritual growth and development. In popular usage, Soul is associated with the capacity for deep feeling (as in the expression "soulful"), or, as in "soul-loss," with the sense (or the loss of such a sense) of meaning, value, and purpose.[1]

It is not necessary to believe in God in a conventionally religious sense or even to believe in an afterlife to develop our Souls. We move to a concern with Soul when we feel the need to know the meaning of life or of our own lives, when we feel a yearning for some connection with the cosmos, or when we contemplate our mortality.

Sometimes the Soul makes possible a sense of Oneness or spiritual connection, or, more often, a sense of intimacy with another human being. Paradoxically, the Ego's accomplishment of boundaries allows us to risk connection—because we no longer fear we will be swallowed up and lose ourselves.

The Ego is great at building a sense of discrete, individual boundaries, but we need the Soul to experience meaning.

In the modern world, we often lack even respectable categories in which to think about our Souls. Our main experience of Soul may be negative, a sense that something is missing in our lives. Because our society denies Soul, we experience it primarily between the cracks—the cracks in our health and our morality, and the cracks brought on by crises. Many people, for example, experience Soul only through self-destructiveness: addictions, cravings, obsessive behaviors. Yet it is during the great crises of life that the individual suddenly yearns for meaning and cosmic connection.

Soul is evident in the transitions of human life from childhood to puberty, from adolescence to young adulthood, to parenthood, mid-life, advancing age, and finally death. These are the moments of "liminality" or "standing on the threshold," having shed one identity but not having attained another. These also are the moments when we most predictably and assuredly yearn for contact with some transcendent element.

Many cultures have developed rituals and sacred myths to mediate and help soften these transitions, to ease our movement from one reality to another. It is certainly the lack of such rituals and the relative lack of regard for the spiritual dimension in modern secular society that make these passages so difficult and lonely. Although to some degree suffering and loneliness are inevitable in all cultures, the pain can be lessened if we have a framework that helps us understand what is happening to us.

Initiation

Some cultures have provided special initiatory experiences, unrelated to other life passages, into the sacred mysteries of the Soul. The great mystery cults of the Hellenistic period in Greece, Syria, Anatolia, Egypt, and Persia, for example, were secret initiations meant to help people disengage from ordinary, consensual realities and see and hear ancient spiritual truths.

The purpose of initiation is to help us recognize the meaning and significance of the experiences it symbolizes in our own lives. The uninitiated do not lack the experience of Soul, but they fail to recognize its power and meaning. Initiation makes such experiences conscious, not in the language of the Ego but in the language of the Soul—through myth, symbol, song, art, literature, ritual.

The hero's journey is an initiation into the realities of the Soul journey. The journey requires us to establish and then let go of control over our lives; to put aside our horror at confronting death, pain, and loss to experience life's wholeness. To do this, we must expand our Ego's narrow view. We must let go of sentiment, safety, and predictability, and even our concern with physical safety, effectiveness, and virtue. In doing so, we move out of the dualisms of good/bad, me/you, us/them, light/dark, right/wrong and into a world of paradox.

The morality of the journey is demanding and absolute, but it is a different morality than the Ego's. Our normal Ego consciousness wants to be immortal, to be safe from all suffering, to be successful, prosperous, loved. Above all, the Ego wants the world to make sense.

The journey requires us to put all these desires aside and see the Soul's truth: the essence of life is mystery. The Soul's truth does not necessarily make any sense from a rational Ego point of view. It is good to be "healthy, wealthy, and wise," but what makes us alive and *real* is journeying into the central mysteries

Preparation for the journey is about learning to be strong, moral, and healthy, but the journey itself is about experiencing the great mysteries of life—death, passion, birth, creation—as mysteries.

of life, where we learn about dismemberment, death, dissolution, sex, passion, and ecstasy, and see the beauty of it *all*.

Without Soul, we feel like automatons. We go through the right motions, but it is movement without meaning. We may even walk through many of the experiences of initiation, but we are so out of touch with our Souls that we are unaffected and untransformed. Yet we get many chances. It is genuinely never too late. We enter and reenter the mysteries many times at deeper and deeper levels of understanding. There is no punishment for failing to connect with one's Soul except the ever-present sense of meaninglessness in one's life, which is punishment enough.

Becoming Real

Initiation begins in childhood with our first experiences of confusion, suffering, intense love, longing, and frustration. For children, the readiest metaphor for this initiatory experience is the process of an object or a toy coming alive. Most children, like most adults, relate on some level to stories about objects coming alive; for until we confront our Souls, we may be good, we may even be successful, but we will not feel truly real because we are, in fact, not ourselves.

Pinocchio is a well-known example of children's literature dealing with the process of becoming real. In *Pinocchio,* Gepetto longs for a son and carves the puppet Pinocchio out of a block of wood. Then the Blue Fairy appears and grants the puppet the capacity to move on his own. Together, Gepetto and the Blue Fairy (symbolic respectively of Ego and Spirit) can make a well-behaved puppet, but only Pinocchio can earn the right to be real.

At first, he is a "good" little puppet and does everything he is supposed to do. His first sign of independence is an act of disobedience and betrayal of Gepetto, the Blue Fairy, and his little cricket conscience. He goes off with the rowdy Lampwick to Pleasure Island. Like most of us, when he begins trying to follow his bliss, he is sidetracked by trivial pleasures (eating candy and destroying property).

Pinocchio descends into the depths of instinctual pleasure seeking, but escapes just in time when he recognizes that he and his friends are turning into donkeys. This disorienting experience so shocks Pinocchio that he begins to see the world very differently.

Pinocchio's initiation into the mysteries has four parts. First, he sees the Blue Fairy and learns that he has the potential to become a "real boy." This is his call to the quest. Second, he allows himself to experience his own shadow qualities and the destruction they cause. Third, in the whale's body he becomes aware of how much he loves Gepetto and how much he is loved. Finally, upon his return, the Blue Fairy turns him into a real boy because he has earned it: He has experienced life. He has suffered. He has learned to see with wiser eyes, and therefore to differentiate base pleasures from real bliss, and he has gained a capacity for genuine love. And he has learned to take responsibility for his actions without being debilitated by shame or regret. He has, in short, become real.

On the symbolic level, living life only at the level of the Ego is like being a robot, toy, or other inanimate object. The hunger we feel is for a more genuine experience. The quest with its call to Spirit is only the first step in finding such genuineness. Initiation shakes up our way of seeing the world and requires us to connect with our deeper wisdom to understand what is happening to us. This initiation may in some way anticipate the experiences of suffering, deprivation, and loss brought by the archetype of the Destroyer, the capacity for genuine and passionate love and connection associated with the archetype of the Lover (Eros), and finally, the union with one's Soul, which allows for the birth of the new Self (the Creator).

Entering the Mysteries

Entering the mysteries—through analysis or mysticism, or by directly experiencing death and love in your life—is about learning to accept and love life in the body and on this earth. Being fully present in the body in no way negates the possibility of the immortality of the Soul, because the body is the expression of Soul and hence part of it. Our Souls need our bodies to enable us to participate in the cycle of cosmic birthing and dying and thus become more fully our own Selves. When we let go of everything in our lives and consciousness that needs to die, and when we open to what needs to be born, we learn to feel the awe and wonder that our own willing participation in these cosmic cycles can bring.

It is difficult for our Egos, however, to understand Soul suffering in any form. The Innocent wants to deny unpleasant truths, and just have faith. The Orphan takes death and suffering as further indication that life is not fair. The Caregiver and the Warrior both try to protect the world from suffering—the Warrior through trying to find and slay the cause of that suffering and the Caregiver by taking all suffering on itself to save others.

Even our spirits just want to transcend such experiences and quest for that state of bliss that transcends them all. There is ample testimony from mystics and sages of all times and places that it is possible to do so, but not at first. The only way out of paradox is through it.

Disorientation as Initiatory Experience

A shift of perspective is basic to all initiatory experiences. We must learn to see, hear, and think in ways that make new levels of experience accessible to us.

Various kinds of initiatory practices designed to alter perception are available to those who seek them out. Most of us, however, do not consciously choose our initiation. It appears just to happen, and often is quite a shock.

Sometimes the shock is physical. Paul is struck blind on the way to Damascus. The shaman in Jean Auel's *Clan of the Cave Bear* is struck by lightning as a boy. But the shock may also be psychic. In the book of Genesis, Jacob, fleeing his brother's wrath, goes to sleep and dreams of a ladder to heaven. He is struck with fear, recognizing that he is in the spot where the divine touches earth. Actually, we are all in sacred space all the time, but usually we have to be shocked out of our normal way of seeing to feel or know this.

You may be shocked into disorientation by sudden suffering, loss, or pain. You may have an experience that cannot be explained by our ordinary way of viewing the world, such as a premonition, or an out-of-body experience, or a vivid dream of a spiritual being.

You could also become disoriented through pathology, disability, or betrayal. Some people are initiated through drug-induced highs (not recommended) and some through mental illness. Others become disoriented by an overload of stress and an inability to cope with their lives. Still others become disoriented when someone else undercuts their sense of what is real.

The hectic pace of modern life may be a strategy that we use, as a culture, to overwhelm ourselves into disorientation. Such strategies, however, can backfire. Disorientation by itself is not initiation. Initiation happens only when we are thrown enough that we begin to search for meaning at a deeper level. The challenge to the initiate is not to try to pretend that your life at that moment is under control, but to stay with the sense of disorientation and powerlessness and open to a deep inner knowing of what you need to see that you have not been seeing.

In these moments the rational mind is tempted to try to figure it all out. There is nothing wrong with analyzing and rationally thinking things through, but this skill is part of Ego development. Rationalize as we will, the Ego's hard won strategies are simply inadequate to understanding life at a Soul level.

Most of us do not consciously choose our initiation. It appears just to happen, and often is quite a shock.

If you are unsettled by an initiatory experience, you can quiet your mind by saying, "This seems like an initiatory experience to me. I know I cannot figure it out. I also cannot push harder and get the situation under control. I can use my Ego to act responsibly in the world while this is going on: take care of my kids, get to my job on time, be kind to my friends. But it is my Soul that is being awakened by these experiences. All I can do to deal with this is to wait until the learning I need comes to me."

And come it always does. Sometimes it is a new insight, percolating up from within, expressed in dreams or in a waking "Aha!" or "Oh yes!" experience. Sometimes it comes to us, by synchronicity, through a friend, a book, a letter, a speaker who "just happens" to say what we need to hear. Or may come to us through a natural object or symbol. We look at it, and suddenly we just know what we need to know.

The language of the Soul is right-brain, metaphorical, narrative, and paradoxical, very unlike the left-brain, logical, discursive, dualistic language of the Ego. Soul insights usually come not as a result of hard work but as a gestalt born out of one's yearning to know an answer. Staying in one's confusion and feeling one's powerlessness and frustration help open us to such moments of sudden clarity. We cannot control what is happening to us at such times; but if we are lucky, we learn to sink beneath the confusion to a deeper level of wisdom that is always available to each of us.

The Ancient Mystery Religions and Alchemy

In the modern world, we are not generally encouraged to talk about our initiatory experiences. And, although Jungian analysis is a modern form of initiation, most people who go to psychologists today go to Ego psychologists and just learn to accommodate better to the world around them. Archaic practices in many other times and places, paid more attention to initiation, its role, and its function. I want to describe just two such practices: the ancient mystery religions and the "science" of alchemy.

Ancient Mystery Religions as Sources of Psychological Truth

The mysteries were the mystic aspect of fertility religions that celebrated sexuality, birth, and death. Essential to all mystery religions is an assumed parallel between the cycles of nature and of spiritual and psychological life. That is, individual and family life, the processes of nature, and the reality of the divine all were seen to mirror one another, and all were seen as part of an ongoing process that was beautiful.

Some cultures celebrated solar cycles (spring, summer, fall, and winter), and others the lunar cycle (waxing, waning, and full moons). The cycles of nature paralleled sacred events, of birthing, coupling, and dying. Initially the great spiritual principle was a goddess, and later a god. This divine being gave birth to a son (who in the early goddess stories becomes his mother's consort) or a daughter (as in the myth of Demeter and Kore) who was prized by this parent. Yet this child had to be sacrificed: Kore is abducted to Hades and forever must live there half the year; Dionysus is torn apart by his followers in an orgiastic revel; Christ is crucified.

In these stories, death or sacrifice is followed by images of rebirth or resur-rection. The old god dies, and is reborn in the new year. Christ is resurrected; Osiris is pieced back together; Kore returns to earth, and winter turns to spring. Such patterns of death and rebirth not only parallel seasonal changes, they also mirror the psychological pattern of renewal, as we die to what we were, we can then give birth to what we could be.

Later patriarchal religious stories, such as those of Christianity, retained the sense of mystery around the pattern of death and resurrection, but lost the equally important focus on the great miracle of sexuality. The earlier fertility reli-gions celebrated not only death and rebirth but the great miracle that birth results from sexual union. Thus, the most sacred objects of the earlier mystery religions celebrated male and female erotic energy in quite explicit ways. Some of this symbolism has carried over into Christian liturgy. For example, as Esther Harding has noted, the "holy font of baptism fertilized by plunging in the lighted candle" is a version of ancient erotic symbolism.[2] But the veneration of the miracle of sexual union at the base of such symbolism has been lost.

In modern life, we may experience initia-tion through love ini-tially as sexual passion and later by experi-encing any passionate connection (with our work, with God, with a cause or an idea), by experiencing divine redemptive love, or by experiencing a pro-found inner union in which love brings the dispersed parts of the psyche together and makes them one.

Indeed, in the present day, it might seem heretical to some to think of sexual intercourse as a major spiritual mystery, especially since the notion of the virgin birth became dogma. To the ancients, however, the celebration of passion, Eros, was as essential as the celebration of rebirth. In some traditions, as with the Hindu Shiva and Shakti, creation comes as a frankly erotic coupling of the gods. And as Harding has also demonstrated, the importance of the God being born of a "Virgin" did not come originally from any puritanical impulses. Classically, the term *Virgin* meant a woman who was "one-in-herself," who owned herself. She could be sexual and could have children, but she could not be someone else's wife or property. Generally, this meant that she knew the goddess within her and honored herself.

The process of initiation into the mysteries of death, passion, and birth venerated by the ancient mystery religions and by native people everywhere reflects the Soul archetypes of Seeker, Destroyer, Lover, and Creator.

Alchemy as Encoded Psychological Truth

Most people think that the alchemists were simply failed chemists, but their attempts to change lead into gold in the laboratory were not truly their pri-mary purpose—at least not the primary purpose of those who genuinely knew the tradition. Actually, alchemical processes and journey myths encode key stages of psychological growth and development.

Like many mystical, initiatory traditions, alchemy was handed down from master to student primarily in an oral fashion. Documents about alchemy writ-ten by masters of the alchemical tradition were purposely obscure so that only those initiated into its language could grasp the meaning. The alchemical masters were being appropriately careful that people who lacked a good Ego structure and a sense of ethics and morality would not stumble upon these techniques and injure either themselves or another.[3]

The goal of changing lead into gold on the physical plane was always secondary, for genuine alchemists, to the greater spiritual goal of raising leaden consciousness to golden consciousness. That is, we expand Ego consciousness to experience Soul, and in the process give birth to the Self. The achievement of changing lead to gold on the physical plane was thought to be an outer sign of the more important inward, spiritual accomplishment. The various chemical procedures that separate out the essence of the gold (Spirit) from lesser elements (matter) parallel the stages of the hero's spiritual journey out of consensual, Ego-dominated reality into the transmutable, spiritual domain, and then back, to transform physical reality as Spirit is made manifest on earth. The final stage of the alchemical process—symbolized by royalty, gold, and the sun—signifies the successful ability to manifest a spiritual truth on the physical plane.

Archetypal Influences on Soul Development in the Modern World

The four archetypes most active on the journey to becoming real—the Seeker, the Destroyer, the Lover, and the Creator—spoke to humankind through the ancient mystery cults and through alchemy, and they speak to us today through analysis and other processes that connect us to our depths. Together, they help us experience meaning and authenticity in our lives.

Each parallels a different element or aspect of the Soul. The Seeker corresponds to the Spirit; the Destroyer to Thanatos, the death wish; the Lover to Eros, the life force; and the Creator to the imagination (as focused by our own uniqueness). The direction of Spirit is upward. Spirit yearns to transcend physical existence and calls us to the quest to encounter our own Souls. The direction of Thanatos is downward and inward, exemplified in the mythic journey to the underworld and symbolized by the cocooning of a caterpillar in process of transformation into a butterfly. Eros presides over the Soul's outward motion and serves to connect us with others. The imagination is that part of the Soul that is the meaning-maker, the spinner of stories, images, and possibilities; its motion is expansive.

The Seeker

The Seeker seeks enlightenment and transformation, but initially is very controlled by the thinking process of the Ego. Seekers thus assume enlightenment is about becoming "better," more "accomplished," more "perfect." Questing is about transcending our mere humanity. This, as we have seen, is the call of Spirit, upward, onward, a constant challenge for self-improvement. Initiation eventually requires us to give up ascending so that we can descend into the depths of the Soul and the Soul's truth.

The Seeker's journey requires courage to break away from dependency and leap ahead into the unknown. We always fear what we do not understand or know. The person who is ignorant of his or her inner reality lives in terror of being alone and being thrust into confrontation with inner demons. The person who is ignorant of the outer world and how it operates lives in terror of being out in the world. Both are afraid of not knowing how to handle what might happen.

As Jung taught us, some of us are relatively more introverted and more at home in the inner world and love to explore it. Others are more at home in the outer world and love to explore that. We tend to be most risk-taking in the world we at least think we understand. The Seeker in each of us challenges us to explore what we most fear, so that by braving the unknown, we ourselves are transformed.

The Seeker's journey requires courage to break away from dependency and leap ahead into the unknown.

The Destroyer

In our inner journeys, we may first experience the Destroyer within the psyche as the negative Shadow, the potential selves we have repressed. Because they have been oppressed, locked up, hated, and reviled, they have not had a chance to grow and develop, so they become twisted, harmful in their expression.

Jung explains that the Shadow provides an opening to the unconscious. Taking responsibility for our own Shadows gives us access to the great riches of the underworld. That is why the underworld often is portrayed as filled with fine jewels and treasures guarded by great monsters. All heroes know we cannot gain the treasure without the willingness to confront the dragon. Where first we do so, we come as Warriors, believing the dragon is outside ourselves. We slay it and win the treasure and, of course, Ego strength. When we confront it again, we recognize that the dragon is ourselves, and we gain access to the treasures of our Souls.

All heroes know we cannot gain the treasure without the willingness to confront the dragon.

Actually, the Shadow is a benign form of the Destroyer, even though its eruption in the psyche may be terrifying; when integrated and thereby transformed, it always gives us a great gift. However, the Destroyer also comes as Thanatos, the death wish. Thanatos may erupt by way of the Shadow, destroying whatever we believed to be true about ourselves, but it is also the part of our psyche that causes us to age, sicken, and die. It is in league with death in its positive and negative guises.

The Lover

The inner Lover archetype is found in erotic life-force energy, symbolized by the marriage of the god and goddess within. A connection has often been made between marriage, psychological unity, and the nature of the cosmos.[4] June Singer explains that the primal separation expressed as sky/earth, male/female, light/darkness needs to be reunified. The symbol of this is the sacred marriage, which gives birth to the Self.[5] That is why genuine androgyny is more than just taping male and female roles together; it involves a fundamental reintegration of the psyche that moves beyond duality.

Jung taught that our entry into the world of the Soul came by way of the contrasexual element within the psyche; for men this is the anima, for women the animus. We can recognize this psychic figure in a number of ways: the anima or animus often figures prominently in our dreams; if we engage in an art form, it often figures in our art as well; and we find ourselves attracted to real men or women who embody the qualities of our inner animus or anima.

The inner Lover archetype is found in erotic life-force energy, symbolized by the marriage of the god and goddess within.

We often know about what is going on within us by looking at our external world. We learn to love the woman within through learning to love and respect women outside ourselves, individually and collectively. We learn to love the man within by learning to love and respect men outside ourselves, individually and collectively.

Although the sacred marriage of the god and the goddess is no longer a symbol in major Western religions, it is a fact of psychological life. The sacred marriage within the psyche is variously imaged as the union of opposing psychological attributes: male and female, body and Spirit, Soul and Ego, conscious and unconscious minds. The unification of each of these polarities—which comes when we are capable of feeling redemptive, compassionate love (agape) not only for another, but for ourselves—results in a deeper and more unified experience of the Self, characterized by greater and greater aspects of wholeness, potency, and power.

The Creator

The Creator archetype helps awaken the seed of our genuine identities deep within us. It presides over the process of birthing our lives. It is part of what we call our "imagination," and it provides focus to our imaginative efforts. Without imagination, we cannot create a life; but without a sense of genuine Self, our imagination is unfocused. It creates many projects and ideas, but they are all over the place, and ultimately unsatisfying.

Jean Houston calls this seed the "entelechy," emphasizing not its cosmic identity, but each person's unique, encoded life mission. Connection to the entelechy has always distinguished great men and women—whether artists,

It is the entelechy of an acorn to be an oak, it is the entelechy of a baby to be an adult, and of you to be the God only knows who or what. What happens in sacred psychology is the tapping into the entelechy of the self, the level most directly related to the Divine Self.
—Jean Houston

musicians, scientists, philosophers, or spiritual teachers. They have a sense of genuine uniqueness and mission.

Connecting with our Souls is most deeply about making the connection with the entelechy—our individual destinies—so that we live out what is our own to do and make our unique contribution to the planet. The technology of the entelechy is creative, tapping into our imaginative potential to create lives that emerge out of the truth about who we are.

●

You may experience these four Soul-related archetypes consciously in analysis (perhaps as they emerge in your dreams); through spiritual searching; or simply through the day-to-day experiences of your life—yearning for more, experiencing great loss or suffering, falling passionately in love, or experiencing great and unconscious authenticity, when suddenly what you are doing emerges organically and easily from who you are. In each of these cases, such experiences cause us, at least for the moment they are happening, to enter the mysteries of the Soul. Almost all of us have had these experiences. If we allow them to change us, we experience initiation.

In analysis or other analogous ways of making the inner journey, these archetypes mark different stages of the individuation process, that is, the process by which we explore our inner psychological world, clarifying our yearnings, integrating shadow elements in the psyche, balancing masculine and feminine aspects, and coming to terms with a deep and profound sense of who we are. The outcome of this process—if we have been conscious as we experienced it—is the birth of the Self. This accomplishment marks the return from the journey, which culminates in the transformation of the kingdom, a transformation that can happen only when we not only give birth to the Self but manifest that Self in real and tangible ways in the world. The process of doing so is the subject of the next chapter.

4

The Self:
Expressing Ourselves
in the World

The Self is an expression of wholeness, the end point of the individuation process. The journey has been completed, the treasure gained, and the kingdom—one's life—is being transformed based upon the new ordering principle.

The essence of the Self is paradox; for it is at one and the same time what is most unique about each of us and what connects our Ego to the transpersonal. The Self is also the entry point into a whole new way of living, moving us out of "life as struggle" and into abundance. Thus, the image of royalty is appropriate for the achievement of this stage. We become Kings and Queens of our kingdoms, and to the degree that we are true to our inner Selves, the areas of wasteland in our lives begin to blossom.

Rulers often hold fast to old ideas about how things should be done or even outdated notions about who we are. But the hero's journey is spiral, not linear. We need to keep journeying to renew ourselves and our kingdoms. The Ruler who clings too long to the old truth or identity turns into the evil tyrant, strangling the lifeblood out of the kingdom or the individual psyche. To avoid this, we must once again sacrifice the old Ruler and allow the new hero—returned fresh from the journey—to rule instead so that our kingdoms will be abundant and prosperous.[1]

We all have a kingdom: the life we are manifesting in the world.

The Grail Story

Many ancient cultures had a regular tradition of sacrificing the Ruler (or some surrogate) to renew the health of the kingdom. Such practices were a literal acting-out of a metaphorical, psychological truth about the necessity for renewal and change. The sense of death and rebirth inherent in the cycle of leadership is encoded in the traditional shout: "The King (Queen) is dead. Long live the King (Queen)!"

The Fisher King legends were part of the great grail stories, popular in the twelfth century. Psychologically, they are also about the necessity of constant renewal. In these stories, the Ruler is wounded and suffering. It is assumed that the King's wound is responsible for the kingdom having become a wasteland. The King must be healed for the kingdom to become healthy and prosperous again.

The King lives in the Grail Castle. He can be restored only by the actions of a younger knight, who asks the right question or questions to the grail and other related sacred objects. In the Parsifal legend, for example, Parsifal initially fails to ask the magical questions. As a result, he spends years in aimless wandering while the Fisher King continues to suffer and the kingdom remains a wasteland. Eventually, however, Parsifal finds his way back to the castle, he asks the questions, the King is healed, and the kingdom blossoms and prospers once more.

Many times in our lives, we find ourselves in the position of the Fisher King. Something is not right. We feel wounded, disconnected from ourselves, and our kingdoms reflect our inner state. Often, we do not initially notice our own wounding; we just find ourselves unhappy with our lives. Answers that previously worked for us no longer serve.

The story of Parsifal and the Fisher King is part of the larger Camelot story—of King Arthur, the Round Table, and the search for the Holy Grail. Idyllic images of Camelot in the golden years provide a good metaphor for the achievement of selfhood. Images of the suffering Fisher King provide a metaphor for what happens when the Self is wounded and suffering.[2] Jungians have been fascinated by the grail stories, and especially the story of Parsifal, because encoded within them is so much psychological truth—truth that teaches us how to heal the wounded Ruler within, so that we may experience our own versions of Camelot.

The Grail and the Suffering King

The Knights of the Round Table went in search of the Holy Grail, which was said to have served as a goblet at the Last Supper and was supposed to have captured some of Christ's blood during the Crucifixion. The Grail therefore speaks to the transformative power of blood ("This is my blood, shed for thee") and of suffering.

Often dualistic images in the psyche—such as those of the successful Ruler (King Arthur) and the suffering Ruler (the Fisher King) of the wasteland kingdom—are resolved by a third, inclusive image that transforms the duality into unity. One of the Kings implicit in the Grail myth is Christ. But this is not only the Christ as a Risen Lord, but Christ crucified, wearing a crown of thorns,

We have all the major characters of the Grail story within us. The part of us that is fragmented, split, and wounded—that knows of the splendor of the Soul, but cannot connect that splendor with our everyday lives—is the Fisher King. The young knight is the Seeker in each of us, yearning for the Grail. The Grail offers the capacity for renewal, forgiveness, and transformation. It also is within us.

having been forced to sit on a throne under a sign that read "King of the Jews." It is important here to remember that in addition to the historical and theological significance of all great sacred stories, they generally also have deep psychological, metaphorical meaning.

Metaphorically, the Christ story tells us of the process of the birth, death, and rebirth of the Self. Therefore, it is possible to gain *psychological* insight from the Christ story, whether or not one "believes" in it in any historical or religious sense. This truth has to do with the essential process of moving through suffering into rebirth, wholeness, and redemption.

The experience of "crucifixion" is essential to the Ruler archetype—that is why Christ is envisioned as a King, even when crying out "My God, my God, why hast Thou forsaken me"[3]—and to the psychological component of the birth of the Self. This is what manifesting one's Soul reality in the world often feels like until the resurrection or rebirth, when conflicts between realities on the physical and spiritual planes are resolved. The symbolic meaning, then, of the Resurrection and prophecies of the Second Coming of Christ is the state of consciousness that allows for full expression of one's Soul essence on the physical plane so that there is no contradiction between the two.

The archetype of the Self finds positive expression as wholeness; but much of the time we experience it as inner conflict, so intense it can produce real suffering. Until we have fully birthed the Self in times of transition, as well as in the evolution of that Self over the lifetime, we will always feel some inner suffering. Allowing this inner pain to emerge into genuine and painful conflict between our Souls and Egos, our masculine and feminine natures, or our inner mandate and outer responsibilities and limitations creates the suffering that forges and births the Self. Or to say it more simply, allowing ourselves to feel the pain of our inner conflicts begins a process that generally will resolve them into a new unity.

Peace comes from accepting and opening to the conflict, especially to what modern Christian theologian Parker Palmer calls "the greatest paradox of all: that to live we have to die."[4] Generally, it does not come at all until we have felt the full extent of the *inner suffering* we all have. Unless we feel that, we do not generate the heat that galvanizes the new unity of the psyche.

The Psychological Meaning of the Cross

In alchemy, too, transformation comes only after a painful experience of inner paradox. The similarity of the symbolism suggests that the psychological truth expressed in both Christian and alchemical symbolism is very deep, powerful, and archetypal. In alchemy, the resolution of the paradox that Parker Palmer identifies as the "cross" is symbolized by a sacred inner marriage of masculine and feminine, consciousness and the unconscious, Spirit and Soul.

Psychologically [the story of the Fisher King] reflects the fact that again and again the outwardly crystallized conception of the Self, after becoming a content of the collective consciousness, grows old and must therefore be transformed, rejuvenated or replaced by another form. This has to happen in order for the eternally self-renewing psychic life to flow up from the depths and for its ungraspable, eternally fresh and unexpected aspects to be retained.—Emma Jung and Marie-Louise von Franz

This symbolic inner marriage is also a death and rebirth experience and is accompanied by profound suffering. It is symbolized, as Titus Burckhardt explains, by "an inverted T" or "cross." The vertical axis of this "T" or "cross" represents the union of consciousness (upper) with unconsciousness (lower). The horizontal axis represents masculine and feminine energy. Consciousness (Ego) and unconsciousness (Soul) are Spirit, which serves as a catalytic agent, and "acts on the original agent like a magic word."

The forces of male and female are "represented by two serpents, winding themselves up the vertical axis of the cross until at the level of the horizontal arms they finally meet and embrace one another in the center, subsequently being transmuted into a single serpent fastened upright to the cross."[5]

Translated into the terms of the Grail myth, this means that we begin by searching for the grail in an active, conscious, and "masculine," or yang, way. Somewhere on the journey, this conscious, active experience becomes an initiation, opening us up so we become receptive, ensouled, and "feminine," or yin, like a grail. Doing so awakens us to Spirit, which heals the dualistic split that characterizes the life of the Ego. This healing not only unifies our consciousness and allows for the birth of the Self (when Ego serves Soul), it also allows us to reconcile the contradictions so we accept with joy the responsibility for being the Lords or Rulers of our own lives. But the only way to do so is to stay with the suffering caused by the internal contradictions and paradox, allowing that suffering to heat up the alchemical vial so that Ego and Soul, masculine and feminine, can be "cooked" in a way that transmutes and unifies both.

The risen Christ is Christ the Lord.[6] The arisen Self, in alchemy, is symbolized by the androgynous monarch. In each of us, the fully realized Self is experienced as a sense of inner depth, peace, and wholeness. Most of us know this state only in fleeting moments when we feel completely whole and ourselves. Such moments, however brief, have a magical quality that speaks to us of what life can, and perhaps will, be like.

> *[The Cross's] very structure suggests the oppositions of life—left and right, up and down. It symbolizes the way we are pulled between this person and that, between our conflicting obligations on life's "horizontal" plane. And the Cross gives mute testimony of the way we are stretched upon the "vertical" dimension of life, between the demands of the divine and the fears of flesh. To walk the way of the cross is to be impaled upon contradictions, torn by oppositions and tension and conflict.—Parker Palmer*

The Responsibility to Be Conscious

When Parsifal visits the Grail Castle for the first time, he is given a Sword. He then sees the Grail procession, which includes a Spear dripping blood, carried by a squire; a Grail that blazes with light, carried by a damsel; and a dish or bowl, carried by a maiden. Parsifal could heal the King were he to ask the meaning of this procession and these objects—but he fails to ask.

The experience of visiting the castle, and the symbolic objects and figures found there, corresponds to the archetypes of Soul initiation. The gift of the Sword represents the call to the Quest (the Seeker); the Spear dripping blood represents Death (the Destroyer); the Grail represents Eros, the feminine aspect of spirituality (the Lover); and the dish or bowl represents the archetype of the Creator, because when we give birth to our true Selves, not only do we feel "fed" and nourished, but our actions naturally nourish others.

Parsifal and the Wounded King represent different parts of a psyche. Parsifal has the great Soul experiences—as all of us do—but he fails to inquire about their meaning, and hence, he does not heal the King. Thus we see that it is not enough to have the experience of the Quest—of Initiation, Death, Eros, and Birth. We must make the experience conscious. Only in that way do we make the meaning known to ourselves and others.[7]

Most of us have experienced calls to the quest—great loves, passions, and losses; internal and external suffering and conflict; and opportunities to create and miscreate our own lives—but if we take them in stride without recognizing their Soul purpose, we may be untouched by these miracles. To be transformed, we have to wake up and experience wonder. We need to ponder such events, ask to have their meaning revealed to us, and allow ourselves to recognize that we have been touched by the transpersonal world.

Both Parsifal and that other great grail knight, Lancelot, initially fail to ask the meaning because they are so overwhelmed by the procession that they get sleepy. As with all of us who are conscious only at the level of the Ego, they were not awake. Even as great knights, they were in some real way sleepwalking.

The Self is not fully realized in the positive image of the healed monarch until we are willing to accept the burden of consciousness and not only have initiatory experiences, but allow the wisdom they bring to be integrated into consciousness. Living royally is accepting the responsibility of knowing what we know—and inquiring what we might know.

All Selves are fundamentally wounded when Ego and Soul are disconnected from each other.

We know we are emerging from the journey when the split stops working for us, and we begin not only to let our conscious minds and Egos know what we have been up to, but to act on what we now know. The Wounded King is, of course, none other than our wounded Self, for all Selves are fundamentally wounded when Ego and Soul are disconnected from each other.

Eros and Knowledge: Beyond Left-Brain Consciousness

The suffering monarch's wound is always located in the genitals.[8] There are many layers of significance here. First is the cultural devaluation of Eros, which spiritually cripples all of us. Healing the wound to Eros—literally and figuratively associated with genitalia—heals the Soul because it is the aspect of Soul that has been systematically devalued and denigrated by the culture.

Eros is associated with Soul and also with the feminine. Marion Zimmer Bradley's best-selling novel *The Mists of Avalon* tells the Camelot story from the point of view of Morgaine le Faye, a priestess of the old goddess religion, which is being destroyed as patriarchal Christianity takes over the Round Table. The denial of the goddess is part of the creation of the new order; it is also responsible for its woundedness. Without the goddess, without the principle of Eros and the feminine as sacred forces, passion becomes destructive (the adulterous love of Guinevere and Lancelot creates a schism in the kingdom). But beyond that there can be no real health or wholeness until Eros, the goddess, and women are restored to their rightful place of honor.[9]

The grail itself is a symbol of the proper relationship of the masculine and the feminine; that is why the knights had to search for it. The kingdom had become overly male and, as Christianity replaced earlier fertility religions, disrespectful of the sacred energy of Eros. The chalice itself symbolizes "feminine" energies, filled with "masculine" spirit. The grail, then represents sexual union between the masculine and the feminine on a psychological rather than bodily level.

The genitals also are associated with generativity and fertility. The wasteland suggests a failure of fertility at every level: barrenness of womb, of land, and of vision.

The grail itself is a symbol of the proper relationship of the masculine and the feminine.

Rulers at this time and in this ancient tradition were seen as symbolically married to the kingdom. Any major problem within the kingdom—and certainly the kingdom's becoming a wasteland—signifies a failure of that marriage. Like the sacred marriage of alchemy or Christ's marriage to the Church, the Ruler's marriage to the land signifies the union of a number of opposite principles: male and female, Ego and Soul, inner reality and outer manifestation. The failure of this marriage is evidenced by a lack of fertility and prosperity in either the outer or the inner life.

The healing of the wound to the genitals begins with connecting all our disparate parts so that one's spirit, mind, emotions, and sexuality will work together and cooperate with one another. Earlier in life, we split off in order to create the Ego so that our sexuality can come under the control of consciousness. We do this for good reason: to develop a sense of discipline or self-restraint, responsibility to self and others—and to be sure we are not all overrun with children.

This is an important and good lesson, but it leaves us all wounded. When we remember that Eros governs relatedness, we understand that we cannot have a fully integrated consciousness until the primary wound in the genitals is healed. It is also Eros, or Love, that connects up the discrete parts of the psyche: Ego and Soul, consciousness and unconsciousness, masculinity and femininity.

Healing this wound restores a unity beyond the split of spirit and flesh, mind and body. A result of this inner connection of heart and genitals, generative and excremental power, is a capacity for relationship based on the knowledge that we cannot create the new (including the new Self) without to some extent destroying or letting go of the old.

The unity that is the result of Eros, healing internal conflicts and tension, provides the capacity for a different kind of consciousness than that which is mental only. The requirement of consciousness, which is the prerequisite to claiming power over one's own life, is not just mind or left-brain knowing. The biblical usage of the verb "to know" as a way of describing sexual intercourse is key here. We need to become conscious in a way that combines mind, body, heart, and Soul. We need to experience our suffering and our transformation with the same body/mind connectedness that characterizes sexual intimacy at its most profound and beautiful. This is the kind of knowing, the kind of consciousness and opening to life and experience that makes alchemical transformation of consciousness possible. In this knowledge, the crucified Lord becomes the Risen King; the alchemical couple disintegrated in the vial become the androgynous Monarch; and you and I fully experience our suffering, make it conscious, and emerge the Rulers of our own lives.

Asking the Sacred Questions

In the Fisher King legends, the King is healed when the grail seeker asks the meaning of the grail and other sacred symbols (signifying the process of making the unconscious conscious). In many versions of the Parsifal story, that question focused on the relationship of humankind to the grail and the grail to God. The traditional question, "Who does the grail serve?" and sometimes also, "Who serves the grail?" remind us that the grail serves us, we serve the grail, and the grail is in the service of God. This has a cautionary meaning. The Ruler must always serve God (rather than rule for Ego gratification), and it is God's grace (symbolized by the grail) that then also preserves the kingdom and the Ruler. On a more psychological level, the grail serves Soul.

Modern seekers need to ask these same questions. As we ask the sacred questions, we open to our Souls and to living life from a deeper level. Each sacred object calls a question from us. The gift of the sword calls us to ask what to do with that sword and with our lives. The wounded Ruler inside ourselves calls us to ask, with compassion, "What ails you?" which signifies our readiness to be healed. The spear dripping blood requires us to ask what we must sacrifice, and the dish or bowl, which gives everyone the food they most love, calls us to ask to know what we truly need so that we can separate that from what we think we need or want. The Grail calls us to open to the sense of enlightenment and wholeness, and to ask what our Souls then require of us.

When we ask the proper question elicited by each of these objects—and hence find their archetypal meaning in our lives—the King or Queen within is healed and the wasteland is transformed.

To be conscious is to wake up and take a new kind of responsibility for being true to ourselves and constructive members of the human race. This is what it means to be royal—to be fully awake, conscious, in your body, feeling your feelings, able to express who you are in the world, and willing to take full responsibility for your life.

Experiencing the Self is not simply about being virtuous. It is also about tapping into the fullness of one's capacities, including one's capacities to do harm. And no integration of conflicting qualities lasts forever. However unified our consciousness, sooner or later that consciousness will split, and the journey will begin again. Even King Arthur's Round Table did not last forever; one epoch in history gave way to another.

Expressing Ourselves in the World

It is not a feeling for the mystery of living, or a sense of awe, wonder, or fear, [which is at the root of religion, but] rather the questions what to do with the feeling for the mystery of living, what to do with awe, wonder, or fear.—Abraham Joshua Heschel

When we commit our lives to the service of our deep Soul purpose, we can never go back to life as we knew it. There is a loss as well as a gain. Emma Jung and Marie-Louise von Franz, however, see the abolition of the Round Table as also resulting from a failure of Parsifal to bring the grail wisdom back to ordinary life. Parsifal was enamored of Soul, and declined the return. "Perceval should not have taken himself into the seclusion of the Grail Castle; in order to remain in the picture, he should have brought the grail to the Round Table, so that instead of Spirit being divorced from the world, the world would have been impregnated by the Spirit."[10]

The issue for us today is not simply to create the unified Self—connecting Ego and Soul, heart and head, male and female—but also to express this Self in the everyday business of living our lives.

The pilgrim, the wandering Soul in each of us, needs to be seduced into developing an expanded, deepened consciousness by awe and mystery, but the Ruler is grounded by the task of ordinary living. The Jewish tradition emphasizes "daily acts" spirituality demonstrated by keeping traditions and laws. The discipline of Zen helps people move out of striving into being, out of a state of childlike becoming into conscious adult living. Zen master Shunyu Suzuki tells how focusing on the task itself helps us become like the Buddha:

When you bow, you should just bow; when you sit, you should just sit; when you eat, you should just eat. If you do this, the universal nature is there. . . . No matter what the situation, you cannot neglect Buddha, because you yourself are Buddha.[11]

Although the traditions and practices of Christianity, Judaism, and Zen Buddhism are quite different in form and emphasis, each calls us to the challenging task of moving from the numinous to the work of day-to-day living—or better yet, integrating the uncommon and the ordinary. It is not the separate, transpersonal experience that ultimately matters, but how such experience informs the ways we live our lives. That is what the return is about.

The Self and Inner Balance

Are we forever doomed in expressing ourselves in the world to experience transient unity and then return to suffering? No. That is why, in psychological terms, certain major figures are present in the classical court. If the Self were only the Ruler, the cycle of suffering and redemption might be endless. Some Rulers developed ways to stay balanced and renewed, so they did not become either tyrants or suffering Fisher Kings. They had a Magician, a Sage, and a Fool. The figures of the classical court keep the kingdom in balance. Each represents wholeness in a number of ways. Each has its own kind of connection to the transpersonal realm. Each is androgynous. Yet each also complements the others, together creating a whole greater than the sum of the parts.

Every great Ruler needs a Magician (think of King Arthur and Merlin) to look into the crystal ball and predict the future, to heal the sick, to create rituals that bond the people of the kingdom in community, and to maintain an ongoing connection with the spiritual dimension of life. Magicians, by looking in their crystal balls, anticipate trouble and warn Rulers if they are getting cut off from their Souls, or simply if danger looms ahead in any way. They heal the Ruler's wounds that are causing problems in the kingdom. Finally, the Magician helps create a positive energy field in the castle, an energy field that attracts positive people and events to the Ruler and hence to the kingdom as well.

Great Rulers are also well advised to have a court Sage to serve as an objective advisor. Rulers often are deceived by flatterers, or let their own feelings and interests interfere with their judgment. The advice of a Sage, who identifies only with truth itself and not at all with the court politics or forces of the moment, keeps Rulers from falling prey to their illusions and vanities.

Finally, every Ruler needs a court Fool or Jester (as with Shakespeare's Fools) to entertain, to bring joy to the castle, and also to say things to the Ruler that might get anyone else hanged. Fools often hear and know things that would be hidden from anyone taken more seriously. Most importantly, they can make fun of the Ruler, and puncture any growing egotism, pomposity, or arrogance.

The metaphor of the court is important here. Certainly there are Sages in ivory towers who do not advise Rulers; there are great shamans or Magicians who work alone and do not lend their aid to the tribe, community, or court; and there are Fools out wandering the earth who do not contribute to community life. The Ruler, Magician, Sage, and Fool of the court help each other and lend their unique talents to the creation of a healthy, prosperous, and joyous kingdom.

On the psychological level, each of the four archetypes is an aspect of the integrated Self. When all four are in balance, the psyche is peaceful, and the cycle of suffering and healing is suspended.

The Ruler

The Ruler is associated with the creation of psychological wholeness and order. The Ruler's goal for the psyche is the creation of a single, unified, fully manifested Self. The main function of a Ruler is to order the kingdom, and the result of the process is a sense of peace, unity, and harmony: all the dispersed pieces come together.

The Ruler is the committee chairperson who sees to the order of the psyche. It is also the reeducated Ego, which, at its highest levels, no longer needs to protect the psyche from the Soul. If the Ruler is highly developed, it will make certain that each of our inner voices, and all the archetypes active in our lives, gets a chance to speak and be heard.

The Ruler's goal for the psyche is the creation of a single, unified, fully manifested Self.

If our Ruler is not very well developed, it will impose order by repressing some parts, creating a split between the accepted and the exiled parts of the psyche. Taken to extremes, this may lead eventually to internal civil war, suffering, and possibly even illness in the psyche. Most of us have Rulers who are somewhere in between. They exclude or repress many potential parts of ourselves, but try for harmonious, orderly expression of many others. In a healthy psyche, there will be significant diversity in the voices heard from.

The Ruler can be the benevolent monarch who can govern well because he or she speaks for Soul or Spirit in the world. In this case, it means that the Ruler archetype is directly connected to the Soul and makes judgments between different aspects of the psyche not only by listening to Ego concerns, but much more fundamentally by consulting the will of his or her Soul.

The Magician

The Magician is the element that can continually heal and transform the Self when the order gets too rigid. It acts within the psyche as an agent of regeneration and renewal, for oneself and others. This is the part of the psyche that can integrate the Shadow and transform it into useful energy.

The Magician is an inner alchemist who is able to transmute base emotions and thoughts into more developed ones, to help us learn new behavior patterns, and to turn primitive behaviors into more sophisticated and adequate ones. And, as the originator of the placebo effect, the Magician can cure illnesses (and create them). When Ego operates in the service of Soul, it is the archetype that helps make the process of creating or transforming our lives a *conscious* one.

Although all the archetypes associated with the Self help provide a link with the numinous, the Magician connects with the power of the divine to save, redeem, or forgive. It also allows for these abilities in ourselves as we learn to forgive ourselves and others and through doing so, completely, to transform negative situations into possibilities for more growth and intimacy.

The Magician is the part of the psyche that can integrate the Shadow and transform it into useful energy.

The Sage

The Sage is the part of the psyche that is experienced in meditation as the objective Self. It watches our thoughts and feelings, but is beyond either. As such, the Sage helps us face whatever is true in our lives and transcend our smaller selves to be one with cosmic truths. When we stop fighting truth, we can be free. In Jung's typology, it is the Wise Old Man or Woman in our dreams who gives trustworthy counsel.

The Sage within is that part of us that observes when we meditate or go through the day-to-day events in our lives. It is that part of us that can watch our thoughts and feelings and allow them to flow without being attached to either.[12]

In therapy, the Sage allows us to notice our pathological patterns, and to see the way we have been projecting our own scripts or perceptions onto the world. It observes those patterns and is capable of experiencing greater truth beyond them. The difference between reflecting reality in a relatively adequate way and through distorted thinking is like the difference between looking at the world reflected in a calm pond and in one in which the water is moving.[13]

The Sage is the Wise Old Man or Woman in our dreams who gives trustworthy counsel.

The Fool

The Fool is the element of the psyche that represents multiplicity of consciousness. Like the Court Fools who make fun of the King or Queen, the internal

Fool (or Trickster) continually undercuts our sense of a unified Self. It is responsible for Freudian slips and other indications that what the conscious mind thinks it wants is not the whole story. The Fool teaches us that we are always expressing our *selves* in the world, not a single Self. The Fool is thus often seen first as a disconcerting shadow Self, the forerunner of the new emerging Self. While it is not the Id, the Fool is the archetype that helps educate, transform, and integrate the Id with other aspects of consciousness—and hence is the repository of psychic energy.

The Self that is not only realized but constantly renewed and renewing, therefore, needs all four of these archetypes. Indeed, there is always some sense of repression in rule only by the Ruler. All that royal order is stabilizing but limiting. The Ruler, for instance, if at a high level, might want us to express all twelve archetypes because doing so increases our success and effectiveness. Theoretically, however, the Ruler would not want an archetype expressed that did not contribute to the overall health of the kingdom or that did not conform to the existing order. The archetype that does not fit in might well be exiled or sent to the dungeon. The Magician focuses on moving any archetype to its more positive manifestation so it will be useful. The Sage helps us see that the essential truth or gift of each is recognized so that rational decisions might be made about them.

The Fool wants them *all* expressed for the joy of it. To the Fool, it does not matter that doing so contributes to individual development, to inner peace or wisdom, or to productivity. The point for the Fool is to express all of one's many selves because it feels good to do so. The Fool, then, provides us space to express our selves in the world, not so much to transform that world as simply to give expression to who we are.

The Fool teaches us that we are always expressing our Selves in the world, not a single Self.

●

Together the four major court figures help us be integrated and responsible, healthy and connected, honest and wise, multifaceted and joyous. They are, indeed, the reward at the end of the journey. As we express our Selves in the world—having experienced suffering and loss, and having discovered that we do survive them—we are no longer controlled by fear. Therefore, we are more free to take risks. Because we have discovered our identities and vocations, we make a genuine contribution to the world. Because we have tapped into our creativity, we are likely to find ways to be rewarded for our efforts. Because we have learned how to love, we tend to receive love from others as well.

When the Ego dominated, we lived in a world of scarcity, but now things feel abundant. We understand, moreover, that the issue is often learning to recognize and let in all the many gifts of life. Having experienced miracles on our journeys, we no longer believe we have to do it all ourselves; indeed, if something is truly ours, nothing or no one can take it away. If it is not, nothing or no one can make it stay.

The more grounded we become in manifesting our unique selves, the less we need to have to be happy. We do not need lots of work, we need only the work that is our own. We may not need many loves, only those that truly will satisfy. We may not need so many possessions, but really treasure the ones we have, because they reflect something in ourselves. We may not even need as much money, because we spend it on things and activities we really enjoy.

Slowly, but surely, we begin to discover that we do not need to climb the ladder of success to be happy; we need only to be fully ourselves. If we do so, we have everything. The cycle of repetitive suffering abates, partly because it comes to be expected and hence not feared, and partly because of the growing realization that we do not always have to be a unified Self to feel whole. The Fool responds to inner plurality, not by suffering, but by offering the discrepant pieces of the psyche the option of dancing with one another. Whether the music of the Soul, which they dance to, is discordant or harmonious, whether the dance is beautiful or awkward, is of little consequence. The dance is for its own sake.

5

Beyond Heroism: The Dance

The last archetype described in this book is the Fool, which is included with the archetypes of the return because it governs the expression of our selves in the world. However, the Fool never really fits neatly into any classification. We find the Fool at the beginning and end of our journeys; but during them we only glimpse the Fool on the margins—we don't usually admit much of it into consciousness. The Ruler symbolizes the achievement of consciousness and of the true Self; the Fool, however, helps us move beyond ourselves, beyond heroism, beyond individuation, beyond consciousness, into ecstasy.

At its earliest levels, the Fool is aligned with a very primitive part of the psyche. It is related to the deepest repository of our instinctual drives and urges, wishes we may not want to acknowledge to ourselves or others. In Freudian terms, it is closely related to the Id and the basic drives and instincts of the species. Even in what are often seen as relatively primitive cultures, Trickster figures, which illustrate this early mode, were usually already outside of the socially acceptable personas, and yet, as we have seen, recognized as contributing to our enjoyment of life.

We do not have theology, we dance.
—Japanese monks to Joseph Campbell

We can learn about the growth and development of the Trickster part of ourselves by looking to myth and legend. Jung saw the Trickster as appearing "in picaresque talks, in carnivals and revels, in sacred and magical rites, in man's religious fears and exaltation" and in the "mythology of all ages." In his view, the Trickster in such myths "is an archetypal psychic structure of extreme antiquity that in its clearest manifestations is a faithful copy of an absolutely undifferentiated human consciousness, corresponding to the psyche that has hardly left the animal level."[1]

Trickster Myths and the Development of the Ego

Trickster figures occurred in myth and ritual so that people could recognize that shadow form of their own consciousness and laugh at it, knowing that it was still theirs, even though much of it had to be sacrificed to the building of culture. But Jung also notes that the Trickster is not just an anachronistic form of human consciousness; it has continuing utility in individual and collective life. At first, it represents completely undifferentiated instinct. Humankind needed to move beyond such an existence to develop consciousness. We can never completely leave the instinctual, or we lose all our energy, our zip!

The Trickster in many native American myths is a creature of great appetites who, like an infant, has not even learned to separate parts of itself from the environment. Paul Radin recounts the adventure of the hero of the Sioux Winnebago Trickster cycle, who takes a nap while roasting some ducks and gives his anus the job of keeping watch over the food. The food, however, is stolen, and when he awakens, he is so mad at his anus that he burns it as punishment for its failure. But then he smells something good cooking, which is, of course, his own flesh, and tasting a bit of the dropping fat, he determines it tastes pretty good. So he ends up eating his own intestines.

While we might laugh at the Trickster, feeling superior to its foolishness, we are all quite capable of letting our appetites get so out of control that they become self-destructive. If you have ever had a hangover, kicked yourself for cheating on your diet, or been too impassioned to remember to use birth control, you know how easy it is to forget the consequences of acting on your impulses.

Young children, of course, slowly learn to distinguish their own bodies from their surroundings, their own emotions from those of their parents, and eventually, as they grow older, to make connections between certain actions and their consequences. Although adults may be able to differentiate easily the parts of their bodies from objects or beings in the external world, they may not be able to sort out the difference between their genuine thoughts, values, feelings, and opinions and those of their parents and friends or those they encounter in the media. Either we get caught up doing what someone else wants us to do because we cannot separate our desires from theirs, or we simply assume that others share our views, without checking out to see if this is, in fact, true.

The Trickster part of us is activated anytime we need to find out what is "me" and what is "not me." Stories of the Trickster teach us to connect up parts of ourselves to become an integrated whole. The Trickster's sexuality, for instance, is initially unbridled, lustful, and disconnected from any sense of love or responsibility. The Winnebago Trickster's penis originally is so big he has to carry it on his back. It is so disconnected from the rest of him that he sends it ahead to have intercourse with the daughter of the chief of the upcoming village. As you might imagine, this creates a huge uproar in the village. The Trickster's sexuality is totally detached from the rest of his identity, not unlike much of adolescent sexuality.

Eventually the Winnebago Trickster's penis is chewed up by a chipmunk the Trickster is aggressively pursuing, giving the penis its present human (diminished) shape. It then can become attached to the body. The chewing up of the primitive, huge, disconnected penis so that it assumes its smaller, more manageable size is similar in significance to male and female circumcision in puberty rituals, the wounding and taming of the Trickster's unbridled and disconnected lust benefit the culture.

The Winnebago Trickster's genitals not only diminish in size and strength, but also become integrated as part of his body; thus their urges are potentially controlled by other elements of his being. However, he is not entirely prepared for a "meaningful relationship" until he also has experienced what it is like to be the other gender. Initially, the Trickster's sexuality is polymorphously perverse and undifferentiated. Hence, he (or she) encompasses both sexes. This is why adolescents, for example, are so attracted to unisex hairstyles and clothes, and why, when not overly contaminated by the homophobia of the culture, they may be erotically attracted to both sexes.

The Trickster in each of us needs some time to wander and explore the world, simply to respond to our hunger for sensations and experiences and to find out who we are, what we like and do not like, what we feel and do not feel, what we think and do not think.

The Winnebago Trickster tricks a chief by becoming a woman and marrying and bearing him several children until he is discovered and escapes. The most powerful Trickster figures are androgynous, and may express this through cross-dressing. They know what it is like to be both a man and a woman, and hence have a kind of wholeness that makes them not need a member of the opposite sex for a sense of completion. They feel turned on by the world and go around in a general state of joyful arousal.

Those who allow their Trickster side charisma and power do not hold in psychic energy out of fear; they can communicate and relate well to both sexes because they have activated both their male and female sides. And they do not repress their sexual feelings, even when those feelings would be deemed socially inappropriate (although the wise Trickster learns not to act on these "inappropriate feelings"). They also waste little energy compromising their own desires in order to please others. They know what pleases and satisfies them, and are not afraid of being eccentric or unusual.

The Fool is never really bound by conventional society, but does learn the rules of that society and how to play the game effectively. This ability includes playing an appropriate social role (or roles) without identifying with those roles.

Fools who take the time to know what they like, and think, and feel can shift roles as situations and circumstances change without experiencing an identity crisis. They know they are not their roles. Near the end of the Winnebago cycle, for example, the Trickster again takes an identity as a male, marries, and has children, but no one for a moment thinks that role will define or tame him.

The Trickster in each of us needs some time to wander and explore the world, simply to respond to our hunger for sensations and experiences and to find out who we are, what we like and do not like, what we feel and do not feel, what we think and do not think. Without this, we never have any true sense of identity.[2] That is why so many of the most powerful and interesting people have sown some wild oats, have made big mistakes, and often have learned from having botched things up.

Tricksters: Exploration and Self-Expression

Tricksters also learn mastery through experimentation: taking machines apart to see how they work; trying to invent new things; beginning an entrepreneurial project; trying out an art form; learning how the politics of an organization work; or trying to find out what makes other people tick. The Trickster's curiosity, expressed in such ways, also helps us learn what kind of work we like to do, and provides us with at least beginning-level skills to start that work.

The Trickster's energy can and should be bound and channeled, but it should never be totally repressed. And, of course, in the individual's life, vacations and frequent time-outs for play and creature comforts the body loves help people stay sane, happy, and well balanced, as does a good sense of humor.

The Trickster's energy can and should be bound and channeled, but it should never be totally repressed.

The mature Trickster in each of us is an iconoclastic epicure who has highly developed and individualistic tastes, and who finds socially acceptable outlets for all the many facets of his or her personality. Highly creative, Tricksters are able to create life-styles that fit them and allow for the full expression of all the things they love to do, even if those things seem unusual to many. Although these life-styles may put them on the boundary of society (think of the life-styles of many artists and musicians, for instance), they are still a positive force within it.

In old age, the Fool teaches us to let go of the need for power and goals and achievement so that we can live each day as it comes. We can feel this way any time in life when the awareness of mortality leads us to savor each moment of life as precious for its own sake.

The Fool and the Hero

The Fool elements of the psyche split off from its heroic elements. That is why the virtuous and good hero, who begins as a pristine Innocent full of integrity, faith, and courage, often has a Trickster sidekick, who can provide the balance of street smarts the hero will need to survive, but who may not be consistent with the heroic self-image.

It is not just the hero's folly, however, but all his or her foolish elements that need to be split off just enough so that they are not in control, yet not repressed, either. They are in the position of the loyal and trusted sidekick. Through the dialogue between the more "heroic" Ego and the Trickster or Fool sidekick, a strategy can be found for saving the victim (Orphan) that is both appropriate to the circumstances (Trickster) and moral (Innocent). Often the Trickster sidekick (or the Trickster hero when both are in one person) is able to find the clever way around obstacles and does not have to take them on directly.

The Ego—buttressed by the Innocent, Orphan, Warrior, and Caregiver— identifies with order. It wants an orderly world and is horrified by chaos, in the culture or the psyche. The Fool, however, is allied with chaos and disorder and hence with the principle of entropy in the universe. Sometimes, the Fool splits off because the Ego would not and could not approve or allow what it plans to do.

The Fool, the Id, and the Dance

It is only when we have developed a long-standing relationship to our internal Fool sidekick that we can "trust the process," even in perilous times. When that trust is well developed, we can enjoy the ride, as children love roller coasters. They just hang on and scream—but the screaming is not real terror, only fun and exhilaration.

It is important to recognize that just as the Innocent, Orphan, Warrior, and Caregiver help develop the Ego, but are not the Ego, the Fool helps to transform the Id, but is not itself the Id. The Fool helps us first dissociate from primary instinctual life so that we can develop consciousness. But it also provides a link with the instinctual and with our Souls, a link that is often outside of consciousness itself.

When consciousness is integrated, the wandering Fool becomes the Court Fool or Jester, with an established and accepted role in the psyche. Prior to this alchemical transformation, the Ego tends to operate to repress instinctual life—if it did not do so, we would not be civilized! However, most of us tend to overdo it; we lose our force, charisma, and power because we are cut off from the instinctual ground of our nature.

People who have taken their journeys and developed an integrated Self can trust their instincts. When they live by their deepest, essential Selves, they can "follow their bliss" without fear of doing harm to themselves or another. They know how to trust the process of life, and when they do so, life can become a dance—an expression of pure joy.

Beyond Individuation: Radical Plurality of the Psyche

James Hillman in *Re-Visioning Psychology* suggests that polytheism is a better model for psychology than monotheism, because the idea of one God creates in us the fantasy that we can become one Self. He reflects the Wise Fool's perspective as he argues for the acceptance of the great diversity of potential ways of being and behaving alive within each of us.

Hillman calls on psychology to "see through its main convictions and assumptions" and thus "dissolve the literal belief in persons by repersonifying them into metaphors." "Then personality," he continues, "may be imagined in a new way: that I am an impersonal person, a metaphor enacting multiple personifications, mimetic to images in the heart that are my fate, and that this Soul which projects me has archetypal depths that are alien, inhuman and impersonal. My so-called personality is a persona through which Soul speaks."

Hillman speaks of the "personified archetypes as Gods," in a polytheistic tradition, who "present themselves each as a guiding spirit (spiritus rector) with ethical positions, instinctual reactions, modes of thought and speech, and claims upon feeling. These persons, by governing my complexes, govern my life."[3]

Except for brief, transcendent moments of unity, each one of us lives with inner plurality—plurality that is usually not even integrated. Indeed, we generally are capable of living with such inner plurality because we repress knowledge of the parts of us that do not fit our image of ourselves. Or, we engage in self-improvement projects to try to get them to fit. Yet it is part of the human condition that we will experience some radical plurality in our lives: different parts of ourselves, for instance, will want different things. The Fool teaches us to stop denying that this is so and learn to enjoy it.

Expressing Ourselves in the World

Hal Stone, in *Embracing Our Selves,* provides a practice for helping people to reexperience the richness of the plurality within them.[4] He has them recognize that their psyches are made up of many potential selves, some of which we repress, deny, or hide. Using Gestalt techniques, Stone has people speak and move from these other selves, reinviting them into consciousness and into rich communion with the world. People literally adopt different body language and different speech patterns, and seem to be different ages and races, as they move from one identity to another. Often each self has a name. This differs from multiple personality disorders because it is a conscious process. It is the Wise Fool who can move past the illusion of a unified Self, to express the diversity of his or her wholeness in the world.

If we are to be large, we must embrace all our conflicting thoughts, feelings, urges—our many Selves. Then we are not foolish but wise Fools. While doing so hardly brings more order to life, it does bring richness and experience.

The Fool in each of us sees through and punctures our sense of self-importance, bringing us down to earth. Certainly, it takes away any sense that we control our fate—and hence takes us beyond a heroic stance toward life. Instead, the Fool simply expresses the plurality within and savors the beauty and joys of each unique and different moment and individual.

Rulers and Magicians work hard to redeem and heal the planet. Sages struggle and strive to attain truth. Only the Fool simply trusts the moment and savors life in its fullness, without judgment, appreciating not only life's joys but also its sorrows. The Fool, then, has the openness, the creativity of the Innocent without the Innocent's propensity for denial or need for protection. The Fool sees clearly enough even to advise the Ruler.

The Fool's recognition and acceptance of human fallibility is to motivate laughter, not judgment, despair, or even social activism. When the Fool is in our lives, we know joy because we are released from all the collective "shoulds" to really live. When we let go of the Ego and the need to be important, we can open up to joy.

This state is not the end of the journey, for it continues throughout our lives. But it does change the *quality* of the journey: once we have moved beyond heroism, into the dance, we experience much less suffering. The Fool, then, is the archetype that connects us to instinctual life and helps us experience greater joy. Perhaps this is because the Fool knows that we "see the divine the only way we can, through the acceptance of the human," no longer needing to strive but just glad to be here on this earth—as it is and as we are.

Part II

Preparation for the Journey

6

The Innocent

The Innocent is the part of us that trusts life, ourselves, and other people. It is the part that has faith and hope, even when on the surface things look impossible. It is the part of us that "keeps the faith" in whatever it is we are hoping for. It is also the part that allows us to trust others enough to learn from them, so it is essential to learning the basic skills of life and work.

We all begin in innocence, totally cared for inside our mother's womb. If we are lucky, our parents love us and care for us, and they are supported by relatives, friends, and social institutions that believe in us and our potential, encourage our efforts at mastering and developing our skills and our individuality, and help keep us safe and secure until we are old enough to care for ourselves.

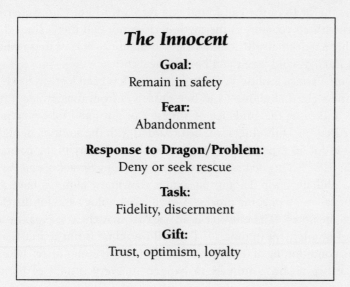

The Innocent

Goal:
Remain in safety

Fear:
Abandonment

Response to Dragon/Problem:
Deny or seek rescue

Task:
Fidelity, discernment

Gift:
Trust, optimism, loyalty

My HMI score for
the Innocent
archetype
is _____
(high = 30/low = 0).

It is my _____
highest score
(highest = 12th/lowest = 1st).

Children who have been loved and cared for have a wonderful faith that the world is a safe place for them and they can count on others to give them the physical, intellectual, and emotional support and help they need to grow and mature. The trust they feel in others, and as a result also in themselves, allows them to learn the skills they need for life—basic socialization to the culture, as well as life and vocational skills and knowledge. Someday, they know, they will be providing that safety to others, and passing on what they have learned, even though that may be difficult to believe at the time.

We all begin in innocence, believing what those in authority teach us, regardless of whether those authorities have our best interests in mind. The Innocent in us trusts even when trust is not warranted. The Innocent believes it if a parent tells us we are ugly, naughty, selfish, uncoordinated, stupid, or lazy. It is the Innocent who gets a bad grade and concludes he or she is dumb. It is also the Innocent who internalizes racism or sexism, or homophobia, or class bias, who believes it is fundamentally not OK to be anything that others condemn.

Although a secure, happy childhood helps produce an optimistic and trusting outlook on life, its absence does not necessarily mean you cannot gain the Innocent's gifts. Some people come out of awful childhoods and become productive and eventually, happy adults, while others remain dysfunctional throughout life.

Paradise Lost, Paradise Regained

Many traditions celebrate the myth of the Fall from innocence. In Christianity, it is the myth of the Fall from Eden into a world of pain, suffering, and toil. But as with all versions of the myth, it does not end there, since the myth also says that a redeemer will come and save humanity—at least those who retain their faith in God—and take them back to heaven.

In some Eastern traditions, the Paradise that has been lost is a mode of perception, true sight that allows us to free ourselves from illusion. As a result of innocently following the guidance of a master or guru and following practices such as meditation, faithfulness will be rewarded with the attainment of nirvana, which allows for an experience of oneness with the beauty of the cosmos.

In *The Time Falling Bodies Take to Light: Mythology, Sexuality, and the Origins of Culture,* William Irwin Thompson argues that many cultures have a strong sense of the fall as an ongoing process. In Vedic cosmology and for the Dogon of West Africa, he notes, "The universe is an egg that shatters as it expands to begin its career of unfoldment in time. . . . The Fall into time is not so much an event itself as the conditioning of time-space out of which all events arise." It happened before time began and continues to happen in every instant of human life.

Both the chaos of the fall and the original cosmic egg of wholeness exist simultaneously.

The Hopi and the Maya have an evolutionary worldview. Their gods "labor to create humanity, but time after time their efforts are met with failure." And they have to "try again." Whether gods or humankind, the rhythm of Paradise lost and Paradise regained speaks of our continual attempt to realize the ideal in the actual, the "fall" of inevitable failure, and the renewed effort to try again—an effort that does, most of the time, bring some improvement, if not actual Paradise, in our lives.[1]

The Greeks had a wonderful legend of an original state of wholeness, in which men and women were one being. However, that being was so complete and whole, it threatened the gods, who then split that original androgyne into men and women. As a result, they speculated, men and women have forever felt fragmented and partial without the other. Archetypal psychologists such as June Singer, in her fine book, *Androgyny,* use this story as a version of Paradise lost, Paradise regained. Once we were whole and androgynous, but now we are partial. We regain wholeness when we are able to develop and balance the male and female (anima and animus in Jung's terms) within us.

Virtually every culture, moreover, has a myth of a golden age, seen as an actual historical period of time. Riane Eisler, in *The Chalice and the Blade: Our History, Our Future,* argues on the basis of anthropological data that the myth of the Fall from Paradise is, in fact, a version of actual history: "The Garden is an allegorical description of the Neolithic, of when women and men first cultivated the soil, thus creating the first 'garden'."

Eisler maintains that at one time in history, goddess-worshiping cultures in which there were no wars, no classes, no sexism or racism existed worldwide. That such cultures operated on a partnership model meant there needed to be no hierarchies between people and no hierarchy in the psyche. In this world, people's Egos, Souls, and Spirits worked together in harmony. Eisler further argues that we can reclaim this earlier Paradise when we reclaim our faith that living in a peaceful, equalitarian way is possible.[2]

The Journey of the Innocent

The journey of the Innocent, in all its versions, begins in a kind of utopia, a safe, secure, peaceful, loving environment. Suddenly, we are thrown from that environment and enter a world where we are judged, where unfair discriminations are made, where conflict and violence are rampant and illusions are shattered.

The Innocent in each of us, however, knows that if that safe garden was possible anywhere or anytime, even if we personally never remember experiencing it, then it can be recreated sometime, by someone. Whether the Innocent in us is active or dormant, it has a primal memory that life can be better than it now is. When we first experienced innocence, we did so because it was just what was there. Returning to innocence is a different matter. Now we choose one option out of a universe that offers many others. This is why the Innocent is both the beginning and the end of the journey; way down inside, each of us is motivated to undertake the journey precisely to revisit, find, or create that world we all know at some level to be possible. Only at the end, we are Wise Innocents, knowing the whole breadth of life's experiences, and choosing to create a peaceful, egalitarian world where all creatures can be known, honored, and empowered.

The hero often begins as an Innocent, but soon becomes an orphan, outcast, slave, or stranger in a strange land. In the classic version of the hero's journey, the hero is an orphan and also an alien, almost always raised by people other than his or her biological parents. The quest is motivated by a search to find the true parents.

Whether we succeed in finding our "real family," returning to our home planet, or finding our real species, the plot is the same. All the problems that we have experienced are a result of somehow being in the wrong place—like a puzzle piece someone has forced into an ill-fitting hole in the wrong puzzle. The return to Paradise comes when we find the family, planet, or species in which we are really at home.

Many love stories follow a similar pattern. We fall in love and for a little while experience Paradise. Then something happens that causes us to realize that our lover is not perfect, but merely mortal (even ordinary). Just as no parents can live up to the archetypes of the perfect Great Mother or Great Father, no man or woman can live up to the image of the perfect lover or soul mate. Whether or not the relationship actually breaks up, most relationships—however romantic and idyllic as they begin—sooner or later "fall" from that initial sense of infatuation.

Whether the myth of innocence lost and regained is a variation on Paradise lost and regained, true home/species rediscovered, or the love story, its plot is profoundly hopeful, and it helps awaken in us the innocent pure child that believes as only a child can believe.

It is only in the Ego state of the Innocent that miracles happen.

The awakening of this childlike faith is undoubtedly what Christ meant when he said, "Except as ye become like little children, ye shall never enter the kingdom of heaven." It is this capacity for faith that allows us to hold on to our dreams, hopes, and visions even when things look the worst, and thereby to bring them to fruition.

Ideally, we begin each new endeavor with some innocence—that is, open-ness, optimism, excitement. Because we do not know what is coming, we have to trust. As we enter each new spiral on the journey, we are wiser and less naive.

It is also only in the Ego state of the Innocent that miracles happen. All the other archetypes are too busy trying to control the outcome! Books like *A Course in Miracles* or the many spin-offs (such as *Love Is Letting Go of Fear* and *A Book of Spiritual Games*) teach people that all suffering is an illusion, that the only reality is goodness, so that people will have enough trust and faith in the universe to allow miracles to happen. So many religions envision God as a heavenly, loving parent because such an image allows us to trust that we are safe in the universe.

Disobedience and Faith

Often the archetypal Innocent is seen as somehow to blame for the fall, with some restitution or atonement called for. In the story of Adam and Eve, for instance, it is Eve's disobedience in eating the apple of the knowledge of good and evil that results in their expulsion from Paradise and the curse of suffering.

This fall is paradoxically seen as a "fortunate" fall, and it is clearly a fall from wholeness into dualism (the knowledge of good and evil). In Judaism, redemption comes through a covenant between the Jewish people and God, which results not so much because of humankind's love for God, as God's love for humanity. The human responsibility required by the covenant is to keep God's laws. In Christianity, God is seen as sending his son to atone for their sin. Atonement means "at-one-ment"—restoring a sense of unity beyond fragmenta-tion and dualism. In both Judaism and Christianity, oneness with God is restored and paradise is regained, whether on earth (through the founding of a society based on God's law) or in an afterlife.

A modern Disney movie, *The Land Before Time,* recounts the story of a little dinosaur traveling with his mother and grandparents. Drought has destroyed their Paradise, but his mother knows there is a luxuriant green valley far away, and if they just travel far and long enough, they will find it. On the way, the mother dies. Heartbroken, the little dinosaur travels on alone (picking up con-temporaries of all sizes and shapes as he goes). He has every reason to give up hope, but retains his faith that his mother's words were true. Finally, he finds the green valley, just as she said it would be.

All these stories and many more remind us that it is safe to trust. Our faith-fulness will be rewarded. When the Innocent archetype is dominant in our lives, it seems impossible for us to find or recreate Paradise; often the atonement or restitution called for is beyond our capacity to fulfill. Our job is simply to have faith. Doing so opens the doors for miracles.

Virginity and Fidelity

Often the classical hero pledges fidelity to a King or Queen, a cause, a god or goddess, or a great love. Keeping this pledge—and remaining true to this primal commitment—is a central aspect of heroism. Each one of us has such promises we made to ourselves or to others in our youth, and they remain sacred to the Innocent within us.

Many stories in medieval literature celebrate women who were willing to die to protect their virginity. The Virgin is a symbol of that Innocent in each one of us that is totally undefiled and pure no matter what we have done or what has been done to us. The ancient meaning of "virgin" is the woman who is "one-in-herself" and whole, not the property of any man. It can be interpreted as an inner state of wholeness, not necessarily the state of physical chastity.

On a cultural level, while women have primarily borne the social burden of the double standard about physical chastity, male heroes like Parsifal were also enjoined to be virgins before marriage and faithful thereafter. In terms of a psychological reality (rather than physical celibacy) they were to retain the primal wholeness of the Innocent and remain faithful to the childhood vows they made in innocence, until they were ready to make new vows in maturity. Saving yourself for the great love of your life is about holding out for your dreams—romantic, vocational, political—and not just settling for the pleasures of the moment.

Each one of us has such promises we made to ourselves or to others in our youth, and they remain sacred to the Innocent within us.

The Shadow Side of Innocence

The Innocent often wants to protect the innocent state of trust and optimism, and so refuses the fall. In doing so, however, it may cause the shadow Innocent to take hold. For example, pathologically refusing the fall and holding on to innocence can even be related to eating disorders. As Marion Woodman has suggested, in a society that denigrates the body and sees women as inferior, one way of clinging to innocence is to refuse the fall into puberty—into having a woman's (and that means sexual) body.[3]

The Innocent, who is prone to denial, simply does not want to see that the parent, teacher, or lover cannot be trusted. For that reason, the Innocent in us keeps walking into the same abusive situations and getting battered and mistreated time and time again.

This is, of course, true of children in battering homes, women and men in physically or emotionally battering marriages or relationships, and enormous numbers of people in emotionally battering work environments. Many of us who would never stay in a physically battering relationship or even an egregiously emotionally battering situation find that over time we begin to be aware of ways we are being mistreated.

The Innocent in us can also move easily into denial about our own actions, failing to take responsibility for our own part in our problems. Since Innocents, at least initially, are absolutist and dualistic, they cannot admit they are imperfect without feeling horrible about themselves, so they either get locked into denial about their own inadequacies or are controlled by guilt or shame.

The Innocent in us keeps walking into the same abusive situations and getting battered and mistreated time and time again.

When healthy Innocents transgress, they forgive themselves, moderate their behavior, and go on. If others hurt them or violate their principles, they are quick to forgive and to believe they will do differently next time.

When Innocents are afraid of others, however, they avoid facing that fear by blaming themselves. Young children, for example, will feel at fault for being molested or beaten by their parents because it is easier to accept their own inadequacy than to face the more terrifying irrational and harmful parents. When wounded Innocents are afraid of facing their own inadequacies (which is more likely in adulthood), they will project them onto others and blame others for their own inadequacies.

These strategies save us from the responsibility to act. If we deny we are being abused, we do not have to stand up for ourselves. If we project our own faults onto others, we do not have to change. If we internalize other people's discriminatory, hostile, or otherwise harmful attitudes, we can continue to wage war on ourselves without having either to figure out how to escape the situation or to experience fully our powerlessness in it.

The Innocent believes it is important to stay defined by one's persona, or social role, and not have secrets from the world—for beyond that surface reality lie dragons. All the archetypes in the unconscious tend to express themselves— in dreams and in our waking lives—in their shadow forms, which possess us if we have not shed the light of consciousness on them. So the person who is an Innocent only will be surrounded by psychological terrors. The shadow Orphan will tempt the Innocent to cross the physical and metaphorical street and to flout the rules. The shadow Warrior will wage war on the Innocent, criticizing unmercifully. The shadow Caregiver will demand sacrifice and accuse the Innocent of selfishness if he or she shows the slightest regard for personal wishes or welfare.

The archetypes related to soul development will be so threatening that the Innocent will almost entirely project them onto others: the Seeker will be seen as the heretic; the Destroyer as the enemy; the Lover as an immoral seducer; and the Creator as guilty of dangerous hubris. The Innocent then lives with a dull void in the solar plexus, obsessive self-destructive habits and sexual urges, and an unconscious compulsion to create drama and difficulty.

The Growth and Development of the Innocent

Innocents, who often feel special, can be charismatic because of the purity of their beliefs and vision. They also assume that they will be cared for by the universe and other people, because they are so special and so good.

People who remain in this initial mode of innocence may pretend to be independent, but underneath, they expect institutions, employers, friends, and spouses to take care of them. They rarely carry their own share of responsibility, although they are "very good" and may work hard. Others often do love and instinctively care for them, as we do for little children. So in this way, the Innocents' lives often work—at least until they lose their job or their spouse, or their friends and colleagues stop taking care of them and expect them to grow up.

Yet at another level, their lives never work well in adulthood, for they never really grow up. Unless they fall—which means losing, to some degree, at least, this sense of favored status in the universe—they may never really accomplish much that is real or lasting. And it is not just their work that is affected, but also their personal relationships. Innocents want relationships to replicate the original symbiotic relationship with their mothers. They assume that others want what they want because they often do not see the other person as real and separate.

When the Innocent in any of us becomes aware that someone else does not want what we want and that our desires might be thwarted, we usually vacillate between showing the infantile rage we really feel and trying to be charming enough to get what we want next time. In other words, the Innocent in each of us is as vulnerable and dependent as a little child who finds a way to manipulate his or her parents to get needs met.

Our inner Innocent is often stricken when life turns out to be more cruel than had been expected. But the Innocent is also resilient, and is, as we have seen, the inner part of each of us that has faith when the world seems the bleakest and that holds on to our dreams even when they seem most unlikely to come true.

The ability of the Innocent to grow up often depends upon the degree to which the Innocent can learn to say that even though everything looks lost on the surface, hope will come. Even though I'm presently lost in the desert, God will bring me to the Holy Land. The Innocent needs to learn paradox: that at the deepest spiritual level, it is safe to trust; yet I'd better not leave my wallet unattended!

Levels of the Innocent

Shadow	Denial, repression, blaming, conformity, irrational optimism, and risk taking
Call	Safe, secure environment; a desire to be protected, to experience unconditional love and acceptance
Level One	Unquestioning acceptance of environment, authorities; belief that the world as it is being experienced is all there is; dependence
Level Two	Experience of the "fall"—disillusionment, disappointment—but retention of faith and goodness in adversity
Level Three	Return to Paradise, this time as a Wise Innocent; trust and optimism without denial, naïveté, or dependence

Initially, Innocents see life as an either/or proposition: either it is safe or they are not. Either authorities know what they are talking about or they do not. People are either perfect or no good. Worse, we often feel we have to be perfect or we are worthless. Therefore, Innocents are tossed back and forth from idealism and perfectionism to disillusionment and cynicism.

Years later, at a higher level of development, Innocents will know that some things are safe and some are not. Authorities know what they are talking about— sometimes. Even the best and the worst of people mix good and bad traits. When Innocents are lucky, they come to accept their own human mix of good and bad motives, strength and vulnerability, and to feel safe partly as a result of a basic faith in the universe, but also because they have become wise in the ways of the world.

At first the Innocent sees safety as contingent: "I am safe unless I try to cross the street." "I am safe as long as I do what others say." The safe world is small and confined, and the world outside is full of unseen, unknown dangers. The more we experience those dangers, the bigger our world becomes. Yet this also requires us to experience pain, defeat, or disillusionment. The fall does not happen just once in life. We experience disillusionment, abandonment, and betrayal by others and ourselves many times during our lives. If we are fortunate, each experience leads us back to innocence (Paradise, Eden, the promised land) not only at a new level, but in a way that allows us to bless more of our world with a kind of innocence that is a product not of denial, but of wisdom.

As we lose and regain faith through experience, larger parts of reality move into the realm of safety. We grow older and find we can cross many streets with safety. We survive the death of a love affair, and we discover we no longer have to be afraid to commit to or love others once we have developed some reasonable ability to size up character. We speak our truth in what we thought to be a hostile atmosphere, and we are not fired or killed. So we discover it is safe to be honest, especially since we now can recognize environments in which we simply could not be understood.

Eventually the Innocent learns to understand paradox and also to understand reality metaphorically, rather than literally. So much of what we think when we are Innocents is bound, at least initially, by very literal thinking. What our teachers, our spiritual leaders, and our myths and legends say is all literalized. For example, most world myths tell us that the gods will forgive our transgressions if we sacrifice an Innocent. In many ancient cultures, therefore, the most perfect young lad or maiden or animal was sacrificed to appease the gods.

At a higher level of cognitive complexity, it is understood that the demand of the sacrifice of the Innocent is a psychological requirement. When we have lost a sense of unity and oneness with God, our communities, or our own Souls, we need to sacrifice our innocence, move out of our illusions or denial, and go on our journey to find a new level of truth that will restore us to wholeness.

The journey requires a great paradox. At one level, we must never let go of our dreams and ideals, and in this way every hero remains always an Innocent. But at the same time, we need to be willing to sacrifice our illusions, gladly and daily, so that we may grow and learn. It does not matter that at first we do not know what is a truth and what is a delusion. Among other things, that's what the journey will help us discover. We make the requisite sacrifice of our innocence only that we might someday regain it on a higher level.

Exercises

Give some thought to when, where, how, and how much the Innocent expresses itself in your life.

1. How much or how little is the Innocent expressed in your life? Has it been expressed more in the past or present? Do you see it emerging more in your future? Is it expressed more at work, at home, with friends, in dreams or fantasies?

2. Who are some friends, relatives, co-workers, and others who seem influenced by the archetype of the Innocent?

3. Is there anything you wish were different about the expression of the Innocent in your life?

4. Since each archetype expresses itself in many different ways, take some time to describe or otherwise portray (e.g., draw, make a collage, use a picture of yourself in a particular costume or pose) the Innocent as it is expressed or could be expressed in your life. What does or would it look like? How does or would it act? In what setting does or would it feel most at home?

Daydreams

In your daydream, allow yourself to experience a perfect childhood, one in which you have everything you need: love, possessions, security, stimulation, encouragement to your growth in every possible way. Allow yourself some time to process your feelings. Be aware that no matter what the reality of your actual childhood, you can give yourself a perfect childhood anytime you wish in your fantasy life.

●

Allow yourself to indulge in fantasies of rescue, whether it is "someday my prince (or princess) will come," or dreams of the perfect therapist, the great boss, or the political leader who will restore Camelot. Imagine how faithfully you wait for rescue, how good and deserving you are. Allow yourself to experience being rescued and taken care of by this caring, benevolent, and powerful person. Then imagine yourself becoming like that person. What does that feel like for you?

7

The Orphan

The Orphan experiences the same "fall" as the Innocent, but to different effect. The Innocent uses the experience to try harder, to have greater faith, to be more perfect and lovable, to be more worthy. The Orphan sees it as demonstrating the essential truth that we are all on our own.

The Orphan

Goal:
Regain safety

Fear:
Exploitation, victimization

Response to Dragon/Problem:
Powerlessness, wish for rescue, cynical compliance

Task:
Process pain and disillusionment fully
and be open to receive help from others

Gift:
Interdependence, empathy, realism

On the most literal level, Orphans are children who are deprived of parental protection and nurture while too young and unskilled to take care of themselves. Perhaps the parents die, literally abandoning the child, or remain on the scene but neglect, victimize, or abuse the child. Many Orphans live in what appear to be intact families, but the children are not cherished, nurtured, or guided and do not feel emotionally or physically safe.

The Orphan archetype in each of us is activated by all the experiences in which the child in us feels abandoned, betrayed, victimized, neglected, or disillusioned. These include occasions when teachers were unfair; playmates made fun of us; friends talked behind our backs; lovers said they would never leave, but did; and employers expected us to be complicit in unprofessional practices. They also include a growing knowledge about the world: that TV ads lie; that some police are dishonest; that some doctors may fail to treat the sick if they are poor; that the businessman may pollute the environment to make a buck; and that even in our democratic society, some people are more equal than others.

To the degree that we do not acknowledge the Orphan inside us, that Orphan is abandoned by us as well as the world. Unfortunately, we live in a society in which being hurt or vulnerable is not socially acceptable. We are all supposed to be OK all the time, which means that most of us hide our vulnerable, lost, hurt inner child for fear of being judged by others—who, ironically, are also hiding their own wounded child. The result is that this child is not only wounded, but very lonely.

My HMI score for the Orphan archetype is

———

(high = 30/low = 0).

It is my ———— highest score

(highest = 12th/lowest = 1st).

The Making of an Orphan

Life is full of orphaning experiences, and some people have more than their share of them. The more we have, the more likely it is that the Orphan archetype will predominate over the Innocent.

Just as we learn innocence from positive and safe experiences, the Orphan in each of us is activated by painful experiences, especially childhood ones. The large number of people now in groups for adult children of alcoholics or other dysfunctional families indicates that many people are orphaned in intact families from very early ages. However, to the degree that the Innocent in each of us wants and expects our parents to enact the positive, ideal image of the nurturing, loving Caregiver, we are all orphaned because our parents were simply human and fallible. Just as we are all wounded, we are also all raised by wounded parents at various stages on their own journeys. We are lucky if we have parents who have acknowledged their own wounding and found some means to begin the process of healing.

We are all, then, on a continuum; some of us come from pretty good families, and some come from just awful families, and the rest come from every kind in between. The child in each of us has been orphaned somewhere. It is simply

Just as we are all wounded, we are also all raised by wounded parents at various stages on their own journeys.

part of growing up. We go to school seeking truth and discover that even the experts disagree. We go to the courts seeking justice and discover they are not always just. We are unfairly judged by the way we look or talk or by where we come from. In short, we discover that life is not always fair, authorities are not always right, and there are no infallible absolutes.

In this way, the Orphan is the disappointed idealist, the disillusioned Innocent. Whereas the Innocent believes that purity and courage will be rewarded, the Orphan knows that is not necessarily the case, that indeed, it is the wicked who often prosper.

From Orphan to Exile to Rebel

When the Orphan is dominant in our lives, the world seems a pretty hopeless place. We have been abandoned by whatever paternal figure might rescue us and are left with a landscape inhabited by only two kinds of people: the weak, who are victims, and the strong, who either ignore or victimize the weak. The emotional experience of the Orphan's life is that of an infant crying in a crib, knowing that no one will come. Finally, the child stops crying, but the pain and loneliness inside do not go away. Sometimes Orphans feel like exiles.

When the Innocents, Adam and Eve, are cast out of Eden for disobedience, God promises them redemption through faith and perseverance in hardship. Other figures guilty of similar sins are cast out more finally as Orphans: Cain, Ishmael, Lilith, Lucifer. The fate of such Orphans is to be shut forever out of Eden, the homeland, or heaven itself.

Such Orphans may remain exiles, traveling through the world without ever finding a home, like Cain or the legendary Wandering Jew. Or the hopelessness of their situation may make them Rebels, turning against the very powers that rejected and exiled them, like Lucifer.

In the twentieth century, when the "death of God" has been widely pronounced, the Orphan has been the dominant philosophical position. Existentialists such as Albert Camus, in *The Myth of Sisyphus*, identify the essential absurdity of modern life as resulting from the death of God and with that death, the death of inherent meaning in life. Without experiencing any inherent meaning in life, and without the benefit of hopeful and optimistic emotions, Camus asks, Why live? Why not simply kill oneself?

In *The Rebel*, Camus goes on to find a kind of meaning within absurdity, which comes from solidarity with all the oppressed, victimized Orphans of the world. "If all are not saved, what good is the salvation of one only?" The rebel gives up the promise of Paradise and of specialness, and thus must give up illusions of immortality "to learn to live and to die, and, in order to be a man, to refuse to be a god."[1] This is his resolution to the problem of suicide as one possible response to a sense of life's meaninglessness. When we give up the childlike wish for Paradise, the longing for immortality, and the belief that there is a parental God, somehow caring for all of us, we begin to grow up. We realize that we are all mortal, all wounded, all in need of each other's help.

The redemption of the Orphan ultimately cannot come from above—God, church, state, history—but must come from collective action. At some point, Orphans give up on failed authorities and take control of their own lives, and when they do so, they become Rebels.

The Orphan as Rebel works for justice and claims solidarity with all other oppressed, wounded, or suffering people, not because of any universal truth, but in response to an inner command. Recognizing no absolute, objective verities, the Rebel comes to affirm relativistic, subjective ones. There is no meaning but the meaning we create through our care for one another.

The gift of the Orphan archetype is a freedom from dependence, a form of interdependent self-reliance. We no longer rely on external authority figures, but rather learn to help ourselves and one another.

Camus's image of the Rebel combines elements of the Orphan with the Warrior, and reflects a male developmental progression. Women, however, are more likely to do so through the Caregiver. Feminist writer Madonna Kolbenschlag expresses this image as a band of interdependent caretakers, each a part of the divine spiritual presence of Gaia, and each taking care of one another. She says that "in order to recover personal wholeness and political equilibrium, we must learn to 'befriend' the orphan in each of us."[2]

Both Camus and Kolbenschlag show us that at the highest level, the Orphan learns that there is no power more powerful and responsible than we are. There is not anything or anyone out there who is going to fix it for us. Whether we envision the responsible alternative in existential or spiritual terms, in masculine or feminine terms, the answer is for us to take responsibility for our lives, lived in interdependence with others, who are as Orphaned as we are.

The gift of the Orphan archetype is a form of interdependent self-reliance.

Resisting Rescue

Because their developmental task is to learn to band together with others and, at best, to both rebel against authority and nurture and care for one another, Orphans are very resistant to rescue. Although Orphans seem to want to be rescued and even believe they want to be rescued, they rarely let anyone help them.

They may say they want help, but then play "yes but." They can often catalog the inadequacies of whatever institution or person you think might be able to help.

The Innocent wants a strong parental figure or institution to provide rescue and create safety for it. To the Orphan, who has usually just left the Innocent stage, trusting individuals or institutions is just asking to be cruelly duped again.

Developmentally, the Orphan stage is the time children turn away from reliance on the parents, to reliance on siblings or friends. In a healthy family, they may not be terribly critical of their parents, but they do begin to recognize and chronicle the tendencies of the parents toward dogmatism, rigidity, or clumsiness and ineptitude.

In politics, the Orphan stage is the time we begin to develop the capacity to identify with the oppressed and seek solutions in unified, populist actions. It is also the time we are most suspicious of people in any kind of position of power or authority. Spiritually, it is the time of agnosticism, a turning away from reliance on God to a practical concern for what people can do to help one another. In education, it is the time we begin to question authorities and start to be able to critique others' ideas.

In an individual human life, it is also the time of living life as an outsider. When the Orphan is strong in us, we see the problems with society and institutions and how they harm us or others. We are critical of people and organizations, but initially feel powerless to do anything about them. We may simply feel alienated. If eventually we do attempt to make changes, it will be by collective action, with those we judge to be similarly powerless individually, but potentially more powerful collectively.

The Orphan calls us to wake up, let go of our illusions, and face painful realities.

Ultimately, the Orphan learns that it is a source of power to face one's victimization and limitations and to feel fully the pain caused by them. Doing so frees us up to work together to create a better world, for the Orphan says there is no one who will do it but us.

Self-Orphaning

Originally betrayed by others, Orphans (especially at the lower levels) often go beyond what might be seen as a healthy skepticism about life and betray their own hopes and dreams because they see them as just the kind of innocence that is, in their minds, asking for disappointment. This means that they often settle for work that is not the work they love, for lovers and friends who do not treat them very well, and in every other way restrict their dreams to a very limited sense of the possible.

It is important to remember that the Orphan is reacting to the unrealistic grandiosity of the Innocent, who firmly believes that anything is possible with enough faith, imagination, and hard work—or maybe just with faith alone. When the Innocent is dominant in our lives, we are often unrealistic in our optimism. When the Orphan dominates, we tend to be overly pessimistic, and hence do not even try for what we really want. Or we try, but we are so convinced that what we want is impossible that we undercut our chances in order to reinforce our own scripts. The Orphan, for example, may do something to provoke rejection simply to have a greater sense of control over life. Since disappointment, rejection, and abandonment are seen as inevitable, we feel just a bit better by leaving first.

Whereas the Innocent in each of us would stay in the most negative circumstances, convinced that if we worked hard enough, "the other" would change, the Orphan says, "Enough." At best, the Orphan leaves and bands together with outsiders and Rebels, or at worst, shuts down and stays in the environment, but without hope.

The Orphan part of us sees greener fields only in relative terms. We do not ask for Paradise or even freedom, only incrementally larger, more comfortable cages. We do not believe we can do work we really love, but we may look for less degrading, alienating, or limiting work. We do not think we can have a really happy love life, but at least we try to find a partner who will not actively mistreat us. We do not expect real happiness, so we settle for buying things.

Having lost faith in authorities, the Orphan in us also strongly wants to bond with peers—and is often quite willing to sacrifice any real separate sense of self to belong to the group. Orphans, in this way, may be as conformist as Innocents, except that whereas Innocents more typically conform to societal and institutional norms (although there are radical Innocents), Orphans either do so cynically or refuse traditional norms while conforming slavishly to outsider norms. We see this, for example, in the unremitting demands for conformity of behavior in teenage gangs or cliques or in most radical political groups, whether on the left or the right. Even in many self-help and support groups, in which people bond around their woundedness and victimization, group norms may preclude getting healthy enough to grow beyond dependency on the group.

When the Orphan is dominant in our lives, we may betray our own values. James Hillman, in his classic article, "Betrayal," talks about those experiences—especially during breakups of friendships, love affairs, marriages—"when suddenly the nastiest and dirtiest appears and one finds oneself acting in the same blind and sordid way that one attributes to the other, and justifying one's own actions with an alien value system. One is truly betrayed, handed over to an enemy within."

It is a self-protectiveness to avoid hurt that leads the Orphan in us to develop a false persona, and to betray our deepest natures. Hillman concludes that self-betrayal is "letting down the essential thing, the essential important demand on the ego: to take on and carry one's own suffering and be what one is no matter how it hurts."[3]

Ironically, the more we live false, inauthentic lives in order to be safe from hurt, the more Orphaned, hurt, and disillusioned we become. At this point, we have essentially turned against ourselves.

When Orphaning Goes Too Far

When we turn against ourselves, Orphaning has gone too far. Many people exhibit few external signs of their self-orphaning, for people living false selves are frequently conventional and fit in very well. Often they seem stereotypical and shallow, or even a bit neurotic; but the condition is so common that it is not seen as alarming or pathological. They settle for pseudolives and pseudoloves, and may substitute consumerism or mindless ambition for any real satisfaction in life. Fundamentally, they lack any sense of who they are. It is not uncommon for them to feel at the visceral level a void in the solar plexus.

They live in a scarcity mentality and are very susceptible to advertising that can convince them that if they do not use the right mouthwash or drive the right car, they will not be respected or loved. They pick loves, work, and homes, not for the intrinsic satisfaction these things give, but simply to achieve the right image. Fundamentally, they are like children, desperate to please and to get love by trying to conform to whatever seems to be rewarded in the culture at a given time. They play at "appropriate" sex roles, work roles, friend roles. They may even play the role of being an individual.

Such people are unlikely to look inward because they fear nothing is there or they fear the monsters (that is, the Shadow) within, so they often fail to seek help, unless their situation deteriorates. At worst, they become so cynical that they no longer even try to please or win friends or influence people, but just attempt to experience some pleasure in some way: through the purchase of things, fine food, and nice clothes; through "winning" and the illusion of control; through alcohol or drugs; through excitement and danger.

More likely to seek help are Orphans who have so much internal pain that life offers little joy except when they can be numbed enough with alcohol, drugs, excitement, or adrenalin to mask the pain. In such cases, oppressive, abusive figures in early life may have come to inhabit the inner life, so the voice of the critical, unloving parent saying you are worthless and no one will ever love you is always there in consciousness, even though that parent has long ago left, been left, or even died.

Even though the Innocent inside is crying out to have a secure place, Orphans may not be able, initially at least, to "use" that security even when it is available, since wherever they go, their inner voice continues to batter and berate them. No matter how externally safe an environment is, the internal environment is so unsafe that growth continues to be stifled.

Some Orphans' self-esteem is so wounded that it is hard for them to progress at anything—school, athletics, work, therapy, a spiritual path. Any small failing is seen as a sign of their total inadequacy, and they collapse, berate themselves, or project the blame onto others. They have no knowledge that they could make a mistake and just keep going. The more this syndrome progresses, the more behind their peers they lag, and hence, the lower their self-esteem drops. Such Orphans orphan themselves further by dropping out of school, or therapy, or friendships, or relationships, sure that they are inadequate.

Eventually, such a person might find a niche in life as a victim—excusing unskilled interactions and performance as a result of early trauma or societal injustice, and using incompetency and weakness as a means to gain attention and care. A great danger to any of us when we are in our Orphan stage is that our pain and victimization become too interesting and too good an excuse. Further, if we learn we can work on others' guilt to get what we want, we will never learn to move to the highest level of the Orphan, which is a truly critical step in human development: to be willing to become interdependent with others whom we recognize to be wounded just like ourselves.

Some Orphans have highly developed skills but an internal sense of unworthiness and/or despair about life's possibilities that keeps them locked in limited circumstances. The worse the situation gets, the more powerless they feel and the more paralyzed they become. Often it is not until they become aware that the situation they are in could kill them, that they gain the desperate courage to leave. Whether it is a battered wife, a citizen in an intolerably oppressive regime, an addict or a person working in an addictive organization, or someone simply trapped in a life too small for them, the dynamics are very similar. Many times the people in question are almost hypnotized by the persons, habits, or systems that have captured them, and they literally need to be rescued.

People in this category need love, support, and help to move out of their immobilization. Often this support comes initially from one person, but ideally also includes peer support as soon as that is available. Unaided, Orphans may succumb to cynicism that becomes an excuse for criminal, unethical, or unfeeling behavior, which the Orphans can justify by blaming their early life, society, or the general moral tone of the times ("Everyone does it"). Living in a world of victims and victimizers, Orphans may choose to go over to the other side, feeling that at least victimizers have more power and control than victims.

Levels of the Orphan

Shadow	Cynicism, callousness, masochism or sadism; using the victim role to manipulate the environment
Call	Abandonment, betrayal and self-betrayal, disillusionment, discrimination, victimization
Level One	Learning to acknowledge the truth of one's plight and feel pain, abandonment, victimization, powerlessness, and loss of faith in people and institutions in authority
Level Two	Accepting the need for help; being willing to be rescued and aided by others
Level Three	Replacing dependence on authorities with interdependence with others who help each other and band together against authority; developing realistic expectations

Criminal behavior, addiction, and all unethical and inhumane behavior suggest the individual has such difficulty, has identified with the victimizer, and is abusing oneself and/or others rather than identify with the pain of the inner Orphan. Such people need help, ideally both from trained professionals and from peer groups of people who, like themselves, have begun to process their despair and emotional pain and come out the other side.

Such people need clear limits, "tough love," and models of others like themselves who have changed their lives and found more wholesome and satisfying ways to live; however, they may not even be open to receiving help, at least initially—their despair and cynicism may be so great as to undermine any sense of faith that they can be helped. Sometimes one has to wait until things get so bad (in Alcoholics Anonymous, they call it "hitting bottom") that they cannot avoid seeing that they have to change. It is essential, moreover, that the rest of us not disengage from such profoundly wounded ones, seeing them as "other." If we are tempted to do so, it is almost always a sign of our rejecting and retreating from the perhaps smaller but very real part of each of us that is, of course, capable of the same cynicism, self-destructiveness, and betrayal of self and others.

The Healing Wound

Orphaning, while dysfunctional in excess, is a crucial part of growth and development. Even people who have been Orphaned in exceptionally painful ways may find that the gifts they receive from the process of recovering health and faith are so great that, for them, the pain that triggered their Orphaning seems fully worth it. Woundedness is part of the human condition, the part that motivates all our journeys. If we were not wounded, we would remain in innocence and never mature, grow, or learn.

We long for perfect parents—the archetypal perfect mother and father—and we get real, flawed, simply human parents. We expect immortality, and get mortality. We long to be the center of the universe, and find we are merely one person among many. We have great dreams of what we will be and accomplish in our lives, and in the main, find we have to settle for quite ordinary lives.

Perhaps most difficult of all, we betray our own hopes, values, or dreams, and we come to recognize that we, too, disappoint others, as well as ourselves. James Hillman, in "Betrayal," speaks of the many kinds of betrayals in human life as sparking the birth of Soul. In my view, such betrayals are also initially connected to the birth of the Ego. If we could always trust, then we could safely stay in blissful symbiosis with the world, beginning with our mothers. It is, then, the failure of our external world to meet our needs that motivates the journey in each of us to discover that we have to take responsibility for finding and for getting what we want. No one is just going to give it to us.

If we were not wounded, we would remain in innocence and never mature, grow, or learn.

Jean Houston, in *The Search for the Beloved: Journeys in Sacred Psychology,* argues that the nature of our woundedness defines much of who we are and what we choose to become, like trees that take unique shapes from growing around their scars.[4] Many people's vocations come out of their woundedness. The child who has been badly traumatized by her parents becomes a therapist after having been helped by therapy; the child who feels sinful or sick and is "saved" or healed by a religious experience goes into the ministry; the child with polio becomes a long-distance runner; a young person who feels powerless goes into politics to feel more in control.

The classic shaman's story always begins with a great wound such as epilepsy or insanity, and by healing this psychological or physical illness, the shaman develops magical, healing powers. Unfortunately, in our culture we persist in thinking of the world in terms of the healthy ones and the wounded ones. We want to cure people and make them "normal," which not only keeps them from sharing their woundedness, but also prevents them from finding the potential gift in that wounding. And it keeps all of us from providing the support and love that alone can heal the pain we all share.

Often it is the most highly functional, high-achieving people who feel that they cannot admit their vulnerabilities, especially if they are leaders. It also puts those who do share their pain in a separate category with the ill, the wounded, or the weak. As with children, those having a visible wound may find themselves at the bottom of the pecking order and even get pecked to death, since people with repressed wounds can be sadistic and cruel.

The tradition of confidentiality in support groups and therapy and the traditional anonymity of all Twelve-Step programs testify that we all understand that the knowledge of our wounds, our weaknesses, and our vulnerabilities may be used against us by others, who are, of course, afraid of acknowledging to themselves or others their own brokenness.

At the highest level of Orphan, we learn to welcome all our prodigal children home.

Psychic wounding is not only universal, it is essential to the process of both building the Ego and connecting with our Souls. The gift of the Orphan is to help us acknowledge our wounding and to open enough to share (in places that are safe) our fears, our vulnerabilities, and our wounds. Doing so helps us bond with others out of a grounded, honest, vulnerable place. This provides the bonding that allows intimacy to happen and also to open the heart so we may learn to be compassionate with ourselves and one another.[5]

Healing begins when we really feel the pain and reality of all the times we have been orphaned from outside, and it progresses to include recognizing how we have denied parts of our very selves. Only then can the psyche feel one and whole. As each of us reclaims our Orphaned selves, we no longer need to exile or oppress parts of the population who "carry" those banished qualities for us. We can be like the wise father in the biblical story of the prodigal son, who welcomed back his son who had acted out everything his father despised and scorned and had returned, destitute. Instead of lecturing his son, the father called for a feast to be declared in honor of his return. At the highest level of Orphan, we learn to welcome all our prodigal children home.

Exercises

Give some thought to when, where, how, and how much the Orphan expresses itself in your life.

1.   How much or how little is the Orphan expressed in your life? Has it been expressed more in the past or present? Do you see it emerging more in your future? Is it expressed more at work, at home, with friends, in dreams or fantasies?

2.   Who are some friends, relatives, co-workers, and others who seem influenced by the archetype of the Orphan?

3.   Is there anything you wish were different about the expression of the Orphan in your life?

4.   Since each archetype expresses itself in many different ways, take some time to describe or otherwise portray (e.g., draw, make a collage, use a picture of yourself in a particular costume or pose) the Orphan as it is expressed or could be expressed in your life. What does or would it look like? How does or would it act? In what setting does or would it feel most at home?

Daydreams

Sit in a quiet, comfortable spot where you will not be interrupted, and breathe deeply and slowly. Allow yourself to experience the desire to be cared for by others—a desire natural to the child in each of us. Let yourself know whom you wish would take care of you. (For example, you might imagine a person, a type of person, God.)

Then tell yourself that no one is going to care for or rescue you. You will have to act in your own behalf. Allow yourself to experience any feelings you have of sadness, disappointment, and cynicism, or the sense of your own powerlessness or ineptitude.

●

You may leave the daydream here or go on to imagine yourself joining a group of people who feel just the way you do—people who agree to support each other and share their feelings and knowledge with one another. Be aware of feelings that emerge as you imagine functioning in the context of such peer support.

The Warrior

When most of us think of the hero, we imagine a Warrior. The Warrior escapes from a confining environment and begins the journey in search of a treasure. On the journey, he or she is called upon to face and slay many dragons. Such heroes have courage and subscribe to high ideals, and they are willing to risk their very lives to defend their kingdoms and their honor or to protect the weak from harm.

The Warrior

Goal:
Win, get own way,
make a difference through struggle

Fear:
Weakness, powerlessness, impotence, ineptitude

Response to Dragon/Problem:
Slay, defeat, or convert it

Task:
High-level assertiveness;
fighting for what really matters

Gift:
Courage, discipline, skill

The Warrior within each of us calls us to have courage, strength, and integrity; the capacity to make goals and to stick to them; and the ability to fight, when necessary, for ourselves or others. The Warrior exacts a high level of commitment to our own integrity. Warriors live by, and when necessary fight for, their own principles or values even when doing so is economically or socially costly. In competition, it means doing your utmost best, and striving not only to win, but to play fair.

Warrioring is about claiming our power in the world, establishing our place in the world, and making that world a better place. In practice, this means that as Warriors, we identify the aspects of our individual or collective lives that displease or dissatisfy us, and we seek to change them by force or persuasion. It is about being tough enough not to get pushed around, and forceful enough to have things "one's own sweet way."

The well-developed internal Warrior is necessary, above all, to protect our boundaries. Without courageous, disciplined, and well-trained Warriors, the kingdom is always in danger of being overrun by the barbarians. Without a strong internal Warrior, we have no defense against the demands and intrusions of others. We live in a Warrior culture. Any system based on competition— from competitive sports to politics, to the judicial system, to capitalist economics, to competition in education—is based on Warrior modalities.

Today, when it is so clear that war cannot continue to be the way nations settle their differences, many people have negative feelings about the Warrior archetype. Yet it is not the Warrior archetype that is the problem; it is that we need to move to a higher level of the archetype. Without the ability to defend the boundaries, no civilization, country, organization, or individual is safe.[1] It takes high-level Warriors—whose weapons include skill, wit, and the ability to defend themselves legally and verbally or to organize support for their cause—to keep predatory, primitive Warriors in place.[2]

> My HMI score for the Warrior archetype is
>
> ———
>
> (high = 30/low = 0).
>
> It is my ———
> highest score
> (highest = 12th/lowest = 1st).

Overcoming the Enemy

The Warrior myth tells us how human courage and struggle can overcome evil. The myth is encoded in all the stories of great Warriors who ever stood up to the dragon, the wicked tyrant, the forces of evil or oppressive circumstances, and in so doing, rescued not only themselves but others, especially those weaker than themselves. Its plot requires a hero, a villain, and a victim to be rescued.

Sometimes the victor, like Alexander the Great, Napoleon, or George Washington, is a mature and experienced general. Sometimes, as with David and Goliath, a younger, smaller figure overcomes the older, bigger bully.

The Warrior myth is identified heavily with masculinity. Indeed, there is great confusion over being "macho" and being a "Warrior." There is, however, a difference. A real Warrior fights to protect and ennoble others. Someone who is macho seeks to feel superior to others and keep them down, even if also fighting to protect them from others. Any reasonably high-level Warrior treats others as he or she expects to be treated—with respect.

Although in traditional societies men are socialized to be Warriors and women Caregivers, there have been great women Warriors—beginning with the Amazons and coming down through history to such women as Susan B. Anthony, Elizabeth Cady Stanton, and Sojourner Truth. Indeed, any woman who wants equal rights, or even a separate sense of identity, needs to be able to access the Warrior within.

Anytime we stand up to unfair authority—whether it is a boss, a teacher, or anyone else—and anytime we take action to protect someone else from harm, we are being Warriors. Every time we risk our lives or our livelihoods for a principle, the Warrior myth is active in its positive form in our lives. It is at the root of all revolutionary struggles of all oppressed people everywhere.

The Warrior myth stresses that evil, injustice, and dishonesty *do* exist. Yet if we are smart and skilled enough, if we have enough courage and discipline to take a stand, and if we can enlist enough support, they can be overcome. It tells us, furthermore, that we are not responsible just for ourselves; it is our task to defend the weak and the powerless. We should never use the power of the sword, the pen, or the word to harm another unnecessarily. We should always use the least force necessary, and the least punishing approach that can also appropriately protect the boundaries.

It is also the Warrior in us that when faced with a problem, whether one's own or another's, immediately tackles it and tries to save the day. Finally, it is the Warrior within each of us that is humiliated if we let a wrong or slight go by and do not do anything about it.

Anytime we stand up to unfair authority and anytime we take action to protect someone else from harm, we are being Warriors.

The Negative Warrior

For every Warrior who fights against injustice, there is also a Warrior fighting to preserve it. But not all negative forms of the Warrior are villains.

The Warrior has received a bad name, like many other useful archetypes, because so much of the Warrior behavior we see around us is primitive, unpleasant, and unproductive. Most of us know people for whom every encounter is a contest or who are always crusading for something and trying to enlist others to fight for a cause. This is Warrior possession. The Warrior has them; they do not have the Warrior.

Sometimes people who are new to Warrioring have very rudimentary, primitive skills. Any time anyone says anything with which they disagree or that they do not like, they take it personally and battle as if their life depended upon it.

Some Warriors simply cannot see the world from any other perspective. To them, the world is made up of heroes, villains, and victims to be rescued. If you are not one, you must be another. These are the educators who hold to competition as the only way to promote learning; the doctors who wage war on disease, even if it makes their patients experience their bodies as a battleground; the businesspeople who allow their health and family life to suffer greatly as long as they can close the big deal.

Such single-mindedness can be serious. Indeed, overreliance on the hero/villain/victim plot actually creates a self-fulfilling prophecy in which we always have villains and victims (and hence war, poverty, and oppression) because the hero needs them to feel heroic. The negative side of the archetype is a belief that it is not all right merely to be human. We must prove that we are better than others. The Warrior wants to be the best—and of necessity, this leaves others not the best, and ultimately in the Warrior ethic not OK.

In its most serious and negative manifestations, this desire to be above others is not checked by any humane feeling or higher values. Many people in our society today have lost the heroic, positive aspect of the Warrior entirely. Too often, in business, politics, and other aspects of modern life, we see people who are competitive enough, but their striving is no longer related to any ideals or larger social purpose. Instead, they are just out for number one—and in a shallow and vulgar way at that. All they want is money, status, and power, and they are willing to cheat, lie, and do shoddy things to get them. They have become villains, not heroes.

Critical to the Warrior's path is a choice between good and evil, for Warriors can use their power to make the world a better place, or simply to gain power and control over others.The Warrior who has essentially gone over to the evil side, like Hitler or *Star Wars'* Darth Vader, divides the world into two categories in an egocentric way. People who block their desires or powers must be destroyed, conquered, or converted. The victims may be protected from others, but the negative Warrior's price is that they then will be totally and completely under his or her domination. This is, of course, the case in imperialism of all kinds, whether it is one nation that conquers another, the boss who oppresses his or her workers, or the husband who keeps his wife under his thumb.

Claiming power always brings with it dangers, not the least of which are moral dangers. The problem with the Warrior archetype in our time is that so many so-called Warriors are not true Warriors at all. They are Orphans, calming their own sense of powerlessness by trying to best or control others. These are pseudo-Warriors, not Warriors.

Inevitably, all forms of the negative Warrior need to develop and affirm their own inner Orphan (to increase their empathy) and their own inner Innocent (to be relieved of their cynicism) so they can become positive and powerful Warriors.

The Making of a Warrior

The Warrior is both a dominant and an unpopular archetype today because we are experiencing a culture lag; we need a higher level of the archetype. The high-level Warrior requires that we fight for something beyond our own petty self-interest, that we claim the idealism basic to the archetype in its higher and purer forms and fight for what really matters—which in our generation may mean the survival of the species. It also requires that we fight in a way that is in the larger social interest, and in this generation, that may necessitate a redefinition of identity so that we see not only our own company or nation as on our same "team," but all people everywhere. In this context, the enemy is no longer a person, group, or country, but ignorance, poverty, greed, and small-mindedness.

But none of us starts there. We begin by learning the rudiments of defending ourselves and getting what we want. For most people, the Warrior and the Caregiver are the first adult archetypes to be experienced and integrated into consciousness. Without developing at least one of these, most people emotionally and developmentally remain children.

The inner Innocent dreams big dreams; the Orphan recognizes the impediments to those dreams; but without the Warrior, those dreams seldom come true except by serendipity or the kindness of others. The Warrior takes those dreams and creative ideas and devises a goal and a plan. The Warrior also provides the discipline to stick to the plan, or to advise a strategic retreat if necessary.

The inner Innocent dreams big dreams; the Orphan recognizes the impediments to those dreams; but without the Warrior, those dreams seldom come true.

Warriors who also have highly developed and healthy Innocents do not get caught in the trap of fighting about everything. They fight for what really matters to them, in defense of their deepest values and ideals, not simply for material gain. If they have made friends with their Orphans, they do not have to be so tough every minute of the day or demand such unremitting toughness in others. Often they can work as equals in an interdependent way, with much less need to set themselves above others. If they also have highly developed Caregivers, they will fight willingly for the good of the people, the country, or the cause that they love, not just for self-interest.

When all four archetypes associated with the Ego are developed, the Warrior tends to operate on a very high level, fighting only when it is really called for.

However, if the Innocent and Orphan are badly wounded and the Caregiver not developed, the Warrior's goals, plans, and schemes will be merely self-directed, cynical, and selfish. They will not be oriented for genuine psychological and spiritual development, but simply to assure base survival.

To a person with only the Warrior archetype evidenced in consciousness, every situation seems like a dragon, and the only options are to run, fight, or be destroyed. This is a difficult psychological landscape in which to live. The issue is, of course, always courage, and this extraordinarily difficult landscape is where many of us learn it—even if we visit it less often than those who live there all the time.

Orphans live in this terrain without any conscious ability to defend the Self, so they are constantly looking for someone else to defend them, even at the cost of losing their autonomy. In older societies, for example, in which men were expected to carry the Warrior energy for both sexes, women often traded rights over their very bodies for the economic, social, and physical protection of a man. Although many men under this system were highly developed Warriors who would defend women and children, others were less developed and hence filled with contempt for people they saw as "weak," and they physically or emotionally abused the women and/or children they were supposed to protect. Many women, however, would stay with these men primarily because they could not imagine taking care of themselves, such was the price of bowing to the social pressure that women should repress and deny the Warrior within themselves.

In the past, archetypal functions were assigned to different roles in family systems. Mothers were Caregivers. Fathers were Warriors. Children were taught to be good (Innocents) and honor their parents or risk being disinherited (Orphaned). If the father was the only person to develop Warrior qualities (until his sons did and, as Freud has posited, deposed him), the family had no protection against him if he became a shadow Warrior, or against the world were he to die or leave. If the mother was the only one to do caregiving, the family could fall apart if she took sick or left; and if she evidenced the devouring shadow side of the Caregiver, there would be no one to comfort or help those wounded by her. In short, if anyone fell down on the job, everyone suffered. The more modern emphasis on having each individual develop psychic balance and wholeness does not preclude having any individual in a group "lead" with certain archetypal qualities, but through diversification, it decreases the dependence of the group on the archetypal development of any one individual within it.

In contemporary society, nevertheless, most men have an easier time in our culture with the Warrior than the Caregiver archetype, and most women find it easier to be a Caregiver than to fight. This is most likely a result of centuries of socialization, and perhaps also some biological predisposition; yet it does create

a social challenge as larger and larger numbers of women enter the predominantly male work force defined by the competitive Warrior standards and men
aspire to intimacy with their wives and children.

But even here, the Warrior archetype can help us. It is the Warrior within
that helps us find a sense of individuality within wholeness that is not just
socially programmed. Without the Warrior archetype, it is difficult to develop a
sense of an identity that is one's own and not another's. It is the Warrior that
guards the boundaries and protects that first budding self (Ego) from encroach-
ment by the demands and wishes of others.

Neither Innocent nor the Orphan has any effective sense of their own
boundaries. The Innocent feels a sense of oneness with the universe and other
people. The Orphan understands separateness only as a wound, a lack. The
Orphan feels separate, but vulnerable rather than empowered by that separateness. The Warrior is the archetype that helps us find and create our boundaries
and defend them against attack.

The Warrior's Journey

The would-be Warrior begins the journey often feeling anything but powerful, imprisoned within boundaries of someone else's making. Traditional fairy-
tale heroes, for instance, are often held prisoner as children by a wicked witch or
ogre tyrant, or are mistreated by an evil stepmother or stepfather. Many people
today feel imprisoned or mistreated not only in their childhood homes, but at
many different points in their lives. The challenge is to learn to live in such environments without becoming like them.

In psychological terms, until we have our own boundaries, we need someone else to provide them. We often may feel oppressed by someone else's limits,
yet unable to escape them because we are not yet capable of creating our own.
Parents, good or bad, create boundaries for us; so do institutions and rules. As
long as we are in a child ego state, having boundaries set by others for our benefit
and with our interests in mind makes us feel safe and secure (as long as they are
not really too oppressive). However, when we are ready to become more autonomous, suddenly those rules and restrictions seem much less benign. We feel
imprisoned and struggle against them.

Ideally, parents, schools, and other institutions create more room and
incrementally have fewer and fewer rules as we mature and become capable of
more autonomous functioning. By the time we actually leave home, or the job, or
the traditional marriage, or the halfway house, we have gradually learned to

Levels of the Warrior

Shadow	Ruthlessness, unprincipled and obsessive need to win, use of power for conquest, a view of all difference as a threat
Call	Confrontation of a great challenge or obstacle
Level One	Fight for self or others to win or prevail (anything goes)
Level Two	Principled fight for self or others; abiding by rules of a fair fight or competition; altruistic intent
Level Three	Forthright assertiveness; fighting or competition for what really matters (not simply personal gain); little or no need for violence; preference for win/win solutions; conflict honestly aired; increased communication, honesty

provide appropriate rules and boundaries for ourselves. However, when families, schools, or other institutions are not willing to let people grow up, they continue to treat adolescents and even adults like children. Or worse, they may punish or abuse children who are not properly docile and obedient or neglect the child's need for rules to rebel against, so the child is simply adrift and must act out in very serious ways before any sense of limit is reached. In both cases, a maturing young person needs to jump ship before he or she is developmentally ready.

Until we develop clear boundaries, we will believe, rightly or wrongly, that we are being held prisoner by someone or something. Many times when people are beginning to claim their own identities in the world—especially if it is power based on claiming their own authentic voices—their fantasy is that if they do so, everyone will attack or abandon them. And since the Warrior in us often begins the journey toward speaking our own truths by attacking others' truths, we do provoke attack and abandonment. Only later do we recognize that it was our own attacking, not our power, that provoked such unfriendly responses.

This is doubly troubling to women who have been taught that powerful women are threatening to men, but both men and women get this message in one form or another: "Don't challenge authority"; "Don't rock the boat." By the time we do speak out with some strength, we've muffled our own authentic voices for so long that our first assertions come out as either squeaks or shouts. Women frequently first contact their inner Warrior in the service of their Caregiver by fighting for others; only later do they learn to fight for themselves as well. (Conversely, men often learn to show the Caregiver's warmth and care in the service of the Warrior's determination to achieve the goal, which may be a happy love life, family, or organizational team.)

The budding Warrior has two major defenses: secrecy and strategic retreat. Secrecy is a kind of camouflage. We are safer from attack when we cannot be seen. People who might attack our new interest or idea or sense of Self cannot do so—because they do not know about it. Good Warriors know that we should never enter a battle until we are prepared for it. This means that we often don't want to raise issues that might provoke a conflict with others until we are confident enough in our relationship to know that it's worth risking a separation and until we're sufficiently protected should the battle occur.

Strategic retreat makes good sense. When clearly overwhelmed by superior force, the Warrior retreats and takes time to rebuild strength. Whether it is children beginning to separate from parents, adolescents attempting to separate from their peer groups, or adults finding they differ with their friends, colleagues, or co-workers, if the response from others is too overwhelmingly negative and punishing, they will often retreat for quite a long while, nursing their wounds, healing, and regrouping. In some cases, the damage is so great that they never try to assert themselves again.

In most cases, however, they retreat and think it over. Perhaps they watch and learn new skills. Some children, for example, know they need to leave their parents, but they bide their time, seeking help when and where they can until they graduate from high school. Some people stay in terrible jobs until they complete a degree in night school. Others take karate or practice games of strategy like chess, and then they try again. Often people berate themselves for how long they stay in what seem to be imprisoning environments, but people do so until they are psychologically strong enough to fight for themselves.

Clever Warriors try to control the battle zone and do not fight until they are prepared enough to have a good chance of winning. Taking the time to undergo basic training and to build a battle plan is only sensible. During this time of preparation, we learn self-discipline and the high-Warrior craft of controlling our own impulses and feelings. But eventually we all must fight, and that takes courage.

Some people begin battling practically from birth. They fight their siblings, their parents, their friends, and usually their teachers, and in doing so, sharpen their skills. Over time they may learn to hone them down a bit, to discover that Warrioring is not about fighting about everything—it is about having the wisdom and the courage to know when and where to fight.

But good Warriors eventually learn that to really affect their environment in a way that ultimately gets them what they want, they have to know what they want and be willing to fight for it. Perhaps the most important thing taught in assertiveness training is to have a clear sense of what you want to accomplish, and then to tell others what you want in a clear and respectful way.

It is not just speaking one's truth that is required. Many times we do not need to tell anyone. We simply need to get clear what we want, act on that knowledge, and keep our focus absolutely on the goal, whatever other people think; or when we are stronger, take in other people's advice and concerns, and adjust our strategy (but not the goal) accordingly.

Some people have lost very few battles. Those "favored" ones, whose first assertions of differing opinions, views, and ways of acting were encouraged and praised, will find themselves strengthened and their courage bolstered to try again. However, if they never encounter any resistance, they may become imperialists, asserting themselves no matter what the impact on other people. If they ever do experience defeat, they are demolished, and their whole sense of self is at issue.

If there is never any cost to asserting one's own wishes, then it is very unlikely that one will be able to sort out the demands of identity from narcissistic whims. Ironically, the imperialist whose motto is "I take whatever I want" is as psychologically deprived as the person who is too scared to stand and be counted. Neither can possibly know who they are. There is a price exacted from individuality that motivates each of us to question our whims and our desires in order to discover which ones are essential.

Becoming a High-Level Warrior

For the highest-level Warrior, the real battle is always against the enemies within—sloth, cynicism, despair, irresponsibility, denial. The courage to confront the inner dragons is what ultimately allows us to confront the outer dragons with wisdom, self-discipline, and skill.

The cost of the battle can be very great, for the world is often a tough place. It is important to be tough enough not only to hold your own, but also to pick your battles. Mature Warriors, especially those confident of their skills, do not have to fight about everything. They choose their battles carefully.

Warriors set their goals and devise strategies to achieve them. In doing so, they identify the obstacles and challenges they are likely to meet and how each will be overcome. They also identify opponents who may try to get in the way of the achievement of their goals. Low-level Warriors reduce the complexity of this situation by objectifying their opponents as enemies and using any means to defeat them—in war, even killing them with no sense of remorse for the loss of a human life.

High-level Warriors seek to convince others to support their goals. Warriors understand the politics of organizations or communities and how to martial

For the highest-level Warrior, the real battle is always against the enemies within—sloth, cynicism, despair, irresponsibility, denial.

support for their causes. They know how to avoid the showdown vote or decision until they know they have the support they need. Actual combat is the choice of last resort, after one has thought through all the other options—going around the opposition, confusing them, controlling their response, tricking them, infiltrating their ranks, or converting them. Furthermore, high-level Warriors know how and when to admit defeat and learn from doing so.

The test of the Warrior is not always persisting in the battle, but attaining the goal. High-level Warriors can choose to retreat for a time, develop their strategy, mobilize and regroup their energy, and move only when they are ready. For instance, one woman who was fighting for a cause in the hospital where she worked eventually decided to leave. It might look more like Warrioring to others if she had stayed and fought, but she knew she would not achieve her real ends. By leaving, she had a greater chance of winning the goal itself, and having proven her courage to her own satisfaction, she had no need to continue the fight.

Actually, the most skillful Warriors may not even be recognized as Warriors at all, because there is never any battle but a battle of wits, waged completely behind the scenes. At the higher levels, victory is achieved not only without bloodshed, but also without loss of face for anyone; it is only when everyone feels fairly treated that peace can be maintained.

High-level Warriors always command respect for their toughness and for their intelligent assessment of people and situations, so they can fight when fighting is called for and seek creative compromise when that is possible. High-level Warriors may prefer peace, but they are not afraid of conflict. Indeed, at some level they tend to relish it, even when their better judgment prevails and confrontations are avoided.

As thinkers and learners, Warriors crystallize their own ideas in opposition to others, which they like to discredit as wrong (or even "dangerously," villainously wrong) or inadequate, weak, naive, and unsupported (needing rescue). This process initially predisposes the Warrior in each of us to prove that we are "right" and others are "wrong," a position that carries with it a presumption of superiority.[3]

Warriors are generally most comfortable in a universe in which issues of integrity are fairly simple and straightforward and it is easy to know what and who are right. However, the modern world is not like that. Warrioring in the modern world requires integrity within a morally complex and ambiguous universe.

The contemporary world requires Warriors who can make and commit to decisions and actions when nothing is absolutely wrong or right. The question, then, becomes not simply, "What is the right thing to think or do?" but, "What is right for me?" (and later to balance this with what is right for us) and finally, "What is best for all concerned?"

In this context, an appreciation that we all see the world from a different perspective and that none of us has a corner on the truth helps the Warrior gain comfort in moving from a win/lose to a win/win model of decision making and conflict resolution. If I am "right" and you differ from me, then you must be "wrong." But if I am doing or thinking what is right for me, and you are doing or thinking what is right for you, there is no necessary opposition, even if what we are doing and thinking are in great opposition to one another.

Yet most good Warriors would set some limits on cultural relativism (certainly with criminal or blatantly unethical acts), for it is their job to protect the kingdom from forces within and without that might harm or undermine it. High-level Warriors seek the appropriate balance between situations requiring respect for difference and those requiring swift and forceful redress.

Warriors also have different models for battling based upon their level of development. The first level is a jungle fighter. Battling is dirty, and the goal is to kill, not just defeat, the opposition (inside or outside). The enemy is seen as truly evil and perhaps even inhuman. As the Warrior becomes more civilized and refined, the battle is bound by principles and rules of fair play, and the goal is to beat the opposition, but if possible not to unduly harm them. In religion, for example, it is the movement from killing to converting the infidels.

At the third level, the Warrior's sole interest is achieving a goal that is in the larger social interest. When the Warrior's goals are defined only by the Ego, they are likely to be achieved in competition with others, because as Jung said, the Ego is about proving ourselves in contrast to others. We will then want to achieve our own ends and triumph over people of other views.

Finally, when the will is informed by the Soul and the Warrior is acting in service of the Soul's call of the individual, there is often no conflict between what the individual wants to achieve and what contributes to the general good, particularly if we learn to listen and learn from others, even (or especially) the opposition. The lesson great Warriors eventually learn is that there is no way we can really win unless we are contributing what we are here to give.

When we do so, everyone wins. The highest-level Warriors, therefore, seek such win/win solutions knowing it is in the interest of each of us if everyone achieves what will fulfill them and bring them joy at the deepest level.

Widening Spirals

It is the Warrior in us that protects the culture from any behavior that is harmful to society or the natural world. If the rain forests are depleted, if we have an epidemic of acid rain or drugs, then our Warriors are not functioning in the collective interest. If we are undisciplined and unable to curb the self-destructive patterns in our lives, then our inner Warriors are not functioning properly.

Societies only work well when the Warrior in each of us moves past simple self-interest to the defense of anyone's children and the protection of the common good. People's Warriors have their individual predilections, of course. Some Warriors care most about the environment, some about hunger or housing, some about upholding standards or morals, some about justice.

Some Warriors cannot protect others, while other Warriors, who have been taught to fear selfishness, may not be able to fight for themselves. The healthy, mature Warrior develops the ability to identify in widening spirals the locus of what needs protecting: first self, then loved ones, then others in one's own society, and finally the planet.

As Chogyam Trungpa has said, "The essence of warriorship, or the essence of human bravery, is refusing to give up on anyone or anything." The highest-level Warrior knows that "we can save the world from destruction," and beyond that build an "enlightened society."[4] But to do this, we must have not only courage, but compassion—which is the subject of the chapter that follows.

Exercises

Give some thought to when, where, how, and how much the Warrior expresses itself in your life.

1. How much or how little is the Warrior expressed in your life? Has it been expressed more in the past or present? Do you see it emerging more in your future? Is it expressed more at work, at home, with friends, in dreams or fantasies?

2. Who are some friends, relatives, co-workers, and others who seem influenced by the archetype of the Warrior?

3. Is there anything you wish were different about the expression of the Warrior in your life?

4. Since each archetype expresses itself in many different ways, take some time to describe or otherwise portray (e.g., draw, make a collage, use a picture of yourself in a particular costume or pose) the Warrior as it is expressed or could be expressed in your life. What does or would it look like? How does or would it act? In what setting does or would it feel most at home?

Daydreams

Imagine something of great value that you want very much. It can be an object, a person, an honor or a position, a righting of a social wrong, or anything that has a strong attraction for you. Imagine yourself mounting a campaign to get what you want, using all the firepower you can muster. Your firepower might be guns and tanks and grenades, or it might be words, the wielding of political influence, making others feel guilty. Whatever your means, imagine yourself fighting as long and hard as you need to fight, to attain your goal. If you feel resistance to such no-holds-barred fighting, remember this is only a daydream, not reality. When you have succeeded in attaining your goal, take time to let yourself really enjoy it and to process whatever feelings you may have about doing so.

9

The Caregiver

The ideal of the Caregiver is the perfect, caring parent—generative, loving, attentive to noticing and developing the child's talents and interests, so devoted to this new life that he or she would die, if necessary, that it might thrive. This ideal adapts to the growing child's needs. In infancy, the Caregiver takes care of the baby's every need. As the child grows, however, the Caregiver coaches him or her to learn how to do things and to understand the ways of the world so that, incrementally, the child can become self-sufficient.

The Caregiver

Goal:
Help others; make a difference
through love and sacrifice

Fear:
Selfishness, ingratitude

Response to Dragon/Problem:
Take care of it or those it harms

Task:
Give without maiming self or others

Gift:
Compassion, generosity

The progression is also followed in every analogous situation with Caregivers: teachers, psychotherapists, nurses with patients in life-threatening situations, bosses breaking in inexperienced workers, and other mentors with their protégés. Caregivers begin by taking total responsibility for a learning or healing situation, but as a student or client or protégé gradually grows stronger and more experienced, the relationship changes, until finally the student, client, patient, worker, or protégé is capable of functioning on his or her own.

The Caregiver who already has a well-developed Warrior can set reasonable limits and boundaries on behavior—of a child, of an organization, and in a society. These boundaries create clear and reassuring edges of the container in which collective and individual life grows. The Caregiver archetype's energies, however, are less about setting limits than about nurturing people and creating situations that help them grow and develop.

The Caregiver creates community by helping people feel that they belong and are valued and cared for, and by encouraging nurturing relationships between and among individuals and constituencies. Caregivers create atmospheres and environments in which people feel safe and at home.[1]

The Tree of Life

One symbol of the Caregiver is the Tree of Life, which continually feeds and sustains us. This ancient symbol signifies plenty—that there will be plenty for each one of us: Mother Earth provides what we need. An analogous ancient symbol is the Goddess figurine with a proliferation of breasts, clearly reassuring each of us that there will be enough, so we need not worry.

In the Kabbala, a document of mystical Judaism, the Tree of Life is a symbol for spiritual sustenance, and the nurturance and "food" to be received is "wisdom," not bread. This meaning of the symbol also connects with the Tree of Life in the Garden of Eden, in which it has become the Tree of Knowledge of Good and Evil. In the "fortunate fall," when Adam and Eve choose knowledge over innocence, they open to receive life in all its fullness, which includes both pleasure and pain. It is also the Bodhi tree under which the Buddha sat when he received enlightenment. Later, the Tree of Life appears as the crucifix, which signifies the martyred quality of many Caregivers. Christ is attached to the tree—and indeed becomes the tree—sacrificed so that others might live.

The myth of the Caregiver is the story of the transformative quality of giving and even, at times, of sacrifice. It is first about knowing that we are loved and cared for in the universe, and second about coming to share in the universal

The myth of the Caregiver is the story of the transformative quality of giving and even, at times, of sacrifice.

responsibility to care and give, not just benefiting from the tree but also becoming it.

The images of the many-breasted Goddess and Christ on the Cross suggest two modes of becoming the tree. The first speaks of abundance without notable sacrifice, simply about plenty and joyous, pleasurable giving. The second is about sacrifice and giving that hurts, but that may also bring rebirth and transformation to the giver as well as the beneficiary of the gift.[2]

The Caregiver is the most sublime of all the archetypes associated with Ego development; it also provides the transition from the Ego's concerns to those of Soul. At the higher levels, Caregivers know who they are and what they want, but their compassion is even stronger than their self-interest. They care not because they do not value themselves, but because to do so is the highest expression of that value. The caring within them is even stronger than the instinct for self-preservation.

The Caregiver is the archetype of generosity. To the degree that it is active in the higher levels in our psyches and in our culture, its achievements are greater abundance and freedom for all. Examples of exemplary Caregivers/Martyrs are Christ, Gandhi, Martin Luther King, Florence Nightingale, Mother Teresa, and any number of people who have given their lives to others, either by their willingness to be martyred or by daily sacrifice in the service of a cause or mission. It is also any number of exemplary parents.

The Caregiver has been more associated with the mother than the father, but real flesh and blood fathers are often skilled and devoted caregivers. The archetype of the Caregiver includes both mothering and fathering, and both nurturance and empowerment. Any time one person takes care of or develops another, the Caregiver is there. Men who do not adopt the Caregiver within are prone to seek mothering from all the women in their lives, thus remaining dependent "Mommy's boys." They often compensate for such dependence with misogyny, just as women who cannot access their inner Warrior may hate the men on whom they depend for protection.

The Negative Caregiver

Only the pure archetype can provide such refined, sensitive, and unconditional love as the perfect image of the Caregiver suggests (even Gandhi had his faults). In real life, we are often cast in Caregiver roles before we have entirely grown up. Too many young parents, for instance, get thrown into caregiving roles when they have not yet taken their own journeys or established any genuine sense of a separate identity from their parents or peer group. People whose whole sense of identity comes from the values of their parents or friends or from the fashions and fads of society cannot adequately care for another without maiming themselves.

Young mothers often fall into this category, finding themselves caring for children before they have developed their own boundaries or established their own identities. They may essentially be Innocents, with repressed Orphans and virtually no developed Warriors. If they are more Innocents than Caregivers, they will unconsciously expect their children to take care of them, thus creating a ripple effect in a new generation as their children have difficulty finding their real selves because they were initially fused with the mothers and focused on pleasing and caring for them. These young mothers may also become emotionally or physically abusive out of frustration at lacking the necessary caregiving skills.

If a woman's Caregiver is dominant, however, she may lose herself in meeting the needs of others, lacking the capacity to say no to anything asked of her. Indeed, she may even feel a compulsive need to respond to needs she has noticed whether or not she has been asked for assistance. In fact, what many of us do—male or female—is mask our sense of Orphaning by taking care of others. But what we really need and want is to be taken care of ourselves.

Young fathers who have not found their own identities may feel trapped in the instrumental role of Caregiver—the provider. This means their Warrior is acting in service to the Caregiver role, and feels trapped. Or they may try to be nurturing to their children, but not know how, especially if they came from families in which only the mother performed the caregiving role. The young man may yearn to be more caregiving but retreats because he feels so inept at it. He may pine to be "man the hunter," yet feel entrapped in a boring job in order to feed the family. Some men take out their frustration by withdrawing from their families, invoking patriarchal privilege, expecting to be deferred to and waited on, or even becoming abusive.

Of course, career men and women who are also committed parents may actually develop the Caregiver archetype in their home life and the Warrior archetype in their work, thus developing the capacity both to give and to assert. At best, this combination can create wholeness of the Ego—strength accompanied by compassion. At worst, individuals simply go through the motions of caring for and competing, but without attendant psychological growth.

Little healthy caregiving happens when the Innocent and/or the Orphan are too damaged for the individual to begin expressing the more adult Ego-oriented archetypes. Unhealthy caregiving can also happen when people have overstayed their time in the Warrior and Caregiver modes.

Aside from the problems associated with being thrown into the Caregiver mode too soon, the Caregiver archetype, as all archetypes, has an intrinsically negative side. One expression of it is the Smotherer, the part that wants to maintain indefinitely the symbiotic state experienced by mother and child. Indeed, caring may be a way the archetypal mother or father devours the growing new young self to try to keep it, or make it, part of his or her self.

That smothering potential is always present when the Caregiver energy is evoked, and it is not unusual for people to feel scared when they experience any relationship so loving and accepting that their boundaries begin to disappear. The fear of getting swallowed up by the other can be strong, and if our caregiving is a way of avoiding our own loneliness and hunger for connection, the potential for crippling the other is great; it is as if the hungry child within begins to eat up the other person to fill its own emptiness. The irony, of course, is that such negative Caregivers devour others while also feeling devoured themselves by the caregiving role.

Both men and women use others to feel whole, and both are equally unconscious that they are doing so. For instance, mothers who have sacrificed their own lives and lived only for their husbands and children often live vicariously through them. This means that the husbands and children are often pressured or manipulated into doing what the Caregiver would like to be doing, to live out her unlived life. Caregiver fathers who sacrifice finding themselves are also prone to vicarious achievement through their children (and more rarely through their wives) and to making similar demands upon them either to live out the fathers' unlived dreams or to remain mindlessly faithful to the fathers' values and rules (on the pretext that those values are "right").

Both men and women often bring their neediness to relationships, expecting the person they love to fill their emotional emptiness. Women who do so often express this by wanting to share everything and do everything together, and to reexperience the original symbiosis with the mother with their mate. They often expect the man to also play the role of father, perhaps supporting them financially, but certainly protecting them from difficulty. If he does not care for her in these ways, she falls apart and cries, and he responds, as Caregiver, by comforting and nurturing her.

Both men and women often bring their neediness to relationships, expecting the person they love to fill their emotional emptiness.

Men who look to women to remedy their emotional neediness may feel threatened simultaneously by intimacy and especially by any hint of symbiosis. They want to maintain their freedom while at the same time expecting the woman always to be there waiting for them. They want to be able to come and go and experience sexual union and whatever level of emotional intimacy they can tolerate, but if the woman fails to be available, they withdraw and pout and threaten abandonment until she shows signs of remorse. In the extreme, such men may not want their wives to work, drive, or go out with their women friends, particularly in the evening. They may also act similarly with their children, especially female children.

Another version of the devouring Caregiver is the Suffering Martyr, the type of woman or man, for example, who feels that she or he is always giving to others and never getting enough back. Usually, Martyrs either have difficulty receiving (perhaps because they have learned "it is more blessed to give than receive" or they fear being obligated if they take anything from others), or have low self-esteem, or are deficient in Warrioring ability and cannot say no.

In any of these cases, Suffering Martyrs may use the sense of guilt and obligation they inspire in others to get their own way. Ultimately, they and those they sacrifice for are locked into a prison in which everyone is doing things to please others, but no one really gets what they want or need.

People who are Suffering Martyrs may also have internalized social messages that they have no right to assert themselves.

Initially, Suffering Martyrs need to develop their Warrior aspects, and in that way get their needs met more directly and honestly. The people around such guilt-evoking Martyrs need to stop being immobilized by guilt for benefiting from the unasked-for sacrifices coming their way, and to develop their own Warrioring ability to set limits and boundaries.

Whether male or female, we tend to "devour" others, even against our better judgment, until we also find the Caregiver within ourselves that cares for us as well as for others. However, if we have not ever received adequate care (or if we have received too much), we may not know how to give it.

Learning to Guide and Nurture Ourselves and Others

Each of us has an inner child who is with us all our lives. Unless we develop our own inner Caregiver, we will be always dependent on others to nurture and care for the child inside us. The inner Caregiver is attentive to the needs of the inner child, noticing when the child is being bruised or neglected. The inner Caregiver expresses unconditional love to our inner child, whatever it does. It is the piece of us that suggests taking a warm bath or having some hot chocolate, going to bed with a good book, or indulging in some other pleasurable or renewing activity. It will also help suggest and find ways to learn how to better handle difficult situations so we do not get so bruised the next time.

Often the style of our inner Caregiver is reminiscent of that of our parents or other parental figures in our life. If our parents fed us when we were upset, we may find ourselves suddenly craving or eating milk and cookies or some other of the kinds of foods parents use to comfort children. If they held us, we may look for physical closeness. If they nurtured us but did not give adequate guidance, we may seek "comfort" but not new skills. If they provided guidance but no comfort, we may be good at learning how to do it better the next time but lack the ability to console ourselves.

Unless we develop our own inner Caregiver, we will be always dependent on others to nurture and care for the child inside us.

To compensate for the deficient caregiving by our parents, we also take in caregiving images from the media. People from dysfunctional families, for example, have widely inflated and perfectionist ideals of what is required of them as parents because all they have to go by are the idealized parental figures on TV, in the movies, and in books. To add to the complexity, many TV images of Caregiver figures are in commercials, which leads to a desire to buy things. The hunger to be cared for results in consumerism that masks but does not alleviate the real need. When we find ourselves craving food, or things, or drinks, or money, we need to be a good caregiving parent to ourselves—find out what the real need is beneath these cravings, address ways to alleviate the root cause, and/or find help outside ourselves.

If your inner Caregiver is not very effective, it is important to seek out role models in the external world and consciously model your own behavior on theirs. Simply taking on this project awakens a healthy sense of taking care of oneself. Good parents do not just comfort; they also teach and help the child to recognize and develop talents and abilities. Our inner Caregiver can develop the capability of seeing what our needs are and finding ways to help us grow and develop.

For instance, you come home miserable because you have lost a job, and your inner Caregiver says, "That's OK. Why don't you take a hot bath and relax?" If your inner Warrior is healthy, it will get busy guarding the boundaries, saying, "Don't tell anyone who is going to blame you or get upset until you feel a little better," and suggesting with whom it might be safe to talk. If your inner Warrior is unhealthy, however, it will immediately begin to wage war on you, speaking of your inadequacies (the villain in this case) and how it warned you this would happen (that is, the Warrior tried to save you from yourself).

At this point, if the Caregiver side is healthy, it will say, "Now, Warrior, slow down. It's not his/her fault. He/she hasn't learned yet how to deal with a boss like that. Tomorrow when he/she feels a little better, let's figure out how that can be learned." The Caregiver within us can help us grow up by not only comforting us but also seeing that we learn from each challenge or problem life throws us.

If the Caregiver comforts but does not develop, it may inadvertently be doing what Twelve-Step literature calls "enabling." According to this literature, the partner of the alcoholic or drug addict often caretakes in a way that allows the addiction to continue—essentially picking up the pieces and taking care of things, so the addict does not have to face the addiction. Such behavior helps keep them stuck.

So, too, parents who comfort children but do not help them learn from their mistakes fail to encourage the life skills that make subsequent mistakes less likely. However, it is important that it is the Caregiver, demonstrating an attitude of unquestioned high regard, that does this task, rather than the Warrior, so that the child feels supported, not attacked.

Levels of the Caregiver

Shadow	Suffering martyr; devouring mother or father; "guilt-tripping" or guilt-ridden behavior; enabling behaviors (which aid and abet other people's addiction, irresponsibility, or narcissism)
Call	Responsibilities that require care of others (like parenting, for example), recognition of another's neediness or dependence (or your own)
Level One	Conflict between your own needs and those of others; tendency to sacrifice your own needs to what others need or want from you; rescuing
Level Two	Learning to care for yourself so that caring for others is enriching not maiming; learning "tough love"; empowering—not doing for—others
Level Three	Generativity; willingness to care and be responsible for people (and perhaps also for animals and the earth) beyond your own immediate family and friends; community building

Again, many of our inner Caregivers have trouble with this task and either allow the Warrior to take over (with the Warrior's concern with finding out who and what is to blame here) or simply comfort without addressing the underlying skill deficit that is usually involved in most of our problems. The Caregiver needs to nurture the child within us at various levels: our infant just needs to be held and comforted; our eight-year-old needs to be listened to, to have help figuring out what he or she thinks and feels about what happened; our twelve-year-old needs some nonjudgmental ideas about alternatives; our sixteen-year-old needs to know we still trust his or her ability to handle the situation.

Our own ability to take care of others also comforts our inner child, especially our Orphan, who believes that there is no really safe place in the world. To the degree that we are loving to others and provide a safe place for them to be, our Orphan comes to believe that such safe places exist. However, if we take care of others but not ourselves, that Orphan will conclude, "Well, safe places do exist—but not for me."

Inevitably we will experience the moment when our charges break away from us and are ready to leave and take off on their own. They may leave gracefully, full of thanks, or they may blame their leaving on our inadequacies. If the latter, we need to know it is natural for adolescents, mentees, and others to find the strength to break away by focusing on the negative aspects of the relationship.

At this point, we relive our own dissociation from our parents and mentors, but from the other side.

Experiencing both sides closes the circle and provides us with a complete experience. This is often healing for our own inner Orphan if we use the experience to recognize that, in most cases, at least, we really did not leave our parents or mentors because of their inadequacies, but because we were ready to grow up.

Varieties of Caregiving

Caregiving involves much more than emotional nurturance and guidance. It involves many almost hidden tasks, hidden in the sense that society as a whole tends to take them for granted. We notice them only when they are not done. In the household, this means washing the dishes and the clothes, keeping the place clean and neat, and keeping the dwelling itself in good repair. It also means tending to the needs of the family for community, and providing a social life and connections with the extended family unit.

In organizations, it is maintenance of the physical plant, food services and day care, attention to employee health and morale, and an attitude of care and concern for the individual employee's life, not just for their achievements and productivity.

In terms of the society at large, it is the maintenance of buildings, parks, and bridges; the maintenance of relationships between and among different constituencies and groups; the education of the young; and the care of the very young, the sick or infirm, and the elderly. It means a concern that the weakest and most disadvantaged of the world are not forgotten or forsaken.

In families, organizations, and the society as a whole, these Caregiver functions tend to be terribly undervalued. People who have Caregiver roles are often underpaid, and their efforts are taken for granted. Some of the greatest Caregivers do work that may be considered menial to others. They may sweep the floors, empty the bedpans, do routine clerical tasks while they also minister to the emotional climate and health of the organization. Often they are seen by others as drudges or servants. Yet their contributions are invaluable. Indeed, they are essential, and without them our institutions fall apart.

They are also the bureaucrats who make and enforce those rules the Fool in us hates, who notice that the infrastructure of America is crumbling, that our bridges and our roads need to be repaired. They are the ones who remind us that we cannot take on new projects until we take steps to care for what we have already created.

Caregiving begins with caring for the body and its needs for physical survival and comfort. It extends to include care for the feelings, the development of the mind, relationships between people, and relationships between animals, plants, machinery, and the earth itself. In our culture, these tasks are not always valued, so they do not always get done nor do the people who do them always get thanked or rewarded in any way commensurate with the contribution they make.

Caregiving is, at least at this moment in history, humble and invisible work, often unappreciated or underappreciated. Yet it also has its own rewards, not the least of which is the self-respect that comes from doing what is needed, whether or not it is noticed. There is a kind of nobility in the humility of the role. To know that you can be fair and kind and giving, even if you are not only not rewarded but even penalized for doing so, breeds what people used to call character.

Widening Spirals

As with the Warrior, Caregivers may begin taking care of only their own—their children, their projects, their possessions—and they also learn to care for themselves. As they grow in maturity, they may also have the ability to live in community where they provide some caregiving, but not all of it. The healthiest families, groups, and organizations usually have everyone doing some of the caregiving function so that no one is doing it all. The demands of care are never ending. There is so much need for care in the world that it really does take everyone contributing what they can to the system.

However, there is a step beyond even this stage of caregiving. Although most of our actual caring effort needs to be where we work and live, it is important that we develop the capacity to care for the community as a whole and to feel responsible to minister to the needs of the less fortunate within that community. This sense of widening concern may then grow to include one's country, and eventually the globe.

It is this highly developed Caregiver who, in the words of futurist Hazel Henderson, enjoins us to "think globally—act locally" to care for the planet. We need to concern ourselves with the good of all peoples and the earth itself, while acting in that context to care for people and the earth, where we live and work.

Sacrificing for the common good must never be a substitute for caring for oneself. Caregivers need to learn that care starts with the self and works outward, in expanding spirals of concern: from self, to family, to community, to one's nation, to the globe.

The Caregiver and Identity

The Innocent, the Orphan, the Warrior, and the Caregiver all help us find out who we are. The Innocent helps us know what we want. The Orphan provides a wounding that often defines the shape of our growth. The Warrior sets goals and priorities and fights for them, and in this way struggles to create an identity we have chosen. The Caregiver refines that identity through sacrifice. The Caregiver in us wants to take care of everything, to be responsible and dutiful and be there every time we are needed. Yet we cannot do everything or be everything to all people. The Caregiver has to sacrifice one thing for another.

Life requires choice. Just as there is no end to the battles our Warrior can fight, there is no limit to the demands in this world for care—from inside ourselves, from our loved ones, from our organizations and causes and ordinary people in need. If we were gods and goddesses—pure emanations of the archetype—maybe then we could respond to it all. But as fallible mortals, we cannot. Therefore, we choose.

At the first level, we may refuse responsibility for that choice. Our Caregiver simply attends to whoever is yelling loudest. It simply responds to the demands of the outside environment until exhaustion sets in and one can say no because one is sick, exhausted, burned out, or too depressed. Such Caregivers feel totally devoured by the role.

At the next level, Caregivers may refuse to care for others while they minister to their neglected inner child. At the third level, the Caregiver is willing to give his or her share to the caretaking pool of the family, organization, or community, but not to shoulder it all. It is at this point that conscious choice begins to be invoked, and the Caregiver decides to give here, but not there; nurture this person, but not that one; contribute to this worthy cause, but not that one.

The great lesson of the Caregiver is to be willing to give fully and completely whatever is one's to give, but also to develop the refined self-knowledge required to know one's own limits and one's own priorities. It is also this ability to say no, even to an opportunity to contribute to something very good, that eventually allows the Caregiver to say no to the demands of the Ego if they conflict with the Soul.

At the fourth level, the Caregiver becomes a positive Martyr, willing to give one's life for love of others. Only some of us, like Christ or Gandhi, are asked to die for others, our cause or faith; but all of us are asked to give our unique gifts to the world, whatever sacrifices this requires. Doing so almost always forces us to accept our mortality. And this willingness to do so equips us to enter the mysteries described in Part III.

Exercises

Give some thought to when, where, how, and how much the Caregiver expresses itself in your life.

1. How much or how little is the Caregiver expressed in your life? Has it been expressed more in the past or present? Do you see it emerging more in your future? Is it expressed more at work, at home, with friends, in dreams or fantasies?

2. Who are some friends, relatives, co-workers, and others who seem influenced by the archetype of the Caregiver?

3. Is there anything you wish were different about the expression of the Caregiver in your life?

4. Since each archetype expresses itself in many different ways, take some time to describe or otherwise portray (e.g., draw, make a collage, use a picture of yourself in a particular costume or pose) the Caregiver as it is expressed or could be expressed in your life. What does or would it look like? How does or would it act? In what setting does or would it feel most at home?

Daydreams

Imagine that you had infinite resources to share: time, money, wisdom. You do not have to work, so you spend your time wandering through the world helping anyone in need. Imagine the situations you encounter, the help you provide, the gratitude of the recipients of your generosity.

●

Then expand the fantasy so that you also observe limits. Imagine yourself saying no, too, if giving would make a Martyr of you or if you would be doing for others what they could or should be doing for themselves. Let yourself also imagine others flourishing because you did not rush in to rescue them. Finally, allow yourself to imagine giving to and nurturing yourself. Be as kind to yourself as you are to others.

Part III

The Journey—Becoming Real

10

The Seeker

The quest always begins with yearning. We feel discontented, confined, alienated, or empty. Often we do not even have a name for what is missing, but we long for that mysterious something. Cinderella longs for her prince to come; Gepetto longs to have a child. Telemachus searches for Odysseus; the prince searches for a great treasure.

The urge to seek the grail, to climb the mountain in search of visions, to seek wisdom, to cross new frontiers, to achieve the formerly unachievable in all areas of life seems endemic in the human race. The Seeker responds to the call of Spirit—to ascend.

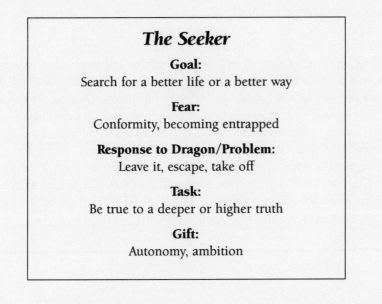

The Seeker

Goal:
Search for a better life or a better way

Fear:
Conformity, becoming entrapped

Response to Dragon/Problem:
Leave it, escape, take off

Task:
Be true to a deeper or higher truth

Gift:
Autonomy, ambition

Life, Liberty, and the Pursuit of Happiness

The Seeker seeks to find a better future or found a more perfect world. The Seeker impulse is evidenced in the beautiful refrain of the Jewish seder ceremony, "Next Year in Jerusalem," and acted out in the desire to literally emigrate to the Holy Land.

A similar impulse is present in the settlement of the New World by people seeking freedom of opportunity, the ladder of success. The impulse is upward and outward, and the goal is to realize a utopian vision. In the twentieth century, John F. Kennedy tapped this energy by aspiring to explore the frontier of outer space and by creating the "new frontier" of social programs designed to promote equality of opportunity.

The utopian dream of a perfect world is behind all dreams of human perfectibility and social justice. Martin Luther King, Jr., in his famous "I Have a Dream" speech, inspired the utopian spirit of going to the mountaintop and returning with a dream of equality. In the 1970s and 1980s, the women's movement, the human potential movement, and the New Age movement all appealed to the desire for liberation and the expansion of opportunity and consciousness.

No one is immune to the call of the unknown—whether we image it as the mountaintop, the frontier, the new frontier of outer space, or a new society, and whether its focus is riches (which we believe will open up a whole new world of opportunity to us), political freedom and economic opportunity, the quest to expand consciousness or reach enlightenment or nirvana, or a simple but unspecified yearning for more.

We begin by longing for a return to the time of innocence before the fall (which may be the primal connectedness of life in the womb or as a small infant). This urge motivates much of our seeking and striving in life; but whatever we attain, it is not satiated. No love, no work, no place, no achievement will give us the paradise we yearn for, although it does motivate our quest and get us going.

We can fulfill this yearning, however, when we become real and give birth to our true selves. Because we feel partial, disconnected, and fragmented, we yearn to become whole and connected. The yearning gets projected onto a desire for an external paradise but can only be satiated when we realize that the real issue is expanding our consciousness beyond the boundaries of Ego reality.[1] We must find what we seek inside ourselves or we will never find it beyond. To do so, we must answer the call to embark on the heroic life.

The Call to the Quest: Crossing the Threshold

The call to the quest can come at any age, but it is clearest and most distinct in late adolescence and early adulthood. This is the time of exploration—exploring new lands, new ideas, new experiences—the time to learn about the world. It is a time for travel, for study, for experimentation.

A young person who has had enough early support in the environment to achieve healthy ego development may respond to this call with excitement, joy, energy. The joy may be so great as to almost overshadow fear of the future and regrets about leaving the womb—Mom, Dad, school—as the excitement of the new adventure calls. The new adventure may be college, a job, a marriage, the military, travels, or virtually anything that offers an opportunity to do something very new, something you have chosen yourself.

In later life, you might look back at that time and say, "I only got married (or joined the army or went to college) in order to leave home"; but whatever the reason, it serves as a start to the grand adventure of living your own life. Ironically, the choices may not be ideal from the Ego's point of view, but are just the avenue that prospers the Soul.

The young Seeker whose ego development is less complete may not have the courage or self-confidence to enter a grand adventure with so much pleasure and ease. The experience may be full of dread, and the first step forward might be more like a walk around the block than a trip around the world. Some of us begin because, like Dorothy in *The Wizard of Oz,* we feel like orphans and want to find a great wizard to help us find a home.

The wandering urge hits as powerfully in mid-life as it does in the transition into adulthood. As young adults, we search for our true vocational call, for true love, for a place we might like enough to settle down in, and for a philosophy of life to sustain us. In mid-life, all these questions surface again (as they may have many times in between). If we are married, we wonder, "Is this the person I want to spend the rest of my life with?" The formerly satisfying job or career may suddenly feel unrewarding, and we consider either a job or a career change.

We reassess our accomplishments in the light of the aspirations of our youth. Whether or not our earlier ambitions have been realized, it is essential to redefine our ambitions in the context of our mortality. Spirituality becomes more important, and our philosophical assumptions need reevaluating once mortality is recognized as not just a philosophical but a personal matter.

For many people in mid-life, and not an insubstantial number of people in young adulthood, the journey is juggled against conflicting responsibilities— children, jobs, mortgage payments, care for parents. Going on the adventure seems impossible. You want to go back to school, but have to work to send your children to college. You want to sail the seven seas, but you have a mortgage payment due.

Self-pity is a form of self-discovery, self-revelation; it reveals my longings to myself.—James Hillman

The call takes different forms for different people. Always the call is to function at a higher or deeper level, to find a way to live that has more significance and depth, to find out who you are beyond the social persona that you and your environment have jointly created.

Often the quest starts with the need to make choices because life feels confining or empty. We experience the call as a sense of alienation and limitation in our present environment. To the Seeker, the issue is conformity versus individuality; the environment feels too small. Yet the desire to please, to fit in, to satisfy the demands of family, peer group, work or school environment is still strong. Most of us know that breaking the unwritten rules causes the greatest reprisals.

We start out by conforming to please authorities and peers, and continue to ensure financial success and status and to please family and friends. But eventually conformity creates a tension between who we really are inside and how we are expected to act. This tension is absolutely necessary to development. "Fitting in" is defined by the ways people are alike; individuality is defined by the ways we are unlike. So it is our very uniqueness—our Self—that does not quite fit in.

We begin our wandering with rather aimless experimentation, trying this and trying that. On the surface, we may be conformists, we alone knowing that we have a source of individuality others do not see. Or alternatively, we are Rebels, defined almost entirely in opposition to the status quo. Usually what this means is that the only way we can hold on to a separate sense of Self is by continually asserting and making it visible. Either way, we are really controlled by our environments.

How many of us have ever thought, "If I said what I really thought right now or did what I really wanted to, I'd lose my job/my family/my friends?" The potential Seeker yearns for something beyond what job, family, and friends provide but believes that to do so one will have to give them up, and in some way one may— at least temporarily. To open up and grow, we have to leave the world and the experiences we know. That does not mean that we cannot have those communities back, and it does not even mean we have to leave them physically behind, but it does mean creating some emotional distance to make our own way and think our own thoughts.

Many of us never feel that we choose to leave. Our Seeker is motivated more by a sense of alienation. Maybe our spouse or lover has left us, we've been fired from our job, we've begun to question an institution and were told to toe the line or leave, or we are in a relationship that is so abusive or addictive that we feel we have to leave to save ourselves. In such cases, we may feel especially lost and unprepared for the journey.

Often we begin knowing what we do not want rather than what we do. In fact, we sometimes enter a period in which we make a radical commitment to our own souls. At this point, leaving may be the major theme of our lives. We encounter every situation looking to see if this is the experience, the person, the work that will satisfy. Each one that fails to satisfy is left, and we are (psychologically at least) on the road again.

The Myth of Exodus

Jungian analyst Pearl Mindell has interpreted the Exodus story as a myth about accepting the call. The psychological territory of Egypt is our slavery to the life we have known. Pharaoh is the part of us attached to staying there, and Moses is our budding new heroic Self. When, for all Moses' heroism and pleading, Pharaoh will not let Moses' people go, God intercedes and sends plagues. Mindell sees this as the time when things get so bad that we have to move out of our numbness and realize the seriousness of our situation. Yet even when we leave Egypt, we do not immediately find the paradise or holy land we seek. Indeed, we wander about the wilderness aimlessly for years, many times wishing we were back in Egypt.[2]

In these years of wandering in the wilderness, we are fortunate if there is some element of our life that remains stable—maybe it is a job, a relationship, a spiritual path. That one stable element makes it easier to make all the other changes the soul requires.

At this point, we may suddenly discover a void where the Ego used to be, and we don't have a clue about what we want to do. The only thing to do then is experiment, trying this and trying that until something strikes a chord of interest. For a student, it may be that a certain course unexpectedly lights a fire; another person may find love, or a job, or the chance to climb a mountain. Sometimes the sense of being lost is so great that people have trouble making the simplest decisions in life, recognizing that every decision they make, from breakfast cereals to television shows, has been programmed by others.

We can discover the image of what we are seeking for if we pay attention to our fantasy life. The images are within us. When we are wandering in the desert, it is essential to remain faithful to our trust in some higher purpose and the journey, to know that manna will come from heaven.

The yearnings of our heart, however, are related to an inner hunger to know who we are at the soul level and to participate in the grandeur of the universe— whether it is through a great love, a great work, the ultimate experience, personal transformation, or the attainment of wisdom. In old age, we may begin to yearn to leave our bodies—especially if our health has begun to fail—and to try out whatever life there might be beyond this one.

It is never too late to respond to the Soul's call to adventure. Often we try many avenues unsuccessfully, some of them perhaps pathological, before we find the one we are looking for.

Sometimes we stop short of committing to our journeys, but it is really too late to go back. Then we become Wanderers only, not Seekers—closed off from others, terrified of intimacy, and mindlessly iconoclastic. We have to be independent and different and moving on. We cannot commit or really bond. Even if we marry, down deep we are still waiting for our prince or princess to come. We may hold a job but know it is not our "real" work. Indeed, our whole life seems empty as we yearn for paradise, or at least something better.

It is never too late to respond to the Soul's call to adventure.

Many people never really commit to themselves or their own journeys. It is only when we are able to do so that we stop being aimless Wanderers and genuinely become Seekers. When we do so, our seeking takes on a different, deeper quality. Suddenly, we are seeking spiritual depth and authenticity, and we know it is not just a change in environment—mates, work, place—we seek but a change in ourselves. Sometimes, this new search begins to have a spiritual quality to it, whether or not we would be comfortable using religious language, for we are seeking something that has deep and eternal meaning.

At the highest level, the Seeker finds the truth he or she sought. In the real world, each of us has found *some* truth, and in this way we can *all* be both Seekers and oracles, sharing our questions and our insights with one another.

The Road of Trials

Once we have made the decision to cross the threshold and undertake our heroic journeys, we experience a number of tests that check whether we are adequately prepared—whether we have learned the lessons of the Innocent, Orphan, Warrior, and Caregiver. If we have learned to balance out the Innocent's naive optimism and the Orphan's knee-jerk pessimism, we will have the street smarts to know who to trust and who not. We can distinguish guides, for instance, from tempters. Some people will support our journeys and provide guidance on the way, and some will try to sabotage them. If we judge wrong, we are usually thrown back into our Orphan until we gain greater powers of discernment. If you continue to find yourself in oppressive relationships, for example, this is the test on which you are working. You have all the time you need.

We are also often faced with a big challenge, or dragon, to test our courage. Again, if we fail, we will keep meeting dragons until our Warrior skills are sharpened. And we will meet opportunities to serve and help others to demonstrate our high-level Caregiving skills. In fairy tale and myth, slaying the dragon gives us a treasure. Aiding someone in need affords us magical protection. The beggar the fairy tale hero helps, for instance, shares a magical object that saves the day at a critical moment on the journey. Knowing when to help and when to stay back, moreover, is a critical skill, for appearances tend to be deceiving. If we help others for our own ego reasons—for self-esteem, to "pass" the test—it always backfires. The help must come spontaneously from the heart without thought of return.

The Seeker experiences the call as a rite of passage, an initiatory experience of the transpersonal without which the real Self cannot be born.

Spiritual Seeking

To some degree, all the forms of the quest reduce to a basic desire to encounter authenticity—in oneself, in the world outside, and in the cosmos as a whole. For many, this yearning takes the form of a quest for God. In all times and places, people have given names to the sacred. Native peoples found the sacred in totem animals, in Mother Earth and Father Sky, and in the ancestors. Many cultures, including the Greeks, Romans, and Egyptians, have also been polytheistic, worshiping many gods and goddesses. Sometimes human history has emphasized male deities, and sometimes—especially in very early human history—the sacred has been in female form. Most spiritual traditions have found some way to honor the One and the Many as divine.

Perhaps for the first time in human history, many people today worship no God at all, yet most have something that is sacred to them. Some people feel a connection to the sacred when they are working for peace or justice. Others feel it when they are being creative. Some like to walk in nature; others enjoy family traditions, or those moments when deeply felt truth—the truth of the heart—is expressed. Others find the sacred in making love when there is deep respect and real intimacy, and still others in watching the process of birth or death. In every case, the sacred is associated with some deeply authentic moment when we are being "real."

*We have in common a terrible loneliness. Day after day a question goes up desperately in our minds: Are we alone in the wilderness of the self, alone in this silent universe, of which we are a part, and in which we feel at the same time like strangers? It is such a situation that makes us ready to search for a voice of God.
—Abraham Joshua Heschel*

Whether we speak spiritual or secular language, our Seeker will not be satisfied until we gain some experience of something real beyond ourselves. The Seeker impulse impels us to experience the transpersonal. It is not necessary to find the absolute "right way." It is necessary only to find some way to do so.

Many Christians feel it would be impossible to learn anything about the transpersonal realm from anyone who is not a Christian. I know Jews who would be open to learning about the numinous, not only in Judaism but in other religions as well—but not Christianity. Many people can experience it only as long as no God-language is employed. For them, Jungian or other transpersonal psychologies are helpful. Many women feel more open to learning about the Goddess than about a God envisioned as white, male, and old.

People experience the sacred in so many ways that it seems only reasonable to conclude that the issue is not its availability, but our ability to take it in. The religions of native peoples often allow for the experience of the numinous to enter through discourse with ancestors or with animals or trees or mountains. In Hawaii, the volcano is still reverenced as the Goddess Pele.

As strange as these ideas may seem to many Westerners raised in a monotheistic tradition, they are not really heretical. Whether one is Jewish, Christian, Buddhist, Hindu, or a practitioner of the more spiritual forms of yoga, virtually everyone agrees that God is love and God is everywhere. Thus it follows that one can find God anywhere and God can talk to us through anything.

The spiritual issue for the Seeker does not have to involve a sense of any transcendent God at all. It does, however, require us to determine what we value, what we hold sacred, what puts spirit into our lives.

The Appearance of the Grail

The internal Seeker is a meaning-seeker, who is symbolically represented in the grail myths by the knight in search of the Holy Grail. However comfortable and successful we might be, our inner Seeker is disconsolate unless we find a sense of high meaning and value in our lives.

In the twelfth century, the great grail myths encoded ancient truths of spiritual questing. (See chapter 4 for a more extensive discussion.) The knights of King Arthur's castle swore to search for the grail, an expression of the search for vision or enlightenment.

Like Christmas, the grail legends combine pagan and Christian symbolism. The Holy Grail is sometimes said to be the cup of the Last Supper, which came into the hands of Joseph of Arimathea, who used it to catch blood and sweat from the body of Christ. In this way, it became a holy and magical object. In King Arthur's time, the grail appeared at Camelot, feeding all the assembled with "the food and drink of their choice." According to one source, this was "a symbol of the spiritual food to be obtained from the grail." Many knights go in search of its power, but only the pure and the good can find it.[3]

The inner Seeker will stop at nothing to find the truth about the cosmos and the meaning of our lives. So strong is the urge that the Seeker is willing, if necessary, to sacrifice the most valued relationships and accomplishments— home, work, friends, loved ones—to the quest. Whatever horrible or degrading things we do in life, the inner Seeker remains pure in its fidelity to the quest. Most profoundly, the search for the grail symbolically represents the search for our true selves.

Brian Cleeve says the grail serves each of us in our dying: "The last thing we see before we see no more, communicating to us the gift of eternal life."[4] The inner Seeker is quite willing to die—literally or metaphysically—to experience the ultimate beauty of cosmic truth. But it is not so much physical death that is the issue here, but the willingness to die to our old selves, to give birth to the new.

Most importantly, the quest helps us learn that God is within us. When we discover this truth, we do not "disappear into a never-never land of no return, our duty is to return bearing the gifts of the grail within ourselves, that we might be a cup, a means of regeneration and remembrance to every living creature. We become the Grail that others might drink, for to find the Grail is to become it."[5] This means dying to one's egotism and being reborn in love for all humankind. The inner Seeker is the part of us that is willing to seek not only for ourselves but for all humanity.

[The grail is] a guide, counsellor, helper. [It is] a gateway to the interior life, the inner journey we must all travel to its end, beset by danger and doubt, fear and loss of faith. And, so long as our goal is a true one, and carries no taint of evil, the grail remains at hand like a light in the wilderness.—John Matthews

The Shadow Seeker, Self-Destruction, and Transformation

If we do not respond to our inner Seeker's call, we may experience it in its shadow forms. The shadow Seeker manifests itself as an obsessive need to be independent that keeps us isolated and alone. If the urge is totally denied, it will be expressed through physical or mental symptoms. As James Hillman eloquently states, our pathologies are calls from the gods.[6]

The urge to ascend spiritually can manifest itself in shadow forms as an urge to "get high" with chemicals, the adrenaline rush of crisis and excitement, or an obsessive and ruthless ambition. Usually this is ambition in the world—to climb the ladder of success—but it can also be untempered spiritual ambition. Perhaps the most frightening story of spiritual ambition in its shadow form is the story of Lucifer, who is cast into hell for his audacity in wanting to usurp heavenly power. Lucifer means "light-bringer," and somehow his very search for more light causes him to be thrown down into the outer darkness because he does not want just to ascend—he wants to be better than others. The shadow form of the Seeker archetype often manifests itself in pride.

Many myths warn us that spiritual ambition is dangerous, and not only in its shadow forms. The Seeker is the archetype of transition from Ego to Soul, and often it is our ego aspirations alone that motivate our quests. Prometheus, for example, steals fire from the Gods and is punished by having birds eat his liver. Daedalus warns his son Icarus not to fly too high, but Icarus, whether from pride or simply the recklessness of the aspiring Seeker, flies too near the sun, which melts the wax wings and sends him plummeting into the sea.

The stories of Lucifer and Icarus do not inherently discourage the quest, however. They merely warn against presumption and pride—flying higher than you have the skill or the right to fly. It is not the attempt to ascend that is punished in these stories, but rather presumption and obliviousness to appropriate limits.

Transcendence and Death

The yearning to transcend that motivates all aspiration seems to be as eternal a human need as water, air, food, and warmth. Indeed, in many cases it is so strong that people will jeopardize these basic human needs in the interest of transcendence. Great artists jeopardize their health to pursue the sublime in their art; great mystics have fasted, worn hair shirts, and in other ways abused or deprived their bodies in the service of spirit; mountain climbers risk life and limb to reach the summit; athletes ignore injuries and compete anyway as they strive to achieve the heretofore unachievable; scholars become pale and stooped from living their lives in libraries in search of wisdom.

Levels of the Seeker

Shadow	Excessive ambition, perfectionism, pride, inability to commit, addictiveness in general
Call	Alienation, dissatisfaction, emptiness; opportunity knocking
Level One	Exploring, wandering, experimenting, studying, trying new things
Level Two	Ambition, climbing the ladder of success, becoming the best you can be
Level Three	Spiritual searching, transformation

For many people today, whatever transcendence they do experience is through their work. Giving your all for work you love can produce a high. It has become normative, however, in many businesses and certainly in many professions, to work many more hours than is physically, psychologically, or spiritually healthy.

In a materialistic, secular society, the mountain to be scaled is often professional or vocational success. Just as monks and nuns wore hair shirts, fasted, and otherwise injured their health and comfort to transcend, contemporary people take for granted the need to compromise their own health in the service of the grail of success. While the workaholism that is so prevalent in the culture is unfortunate and unhealthy, its motivation is not, and many people are discovering more fulfilling ways to transcend.

As we aspire to become more successful and prosperous and in control of human life—to live life at a level of material prosperity and individual freedom never before dreamed of—we are sacrificing our health and the health of the earth. Culturally, the archetype of the Seeker is possessing us in its shadow form.

When the Seeker has us enthralled, we will injure our bodies, sacrifice our most loving relationships, throw caution (almost) entirely to the winds in the urge to become greater than we are. Wandering involves pushing the boundaries of what we can know, can experience, can be and do. In short, we are like a seed germinating, ready to burst out and sprout new life; but doing so means cracking the earlier container open. We experience this at every major breakthrough in life, and we experience it in our dying.

But the connection of the Seeker archetype with death is also in the myth's positive form. Adrienne Rich's poem "Fantasia for Elvira Shatayev," for example, was inspired by a team of Russian women mountain climbers who died in a storm on Lenin Peak in August of 1974. It illustrates the simultaneous call to transcendence and death. Their death on the top of the mountain is not tragic. Indeed, it is the culmination of their lives. In the poem, Shatayev speaks of having prepared for months for this climb, leaving behind the world below, which she sees as dangerous, because in the ordinary world they are each trapped in their separateness. On the top of the mountain, they achieve a transcendence.[7]

Death is a small price to pay for having fully realized oneself and one's own capabilities within a human and natural community. The ultimate aim of the Seeker is a fulfillment of the Self through transcendence—to be fully our own best Self and one with the cosmos.

In some Eastern religions, the goal of spiritual practice is to transcend the body and the ego and eventually to merge with God. This essentially means to die to any sense of individual Ego Self and to be entirely submerged in Oneness. This is similar to the Christian goal of achieving immortality and spending eternity with God. This is the goal of Spirit.

The link with death, then, is not only in the pathological but in the positive form of the archetype, and in virtually every place in between. The quest is the call of Spirit to experience rebirth and transformation, to die to the old, and to be reborn to the new. Thus, at some point in the journey, every Seeker becomes an Initiate.

From Seeker to Initiate

The transformation of caterpillar to butterfly traditionally has been a symbol of a spiritual transformation so extreme as to appear to turn one species into another. It symbolizes the death of life at the physical/Ego level only, and rebirth into a life imbued with spirit.

Many people today channel their urge to ascend into various kinds of achievement—academic, athletic, vocational. And initially this is very positive and healthy. That's exactly what adolescents and young adults should be doing. Achieving and also traveling and exploring the world, are what youth requires. In this way, the archetype of the Seeker aids in Ego development. Eventually, however, as we grow and mature, the archetype emerges again at a deeper, more expressly spiritual level. It is at this point that the call of Spirit requires the ability to transcend the Self and to experience cosmic oneness, an experience that carries with it the capacity for rebirth into life as a spiritual being.

Such transformation requires more than active questing. For true transformation to take place, we must die to our former selves. Accordingly, the chapter that follows describes the archetype of the Destroyer and how it begins our initiation into the realm of Soul.

Exercises

Give some thought to when, where, how, and how much the Seeker expresses itself in your life.

1.   How much or how little is the Seeker expressed in your life? Has it been expressed more in the past or present? Do you see it emerging more in your future? Is it expressed more at work, at home, with friends, in dreams or fantasies?

2.   Who are some friends, relatives, co-workers, and others who seem influenced by the archetype of the Seeker?

3.   Is there anything you wish were different about the expression of the Seeker in your life?

4.   Since each archetype expresses itself in many different ways, take some time to describe or otherwise portray (e.g., draw, make a collage, use a picture of yourself in a particular costume or pose) the Seeker as it is expressed or could be expressed in your life. What does or would it look like? How does or would it act? In what setting does or would it feel most at home?

Daydream

Allow yourself to daydream about greener pastures, where you would rather be than where you are. Perhaps it's a different place, a different job or work, a different partner, a different life-style. Then let yourself imagine how you would have to change to make it possible for you to live your fantasy. Are you willing to allow that transformation?

The Destroyer

We have so many ways to be anesthetized to our experiences—by food, shopping, television, alcohol, and drugs—that it often takes fear to wake us up. Sooner or later, loss or fear or pain turns our journey into an initiation. Seeking is active; we feel like we choose it. But initiation, especially under the reign of the Destroyer, chooses us.

The Destroyer

Goal:
Growth, metamorphosis

Fear:
Stagnation or annihilation; death without rebirth

Response to Dragon/Problem:
Be destroyed by it, or destroy it

Task:
Learn to let go, turn it over, accept mortality

Gift:
Humility, acceptance

The initiation experience may be precipitated by the death of a child, lover, or parent and the sudden awareness of mortality.[1] It may be precipitated by a sense of powerlessness, the discovery that everything you have counted on, worked toward, or tried to build in life has come to nothing. It can be an encounter with injustice. You have been good, disciplined, hardworking, and loving, and in return you get kicked in the teeth.

It is the double punch of not only recognizing mortality and limits but doing so in a context in which life itself has no intrinsic meaning. It is bad enough to know you are going to die. But to know that and to feel your *life* has no meaning is difficult to bear. Often, however, the solution to the dilemma is not to escape from the recognition of death, but to give your own life meaning precisely by accepting the inevitability of death.

We all die. We may or may not believe in an afterlife, yet we all must deal with living this mortal earthly life, with its beauties and attachments. The transience of life makes us recognize how precious it is. An awareness of death can free us from the overfixation on achievement, fame, and fortune, because it calls us back to remember what really matters.

Whether we believe in an afterlife or not, until we stop denying the reality of death, it will inevitably possess us. Sigmund Freud understood that Thanatos is as powerful a force in human life as Eros, and that, like Eros, it cannot be denied. If this were not the case, why would people continue to smoke, knowing that the habit is deadly? Why would anyone work at an extremely high-stress job? Why would anyone stay in an abusive relationship? In a peculiar way, many of us actually do subconsciously choose our own deaths, by our life-styles and our own particular forms of self-destructiveness.

There is no way to actually escape our deaths, and for most people I know, there isn't even a way to completely escape some form of self-destructive behavior. Even people who are vehement about giving up their overt addictive behavior are usually still addicted to some socially acceptable forms, such as obesity, promiscuity, or greed. Human beings seem unable to completely dissociate themselves from the Destroyer. The question simply becomes who gets destroyed and by whom.

Scientists tell us that entropy, the tendency to increasing disorder and chaos, is the natural order of the universe. Life imposes order in a disorderly universe; entropy works against this order, an idea recognized by the many religions that venerate gods and goddesses as destroyers as well as creators. In India, for example, the goddess Kali was worshiped as the bringer of death and destruction. Christianity tends to split off the power of death and destruction onto the Devil as a spiritual entity to be resisted or even conquered rather than revered. Yet it is perhaps the Soul's subliminal contract with death that makes it so difficult for people to avoid trafficking with what we would ordinarily think of as evil—death, destruction, self-destructiveness.

My HMI score for the Destroyer archetype is

_____

(high = 30/low = 0).

It is my _____ highest score

(highest = 12th/lowest = 1st).

The Denial of Death

Whatever we deny in our conscious minds will possess us. Not to face the ways we all traffic in death is to cling to innocence—which is, essentially, an Ego-oriented position—and deny Soul. And it is also to be the unconscious and unwitting agent of what we deny. We are often possessed by death and disorder.

Most of us individually, and society collectively, claim to be committed to promoting life and prosperity and to making the world a better place in which to live. Yet our infant mortality rate is astoundingly high, alcoholism and drug addiction are epidemic, and the consumption of fat, sugar, and junk food is unhealthily high for children and adults. We are polluting the air that we breathe, the water that we drink, and the food that we eat, and we continue to store nuclear and other toxic waste in containers that are less durable and long-lived than the hazards they contain. Widespread denial of death has certainly made us its unwitting ally. Our Egos like to see God as a benevolent parent, strong enough to care for us so that we never—however old we get—have to be without a cosmic Caregiver. This is an important part of religion and spirituality; and the belief helps make our inner child feel safe enough to allow growth. However, when we are in a childlike stance in the world, the sacred is often seen simply as an agent to fulfill our human needs.

The childlike Ego state wants to know that God will keep us safe from the many dangers we see around us and keep us safe on our own terms. But the emphasis on safety always leads to denial, which in time leads to psychological numbness.

Coded in our Souls is an attraction to death that is fundamental to metamorphosis. Yet the reality of death and loss raises difficult theological issues. Annie Dillard, for example, likens the mystic's journey to a moth attracted to a flame. She describes how one night she watched as a moth flew into her candle. It was a beautiful, large golden female moth with a two-inch wing span. First, the moth's abdomen got caught in the wax, and the fire began to burn away her body, leaving only her shell, which began to serve as a wick. Dillard watched as the moth burned for two hours until "I blew her out . . . without changing, without bending or leaning—only glowing within, like a building fire glimpsed through silhouetted walls, like a hollow saint, like a flame-faced virgin gone to God."

Dillard continues by recounting the story of Julie Norwich, a lovely young girl horribly burned in an accident, and by trying to reconcile this tragedy with ideas of a loving God. God, she notes, "is mad. . . . Who knows what God loves?"[2] Yet Dillard's response to the recognition of the cruelty at the root of human existence is not to renounce God or to pronounce that God is dead but to affirm the sacred in all its completeness—including such horrors as she recounts.

Julie Norwich, she surmises, will have plastic surgery and undoubtedly live a normal life. "I'll be the nun for you," she imaginatively tells Julie; "I am now." To the Ego consciousness, such a statement sounds almost masochistic; but the Soul knows its meaning, for the Soul longs to love life, God, the Self, and the other in their full reality, not simply the Ego's prettied-up version of life.

Entering the mysteries almost always requires an encounter with fear and recognition that the ultimate reality of the universe is not pretty and neat and in human control. Whether the experience is sexual passion or the mystery of birth or death, it is part of the cycle of nature and is characteristically intricate, profound, and threatening to the Ego.

Each one of us has within a Destroyer that is in league with death, that loves death. It is this shadow Destroyer that in the modern world tries to destroy Soul to the ends of the Ego. The Destroyer tries to save our Ego by attacking Soul to defend who we are. Ultimately, the Destroyer will also attack our defenses, opening the door for us to encounter our deeper selves.

> *Entering the mysteries almost always requires an encounter with fear and recognition that the ultimate reality of the universe is not pretty and neat and in human control.*

Suffering: Its Meaning and Function

The Destroyer is central to metamorphosis. If the Destroyer had only this role, it would seem fairly benign, and we could relax into the basic beneficence of the universe. But the Destroyer often strikes in ways that seem simply irrational and meaningless.

Some people feel that a belief in karma and reincarnation satisfactorily explains pain and injustice, by positing that there really is no injustice since troubles in this life are a result of crimes committed in a past life. John Sanford, in *Evil: The Shadow Side of Reality*, disagrees, "If one contemplates the horrors of Dachau and Auschwitz . . . it seems an affront to human feeling to suggest that these victims of man's barbarity were experiencing their appropriate karma from previous lives."[3]

Many aspects of human life as we know it defy any sense of justice in terms of human feeling. Whether it is the phenomenon of ill-nourished babies, abused children, or victims of brutal torture, or whether it is the victims of so-called "acts of God," like volcanic eruptions, earthquakes, drought, floods, or famine, the sense of irrationality remains. Any karmic justice found in such experiences is not to be found at a rational level but at a deeper level of cosmic mystery.

The void the Destroyer leaves in its wake is more profound and debilitating than the abandonment experienced by the Orphan. The Destroyer often strikes people in the prime of life, who have a fully developed identity and a belief in their ability to cope. It does not come as punishment for wrongdoing; indeed, the biblical story of Job recounts the typical case of such seemingly unprovoked and undeserved misfortune.

Job was a successful man—personally, socially, economically, and ethically. He was rich, caring, good, and yet everything was taken from him—his goods, his children, and even his good name. The Destroyer assaults the successfully created persona (whether it is socially successful is beside the point) and in the best cases makes way for something new. In the case of some mystics, the destruction makes way for the sacred, and they never go back to anything resembling their former life. In the case of Job, after the emptying came the re-creation of his social persona, complete with new riches and children. Job did not go back to his life as if the gratuitous sense of loss and maiming had not happened; he was permanently changed by his encounter with the mysteries.

The Destroyer often strikes people in the prime of life who have a fully developed identity and a belief in their ability to cope.

Many people in the Job story try to explain what is happening to him in terms of causality. He must have done something wrong, they argue, or as Job's wife suggests, it is somehow God's fault, and Job should curse God and die. The point is that the mysteries are never anyone's fault. That would imply that if we could just figure out the answer, we could control the outcome and do away with death and pain and injustice and suffering. The acceptance of both their "is-ness" as part of life and our own human aversion to that reality allows us to both experience the mystery and go ahead seeking to alleviate as much injustice and suffering as we can.

The mystery cycle can be interpreted not in terms of the causal argument (Who is to blame?) but a utilitarian argument (What is suffering for?). Perhaps each of us is incarnated—and experiences the mysteries of love, birth, and death—as an initiation into a higher level of being, one that creates the opportunity for the sacred potential in the unconscious to give shape to an individual, particular expression of the divine in human form.

It is beyond the province of this book to make claims about the nature of God or the immortality of the Soul, but it is critical to its writing to acknowledge how frequently the experience of misfortune feels like a dismemberment. One can start with the survivors of the Holocaust, the survivors of dysfunctional families, especially those who experienced sexual abuse or battering during their childhoods, people who have AIDS or serious bouts with cancer requiring torturous treatments, people who have found themselves bottoming out from chemical abuse. There are people who have lost a loved child; a spouse of many years of interconnected, committed living; access to the career and identity that sustained them and gave them a sense of identity. Then there is the "normal" progress of life, from health and vitality in youth to infirmity and weakness in old age.

The Ego often protects the growing child from having to deal prematurely with events too horrible to face with a child's consciousness. It represses experiences of neglect, physical and emotional abuse, rape, incest, and so on. At some point in life, when the adult has achieved enough Ego development not to be totally destroyed by facing the reality of these events, memories begin to surface. Memories that are devastating enough can actually cause temporary dysfunction. If the trauma is relatively mild, it can be assimilated easily in the therapeutic process.

When the destruction comes from outside forces, we experience our powerlessness—we are caught in the hands of fate. If we have AIDS or cancer, we may feel that our own body or will has joined the other side, which leads to the realization that we are not just innocent victims, but that death, evil, and cruelty live inside the Self. Knowing one's death lives within is a powerful experience of the Shadow.

The Destroyer is at work when we are going about our ordinary life and suddenly the actions are the same, but the meaning is gone. Everything is suddenly hollow inside.

This experience can either cripple or be transformative. Sometimes the walls come tumbling down, and we succumb to madness or cynicism; but when we can name the experience, we can let go of the old and open to the new. People who relive childhood traumas in therapy, for example, are freed from the emotional numbing of denial and are reborn into new life and authenticity. People afflicted with life-threatening illnesses almost always give up attachment to what is inessential to them. Sometimes suffering, pain, and sickness open us up to the healing power of grace. Many religions may claim a monopoly on this experience, but enlightenment and healing are not the province of any one religion, or even of religion. If it were critical to belong to a particular religion to experience such grace or healing, the Twelve-Step programs would not work. Indeed, all over the country, drug addicts, drunks, and other addicted people experience grace and healing when they turn their lives over to a "higher power," even if they have little sense of who or what that higher power might be.

Suffering frequently moves us out of Ego attachments. We are attached to our health, wealth, homes, attitudes, and people we love. Sometimes, in order to open up to learning something new, we have to let go of the old. We may do this willingly, reluctantly, or against our will, but the result is the same.

Committed love often involves an experience of powerlessness and loss. Any time we commit, we are simultaneously letting go of other options, moving from the infinite world of possibilities to the finite world of mortal life. We are then not free. A woman I know and respect fell in love with a man only to discover he was an alcoholic. Much of her life, then, became caught up in their joint recovery as she went to Al-Anon and he to AA. This took time and attention away from their world of accomplishment and striving, and she had to let go of some of her ambition. A man I know married a woman who shortly after the wedding was diagnosed as having terminal cancer. Instead of doing many of the things he had anticipated, he walked with her through the process of dying.

People deal with their sense of powerlessness in such situations differently. Some people simply miss the rebirth that comes after the death because they get stuck in their bitterness. It is important to fully feel our grief and anger about our suffering and then let go at least long enough to see the new reality on the other side. Beliefs that reassure us that everything is in control are helpful.

Most traditional religions teach us to trust that God is in control and has our best interests at heart. Many people believe that each of us, at a deep level (perhaps the Soul level), chooses everything that happens to us and that we do so wisely for our own growth and development (even though our conscious minds, our Egos, perhaps cannot understand why we would choose some of life's more difficult challenges). Both beliefs help the Ego relax its hold, reassuring it that although it may feel it has lost control, some benevolent force is in charge. Such beliefs allow us to experience the mysteries with less fear and suffering.

Ironically, the degree of vision or spirit or grace we have received seems to be related to how empty we have become. That is why most religions see success in the world (at the level of the persona) and success of the Spirit at cross-purposes with one another, and why mystics and ascetics divest themselves of intimacy, possessions, and pride in themselves. The virtue associated with the Destroyer is humility.

At some point in our lives, the Destroyer within or without strikes, and hollows us out, humbles us. It "wounds" us, and through that opening we are able to experience new realities.

The Myth and Its Function

The key to the hero's journey is a willingness to sacrifice and be sacrificed for the healing or betterment of the world. Christ, Osiris, and Dionysus are all sacrificed so that others might have more life. This sacrifice is necessary for a variety of reasons: by facing our worst fears, we gain freedom from attachment; by being open to transformation, we call forth compassion in ourselves and others.

Sylvia Brinton Perera's book, *Descent to the Goddess: A Way of Initiation for Women,* recounts the myth of the Goddess Inanna, who voluntarily left all her power to descend into the underworld and experience initiation. On the way down, she is divested of all her belongings, jewelry, and clothes, until she arrives quite naked. She is then divested of her very life, and her body is hung to rot.

As with all of us, when the Destroyer descends, Inanna is helpless. She cannot save herself. It remains for someone else to save her. She is saved by the good graces of Enki, the earth god, who creates and sends two creatures (made from the dirt under his nails) whose major attribute is empathy. These creatures show sympathy and compassion for the queen of the underworld, Ereshkigal (who is in labor), and are rewarded with Inanna's corpse, a process that Perera likens to the rebirth through empathy typical of therapy. Inanna is finally reborn when she is sprinkled with the food and water of life.[4]

It is the hero, Christ, Inanna, going before, showing us that we do need to die but that death is always followed by the rebirth that gives us the courage to stay with our journey even when it means entering the underworld.

The Destroyer with a Thousand Faces

The hero aims to balance Ego, Self, and Soul, but many people at different times and places have determined to develop the Soul at the expense of the Ego and the Self. What this has often meant is the renunciation of worldly goods and relationships in the service of a monastic spiritual life.

For most of us, however, renunciation is not so complete. We want a balanced life, including success in the world as well as spiritual or soul development. Even so, we can benefit from the meditative techniques, perfected by mystics and ascetics, that help us empty out and open up without having to experience loss. Emptying out frees us from regrets about the past or ambitions or fears for the future.

Here the Destroyer becomes our ally. We learn to give up and let go of everything that no longer serves our journey. Furthermore, as Stephen Levine explains in *Who Dies?*, all the losses of life, large and small, are rehearsals for death. In other times and places, the mark of a well-lived life was the ability to die with grace. Meditation and other such spiritual practices help us prepare for death by helping us to let go of desire and experience the moment for its own sake.

We learn to die well by acquiring ability to accept all of life's losses and disappointments and to recognize the loss inherent in all change. Every change we experience in life is practice for the ultimate transition of death.

The Destroyer begins to become our ally when we recognize the need to change or give something up without denying the pain or grief involved. The Destroyer can also become our advisor, for we can learn in making every major decision to consult our deaths. If we allow death—rather than our fears or ambitions—to guide us, we make fewer frivolous decisions. If you were going to die tomorrow, what would you choose to do today?

The Destroyer is also the transformer. The sacred mysteries of the nature religions always remind us that rebirth follows death. This is literally true of the seasons. However cold and dark the winter might be, the spring does come. Such religions have always taught that the god who was crucified or dismembered in winter, for example, is born again in the spring. Although different religions have

The Destroyer begins to become our ally when we recognize the need to change or give something up without denying the pain or grief involved.

defined the details of this rebirth differently, the ultimate reassurance is the same: death always leads to new life.

Our encounters with the mysteries tend to strip away layers until the essential within us is revealed, just as they strip away pretense and illusion so we can see into the essence of the cosmos. This element of truth includes the whole range of experiences, from the most sublime to the most depraved. All are, of course, part of each person's Soul—at least in potential form—and in the world around us.

Accepting Mortality and Pain

What part of this reality we see when those layers are stripped away depends upon the direction of our gaze and the range of our vision. It can lead us, as it did Kurtz in Joseph Conrad's *The Heart of Darkness,* to confront humanity at its most evil, and to say, "The Horror, the Horror." Or, like Mrs. Ramsay in Virginia Woolf's *To the Lighthouse,* to be overcome with the grandeur and beauty of it all, with no need to deny the more painful elements of life, and to say, "It is enough! It is enough!" Neither response is more or less a part of experiencing the mysteries, for the extremes fill us with awe because they help us see some deep truth about reality.

All the mystery religions call our attention to the awe in life and death, grace and spiritual deprivation. The passion of Christ included the moment on the cross during which he cried out, "My God, my God, Why hast thou forsaken me?" Poet Theodore Roethke writes, "In a dark time, the eye begins to see."

The story of Dionysus teaches us of the interconnection of ecstasy and great pain. Dionysus—the god of wine, joy, and ecstasy—is not only worshiped in orgiastic revel, but torn apart by his followers. As Robert Johnson points out, the Dionysian story and the Christian Communion service follow the same basic mythic structure: "betrayal, murder, crucifixion; the god become wine." Johnson goes on to talk about the god Shiva in India, who carries Dionysian energy there. Visiting India, Johnson saw a young man dancing to drumming provided by two accompanists as he danced with a whip. Eventually, he began hitting himself with the whip, digging great chunks of flesh from his body.

As blood flowed and agony showed on his face, "he danced his pain into an ecstatic state with a fury and energy" and "his face was transformed from pain to ecstasy by his dance." The community provided the living for this dancer, whom they saw as transmuting their own suffering and pain, with his own, unto joy.[5]

In a psychological sense, it is only when we are willing to face our own pain that we are willing and able to experience joy. It is only when we are willing to face our ignorance that we stand a chance of gaining wisdom. It is only when we feel our loneliness that we are likely to experience love. Finally, it is only when we are willing to experience our inauthenticity that we are able to open to our Souls.

From Shadow to Ally

Like all archetypes, the Destroyer has negative as well as positive forms. We may become literally possessed by the archetype and become criminals, or we can become revolutionaries and channel that energy to subvert, destroy, or change repressive or harmful systems. Destructive acts such as murder, rape, child molestation, and robbery are the work of the Destroyer in its pathological form, as are all acts of self-destruction.

Even the healthiest individual will do or say things that hurt other people. The Destroyer makes us humble not just because each of us is powerless over the Destroyer; but also because we are also powerless to avoid sometimes being destructive to ourselves or others.

James Hillman sees the moments we harm or betray others as also self-betrayal. The confrontation with ourselves that results from acknowledging and taking responsibility for the harm we have done, he says, opens us to our Souls. In Judaism, between Rosh Hashanah and Yom Kippur, each person is expected to atone for wrongs they have done not just to God but to others. This opens us to the possibilities of the new year. Christians confess their sins either directly to God or through a priest; through "grace" they are forgiven. In both traditions, the process of error and atonement is seen as having a positive effect, just as Hillman, taking a psychological view, finds that transformation happens in our psyches when we confront and atone for our "betrayals."

The Destroyer turns us into villains when we refuse to acknowledge and take responsibility for the harm we do—and we all do harm of some kind. At worst, some people who have failed to develop the Ego strength to control their impulses or a sense of morality or character become totally dominated by the Destroyer and have no power or wish to stop their destructive behavior.

In more positive guise, the Destroyer archetype helps us clean out our closets. In the emotional realm, it helps us break off relationships that are not working. In the psychological realm, it helps us let go of ways of thinking and behaving that no longer fit us. Almost always, however, when the Destroyer acts through us—even to good effect—we feel guilty about the resulting destruction.

Taking the journey opens us up to experience our own power—for destruction and creation. Many people avoid claiming their power because they fear the responsibility for the relationships they might have to leave, the people who might feel hurt, the damage to the status quo that the hero as transformer

---

Levels of the Destroyer

Shadow	Self-destructiveness (including drug and alcohol abuse, suicide) and/or destruction of others (including murder, rape, defamation of character)
Call	Experience of pain, suffering, tragedy, loss
Level One	Confusion, grappling with meaning of death, loss, pain
Level Two	Acceptance of mortality, loss, and relative powerlessness
Level Three	Ability to choose to let go of anything that no longer supports your values, life, and growth, or that of others

---

inevitably inflicts. As long as we feel powerless, we do not have to take responsibility for harming anyone. We just feel stuck in a world we did not create.

If the Seeker energy calls us to ascend, the Destroyer calls us to descend into our depths, and to integrate our capacity for destruction as well as creation.

According to the spiritual version of the Columbus myth, it is possible to fall off the edge of the earth and no longer be in the hands of God. It is not the urge to descend to the depths that keeps us from experiencing the divine. We are cut off from the sacred when we are too attached to being good or socially acceptable to face the truth of our wholeness.

Entering the mysteries leads to death. But if we are fortunate, it also leads to love—both human and divine—and through this experience gives birth to the Self.

Exercises

Give some thought to when, where, how, and how much the Destroyer expresses itself in your life.

1. How much or how little is the Destroyer expressed in your life? Has it been expressed more in the past or present? Do you see it emerging more in your future? Is it expressed more at work, at home, with friends, in dreams or fantasies?

2. Who are some friends, relatives, co-workers, and others who seem influenced by the archetype of the Destroyer?

3. Is there anything you wish were different about the expression of the Destroyer in your life?

4. Since each archetype expresses itself in many different ways, take some time to describe or otherwise portray (e.g., draw, make a collage, use a picture of yourself in a particular costume or pose) the Destroyer as it is expressed or could be expressed in your life. What does or would it look like? How does or would it act? In what setting does or would it feel most at home?

Daydream

Begin by getting centered and quiet, then breathe deeply. Allow yourself to move through the events of your life as if you were watching the main scenes of a movie sped up for easy viewing. Let yourself feel, see, or hear the major events of your childhood, adulthood, mid-life, old age, and finally your death. In this daydream, allow yourself to "remember" events that have not yet happened. When you reach your death, spend time saying good-bye to everything that brings you special pleasure—from the people and places and activities you love to ordinary things like the warmth of the sun on your skin, the feel of a brisk morning shower, the smell of a rose. Then allow yourself to watch your body being buried or cremated. Then, after some interval, allow yourself to experience whatever form of rebirth is consistent with your philosophy or theology.

12

The Lover

Without love, the Soul does not engage itself with life. The first task of the child is to bond with someone or something—initially a parent or parent substitute and later a favorite blanket or toy. As the child grows, the web of attachment develops to include many things and people: home, room, toys, friends, siblings, relatives, particular games, and activities.

The Lover

Goal:
Bliss, oneness, unity

Fear:
Loss of love, disconnection

Response to Dragon/Problem:
Love it

Task:
Follow your bliss, commit to what you love

Gift:
Commitment, passion, ecstasy

The spectrum of problems that results from a failure to bond ranges from autism and narcissism to the more "normal" and everyday failure of people to be able to commit to themselves, the people they love, their work, or a set of ethics and values.

Attachment and bonding come under the protection of Eros. Such attachments are deeply primal, sensual, physical. The initial attachment of mother and child involves the most basic function of suckling, which both satiates the child's physical and emotional hunger and eases the child's discomfort. Later the sexual intimacy of lovers carries some of that quality of extreme physicality, vulnerability, trust, and the slaking of desires—for closeness, for sexual expression and release, for knowing and being known.

We know Eros when we experience a passionate connection to a particular landscape, to our work, to an activity, to a cause, a religion, a way of life. We know Eros is at work when our connection with something is so strong that the thought of losing it brings intolerable pain. Without Eros, we can be born but never really live: our Souls simply never fall to earth. It is Eros—passion, attachment, desire, even lust—that makes us really alive.

Choices made under the influence of Eros are visceral. Our bodies are attached to one person, but recoil from another. We think of a particular activity or idea, and our body lightens up, gets energized, and is ready to go. We think of another, and our body gets heavy, leaden, inert. If our minds and bodies are at odds, we may try to mobilize the body to do what the mind wants, and we move into living life as a struggle. If our minds and our bodies are in harmony, we can easily use our body cues to make decisions, and then life is an easy flow.

The Rule of Eros

As children, we operate initially out of Eros, without the controlling connection with mind. Our passions are simply given; we start with a love affair, happy or tragic, with our parents. If we are like most children, we commit willy-nilly to even the most dreadful parents because they happen to be our parents. We internalize their attitudes about us without being able to sift and evaluate them, and we may end up spending years in therapy working to develop an independent sense of self. And it is our parents as well as other parental figures who teach us to curb our passions and keep them under control. Paradoxically, we learn to restrain our passions because the passionate bond we have with our parents makes us want to please them.

As we become adults, we begin to make a series of choices or commitments. These are the predictable adult choices of whom and if we will marry, what our work will be, what our avocation or hobbies will be, where and how we will live, what political, philosophical, and perhaps religious affiliations we will

My HMI score for the Lover archetype is

――――――

(high= 30/low =0).

It is my ＿＿＿ highest score
(highest = 12th/lowest = 1st).

make. We can, of course, make all these life "choices" on the basis of mind or Ego alone, and if so, they will be prudent and practical. But that usually requires a suppression of Eros.

Eros is about Soul, not Ego. Because our culture has operated primarily at the level of the first five archetypes described in this book, there are powerful cultural prohibitions against Eros. Yet if we are lucky, some of our choices are made through its intervention. They may not feel like choices at all. We feel captured—as in the experience of falling in love, especially with someone "inappropriate," or when there is a cost. Or it might be our life's work. Some people feel a "call" to do a particular work, even when the field is not well paid (ministry or teaching, for example), or when the chance for material success is slim (as in the arts). We often recognize a Soul call because it is at odds with what our more prudent Ego would choose for us.

The Left-Hand Path

Joseph Campbell said there are two basic paths in life. The "right-hand path"—the path described in this book as the Ego's way—is prudent and practical. But Campbell warned that you can follow this path, climb the ladder of success, and find that the ladder is up against the "wrong wall."

The "left-hand path"—what I call the path of the Soul—is riskier. It is the path of following your "bliss," as Campbell famously put it, your rapture, your ecstasy. The culture may not understand this choice, and there is no guarantee to what wall your path will lead you, but the choice of the left-hand path is worth it because the journey itself is its own reward.

Eros is notable for its lack of prudence. For the ancients, a cosmic curse was to be pricked by Cupid's arrows while looking at a totally inappropriate object. We are often most made aware of Eros when we fall in love with someone our Ego would not choose, someone perhaps who is not good-looking, educated, or well-off. When we continue to be smitten against our better judgment, we find out that we are not really as under control as we thought.

Eros is the passion that results when Soul and body are in accord.

Great ennobling loves are also frequently either inappropriate or simply outside the realm of practicality or rationality. The cult of courtly love, for instance, was entirely adulterous, assuming that Eros had nothing to do with marriage. Courtly love was passion so profound that the smitten knight could fade away and die if his love was not reciprocated. The power of such love was not simple affection—the intensity of desire was too great—but it was not just lust either. The knight often "proved" his love to his lady by demonstrating how much he would endure for her sake and how long he would wait for her to take pity on him and take him in her arms. Lust is simply a matter of the body. Eros is passion that results when Soul and body are in accord.

Most of the great love stories of myth and legend, moreover, were tragic simply because others did not approve of them (think of Romeo and Juliet, Tristan and Isolde, Lancelot and Guinevere). The greatest love stories always end in death, as Denis de Rougemont's classic *Love in the Western World* shows. The romantic love story is, he argues, the form in which the ancient nature religions, which celebrated the death and rebirth of a god, have come into modern, Western consciousness.

The Elizabethan understanding of the orgasm as a "little death" also makes that connection, perhaps because sexual passion that includes orgasm involves surrender of control, the temporary suspension of the Ego—a suspension that the Ego may both desire and find threatening. Committing to another person or a work also limits choice, involving a death or loss of options. Any time we find ourselves entirely smitten by an object of erotic love, we lose Ego control—a fact that sends many men and not an insignificant number of women into almost uncontrollable panic.

The answer here is not to ignore the Ego. The panic we feel when we are not entirely under its control is a result of Ego development that is too weak to contain the passion. Shirley Luthman identifies this as a lack of sufficient structure in the psyche. Lovers pull away from each other because one or both lack the Ego structure needed to contain the intensity of the connection without losing his or her self.[1] A strong identity is necessary to contain an intense passion. Lovers need to build connections in their relationships on the concrete, everyday Ego level to sustain their passion. That is why lovers must spend time together, know each other on many levels, and form bonds of friendship as well as passion, so that the deep structures of Self and relationship can hold the intensity of their passion.

Any time we find ourselves entirely smitten by an object of erotic love, we lose Ego control.

Love is the spiritual food of the Soul, and it is the Soul that gives birth to the Ego. Without love, the Ego container eventually begins to dry up and crumble. But when we are in touch with our deepest feelings, we cannot walk by the homeless on the street and be unmoved; we cannot see pictures of starving children on the evening news and not suffer; we cannot watch a co-worker be mistreated and not care. And, we cannot disregard the part of ourselves that feels unloved and yearns for more intimate and honest human connection.

If there is nothing we can do about such things, Eros brings a profound sense of powerlessness, which is associated with the experience of death. If there is something we can or are willing to do, Eros may be backed up by our Warrior or our Caregiver, and we may step in and help. In this case, Eros brings not death, but more life. Contrary to de Rougemont, not all love stories end in death. That is true in tragedy, but the love stories of all the great comedies end in marriage. Beatrice and Benedict (of Shakespeare's *Much Ado About Nothing*) and Elizabeth and Darcy (of Jane Austen's *Pride and Prejudice*) are as great lovers as Shakespeare's

Romeo and Juliet. Marriage signifies an ability to combine prudence and respectability with passion, the beckoning of Eros, and the demands of family and society. The fertility cycle is about love, death, *and* rebirth. It is love that motivates us to more aliveness, to act in the service of life. To do so, however, we often have to let go of the past and our past ways of doing and thinking, and open up to rebirth.

In the typical love story, two people fall in love, but encounter some obstacle to their union. In classical drama, they may believe they are brother and sister and would be violating the incest taboo, or their families may be feuding. In more modern times, they may simply misunderstand one another or be victimized by cultural prejudice against lovers of the same gender or different races or religions. Love stories are called tragedies if the lovers and their surrounding community are not able to find a way for the love to blossom and grow within that community. The story is a comedy if it ends in a marriage that typically unites not only the lovers, but the whole community.

Ultimately, it is Eros that wakes us up to feel the suffering of the earth. The denial of Eros has led to a culture in which our ultimate interconnectedness is denied, in which we are unable to make connections between the ravagement of the rain forests and our own capacity as a species not only to survive, but to live enjoyable and vibrant lives. The challenge of Eros is literally the key today to the survival of our species and to our cultural recovery from an epidemic of workaholism, consumerism, drug and alcohol addiction, and the widespread denial of both Spirit and Soul.

Kinds and Stages of Loving

Motherly love, erotic love, and the highest levels of spiritual compassion are all aspects of love. But Agape differs from Eros in that the loving union is initially with oneself, not a lover, friend, or child. It is this inner union that allows us to develop the capacity not just to love our own loved ones, but to love humanity and the cosmos.

Whether love comes to us as erotic or romantic love, a love for work, for justice, for humanity, or for God, it is a call from our Souls to move away from a disconnected way of living. It requires us to give over our cynicism and believe again. Often in the process, we wake up enough to fear for our Souls at how shallow, loveless, and callous our lives have become. We cannot stay in our old lives, for to do so would be to lose our Souls. Yet in the very awareness of that lifelessness come shame and guilt; whether we are guilty of great crimes or only conventionality, we may mourn the lifelessness of our lives. Whether we are converting to a new religion or entering a new relationship or work, we may feel literally reborn.

Love also comes as compassion, forgiveness, grace. In most religious traditions, this forgiveness comes from God. In a psychological sense, the forgiveness must come from ourselves. Paradoxically, it is love that calls us to life and deep feeling, and judges our prior lifelessness and lovelessness. It is love that allows us to forgive ourselves so that we can be alive in a new way. And it is compassionate love that allows us to forgive the people we love for not living up to our image of them and for their inevitable inability to fulfill all our needs.

Love also always calls us to make a commitment and have faith in that decision. In a relationship with a lover, we may not always feel "in love" after a time. We need to trust that that feeling will return. To do otherwise is to do violence to those we love. So, too, with our love for humankind. Sometimes, for example, working for the betterment of others, we are inspired by our love and vision. Other days, we just need to keep putting one foot in front of the other and trust.

To live by love is to accept that all love—however profane or however spiritual—is a gift.

To live by love is to accept that all love—however profane or however spiritual—is a gift. We may not always choose to accept the gift—we have that much Ego control—but we cannot make love happen or make love stay. If we choose to accept the gift, we can only remain faithful and open so that we are present to receive it when it comes. After a time, we come to recognize the rhythm of love's coming and going. Each relationship will have its own rhythm. Until we come to recognize that rhythm, we may panic when the feelings of love seem to go, and act out or try to "make" love come back. We may think everything is all over just before a breakthrough that ushers in more intensity and intimacy than we have ever experienced before.

When love captures us, we are no longer free to attend to only our own desires and wishes. Instead, we make choices based as much on the good of what and whom we love—a child, a lover, a work—as on what we want to do at the moment. This journey may be a complex one. We begin by attaching to very few things and people, and generally we believe we cannot live without them. It is crucial at this point in the journey that we allow ourselves the freedom to love whom we love and to feel fully the vulnerability that brings. However, if our Ego development is weak, there is a danger we might become addicted to love but unable to help ourselves.

Four processes help us here. First, the Destroyer eventually deprives us of much of what we are attached or even addicted to; although we find that painful, we do survive. Second, we gradually allow more people and things into our circle of love, so we begin to experience love as plentiful rather than scarce; the more love we show, the more love we get back. We may also allow in love from a spiritual source. Third, many Lover types are deficient in Warrior; they can't set limits with people, so they end up being taken advantage of or enabling others' addictions. When we develop our Warrior, we can practice "tough love" for the good of all. Finally, when we really learn to love ourselves, we are free to love without addiction or attachment because love is no longer scarce at all. We always have ourselves, so we are always loved.

The Perversion and Reclamation of Eros:
Passion and Its Shadow

Many ancient religions saw the universe as a by-product of the great love of a sacred couple, sometimes depicted (as in Shiva and Shakti) as dancing together. Love, whether sacred or profane, was seen as all one: Eros, Agape, Shakti, and Grace are aspects of the same reality. Only later, with the development of religions so patriarchal that they had no divine image of the feminine, was the erotic aspect of love seen as sinful or degrading.

Virtually every religion teaches us in one way or another that "God is Love," but religions without an image of the feminine aspect of the divine (at least in their dominant tradition) hasten to dissociate Eros from God. Even so, most modern patriarchal religions have within them a mystic tradition that honors Eros and the feminine.

Edward Hoffman, in *The Way of Splendor: Jewish Mysticism and Modern Psychology,* describes how the Jewish mystic tradition of the Kabbala venerates a heavenly couple, not simply God the Father. Since the beginning of the Kabbalistic tradition, he notes, God the Father has been balanced by a heavenly Mother, the Shekinah (wisdom). "Only when the two are united—depicted in explicit sexual terms—does harmony truly govern the universe." Although by the industrial age, he notes, all traces of this belief disappeared from prayers and rituals, it was an important, compelling view for a time. Key Kabbalist texts such as the Bahir suggested that the Shekinah "draws near this realm whenever sexual intercourse occurs," and consequently the faithful were encouraged within the bounds of marriage to make sexual intercourse a regular spiritual meditation, especially to be practiced on the Sabbath.

Catholic theologian Matthew Fox similarly bemoans the history of the church in denying Eros, but he also cites a countertradition of creation spirituality that honors sexuality, women, and the body—Eros as well as Agape. He calls our attention to the beautiful eroticism of the Song of Solomon, often interpreted as a metaphor for the love of God for humankind, which describes sexual union in beautiful, sensuous, and ecstatic detail. He calls upon the church to recognize sexual intercourse as a sacrament, while decrying the pernicious effects of the church's historical antieroticism.[2]

What happened to Eros, and to modern religion and culture, which seem unaccountably hostile to it? Audre Lorde argues that the rise of the pornographic follows from the devaluation of eroticism. When Eros is banned, it goes underground, and is thus seen only in its shadow forms, which are depraved and destructive rather than life-giving and life-promoting. Banished to the unconscious, where it reigns in its shadow form, Eros, now theologically cast in opposition to Agape, is projected by a Christian culture onto the image of the devil, who reigns in a hell that is seen as punishment for identifying with the body.

The irony is that those who despise Eros are often Eros-possessed: fundamentalist preachers who cannot seem to help having affairs or repressed church fathers who tortured and killed millions of women, calling them witches, fearing that women were close to the devil because their "lust is insatiable." The great curse of those who detest their sexuality is to be possessed by lust, but find sex empty because it provides physical release but no psychological nurturance. Such is the fate of the rapist, the child-molester, the sexual harasser, in whom lust is the child of an urge to power and dominance rather than a reverence for the life force itself.

Starhawk writes in *Truth or Dare* about the tragedy of the worst of male socialization in a society that fears and derides Eros. She quotes a chant of soldiers in Vietnam who patted first their machine guns and then their groins: "This is my rifle/this is my gun/One is for fighting,/one is for fun." The rapist mentality is often present among men who have been socialized to view themselves as machines, women as prey, and their penises as weapons.

Remembering that this would be unthinkable in a time or place in which male and female genitals were symbols of the goddess and the god, Starhawk mourns for a man who was so disconnected from his Soul and the life-giving power of Eros that he molested his own little girl. That man, she notes, "has never made contact with the wellsprings of nurture within himself. His own value has been destroyed. No one will ever sing of his cock that its rising makes the desert green and the grain spring up from the fields. He lives in the dismembered world . . . (and) has himself become a weapon that has no needs except for periodic servicing and is ultimately expendable, whose value is that of a thing, an object, a possession."[3]

Such dehumanization is also the fate of women who have been taught that their bodies are dirty or unclean, who find no pride in menstruation, no true joy in sexuality, no miracle in giving birth. It is true of women who fear they will have no market value without their virginity and of women who feel they need to "put out" so that men will love them. It is true of women who feel inferior to men, whether or not they locate the "blame" for that inferiority in their sexual parts.

All lovemaking (as distinct from "having sex") is Christ meeting Christ. Love beds are altars. People are temples encountering temples, the holy of holies receiving the holy of holies. . . . Go beyond "being in love" to being the presence of cosmic love embodied and reflected in two human lovers.— Matthew Fox

Eros smiles on those who see it as sacred.

The Denial of Eros

The denial of Eros causes sickness, violence, jealousy, the objectification of the Self and others, and ultimately a loss of life force, of energy. Perhaps at one time in the evolution of the human species it was not possible to control erotic urges without repressing them and denigrating them. It was also a time in which people thought in a linear, dualistic fashion. The way to climb the spiritual hierarchy of love, from Eros to Agape, was to give up Eros for Agape, hence the emphasis on chastity in religious life. While some highly developed people have been able to essentially sublimate their sexual energy to spiritual purpose while retaining a respect for Eros, it has been more common for people to try to kill Eros in order to become capable of Agape.

This latter path is too dangerous for our time. The projection of shadow eroticism has resulted in the oppression of women (since men have projected their own lust onto women) as well as dark-skinned people (think of the lynching of black males in the South and the association of "the rapist" with men of color), in the oppression of gays and lesbians, and also in widespread alienation from our own bodies.

Greater knowledge of human psychology tells us that we move to achieve Agape not by suppressing Eros, but by getting its gift, by learning to love passionately and fully while also maintaining our sense of morality and ethics. Moreover, as Irene Claremont de Castillejo, that great theorist of love and its meanings, has helped us to understand, Agape is achieved not by being at war with oneself, but with the inner marriage and wholeness that can only come through complete self-acceptance.[4]

The Gift of Eros

The gift of Eros is not only erotic love and the passionate bonds that connect us to the land we live on, our homes, our major institutions, our friends, and the earth itself, although each of these is a great gift. Eros is also the source of personal power that is not a result of position, or authority in an institution. It is not power over another, but power from within. It is sometimes called *charisma,* but even that word fails to capture its essence. It is the power of someone whose Soul is engaged in life, someone who is not afraid to be true to his or her core nature, for Eros comes directly from the Soul.

We honor Eros, and by so doing place the center of consciousness in our Souls, by loving and honoring ourselves, each other, and the earth. We do so by cultivating an attitude of respect toward our bodies and our sexuality, and the immanence of spirit in nature. When we recognize that whatever is sacred in the universe is not separate and apart and above us, but also below us in the earth and inside ourselves, we can commit to our own journeys by also committing to whatever beckons to us of real beauty. It does not matter if anyone else finds it beautiful and worthy of love. The issue is that we do. That is how we find out who we are—by what we love enough to commit to.

Love and Birth

Love is about joy and pleasure, and it is also about birthing. On the most physical level, sexual passion often results in the conception and birth of a child. But it is not just physical birthing that sex creates. Eros often attends the creative process. Two colleagues working together are aware of an erotic charge. They may confuse this with a romantic or sexual attraction when it actually has to do with birthing their project. Often when the project is completed, the feeling goes away. If they get confused and act out their erotic attraction, they may find that their relationship suddenly becomes confused, complicated, and generally unsatisfactory and their project aborts.

Levels of the Lover

Shadow	Jealousy, envy, obsessive fixation on a love object or relationship, sexual addiction, Don Juanism, promiscuity, obsession with sex or pornography, or (conversely) puritanism
Call	Infatuation, seduction, yearning, falling in love (with a person, an idea, a cause, a work)
Level One	Following your bliss, what you love
Level Two	Bonding with and making commitments to whom and what you love
Level Three	Radical self-acceptance giving birth to the Self and connecting the personal with the transpersonal, the individual with the collective

---

Erotic energy is also often present in primary mentoring relationships between an older, more powerful person and a younger, relatively less empowered person—parent and child, teacher and student, therapist and client, and pastor and parishioner. An awareness of this erotic charge can often confuse people, tempting them to act on it. Doing so, however, causes extraordinary harm to the less powerful person. The incest taboo protects against this in families, and professional standards define sexual relationships as taboo for teachers, therapists, and clergy. Sexual harassment policies discourage such activities in business settings.

Damage comes partly because the less empowered person in the relationship may submit to an unwanted sexual relationship under duress, fearing the consequences of refusal. Whether or not the more vulnerable person is willing, acting on the impulse usually causes harm because it short-circuits the energy that should be used in the mentoring relationship. The child of this erotic bond should be a new sense of Self (rebirth) for the person being mentored. The result of acting out sexually is to retard or abort this growth process.

Adults who betray their trust and make sexual advances to children have a devastating effect on the children's psychological growth and development. To grow and mature, children need an atmosphere in which they feel safe to trust and be, as they are, Innocent, naive. A parent's flagrant and cruel violation of trust sabotages the child's development in such a primary way that many children never fully recover, although the prognosis for the current generation of incest survivors is much brighter than for the last.

The damage is even further complicated by the tendency of children to see such actions as somehow their own fault—a tendency that in lesser form is also evidenced by those who have a deep psychological wish to absolve their mentor from blame. Further, internalizing the blame settles in as a deep-seated sense of inadequacy, a belief that something is really fundamentally "wrong with me" or I wouldn't have been treated that way.

Transformation Through Eros

The popular movie *Educating Rita* chronicles a positive mentoring relationship between a disillusioned, alcoholic college professor and Rita, a young hairdresser who defies family and class attitudes and her own inexperience in her aspiration to grow and become an educated person.

The professor, jaded with the boring academic world, falls in love with her. Despite his generally undisciplined behavior in other areas of his life, he is able to channel his love into grooming Rita for academic success—a feat that is doubly difficult because he actually prefers her uneducated honesty and energy to the more sophisticated, intellectual, and measured woman she aspires to become.

What makes this a story about transformation through Eros rather than a Pygmalion project is that he channels erotic energy into helping her become not what he wants for her, but what she wants for herself. It differs from a Caregiver relationship by the intensity of the erotic energy within it, which ends up transforming both parties.

The birth of the new Rita (who now calls herself Susan) occurs as the joint result of his love and restraint and her refusal to get sidestepped by romance. She knows she is a woman giving birth to herself, and she knows Henry is the midwife, and she is not willing to be dissuaded from her goal. She never really gives up being Rita either. She now has more choices. She can be Rita *and* Susan.

It is the presence of Eros that allows miracles to happen.

Henry's transformation involves both death and love. His own excesses—primarily excessive drinking—invoke the Destroyer, and he is transferred from England to Australia. But it is his experience with Rita that allows him to leave behind his jaded cynicism and to view Australia as a "new world" of opportunity and new beginnings. He cannot be so cynical anymore because in helping to transform Rita, he has participated in a "miracle."

James Hillman, in *The Myth of Analysis,* sees therapy potentially as just such a miracle. It is the presence of Eros that allows miracles to happen, but the analyst or therapist cannot be intent upon healing or changing the client or analysand. It is the therapist's job simply to love the client and be present, not needing a particular outcome. The client, of course, almost always has a strong desire for transformation, having come to the situation out of pain. But that transformation cannot come out of the therapist's need. It has to come out of the client's need. While therapists cannot force themselves to feel love for a client, if they are present and empathic, love usually will descend, as Castillejo says, as "grace," and then that love can heal.

Loving Ourselves

We can also transform ourselves, to the degree that we cultivate a loving acceptance of ourselves. This means forgiving ourselves simply as a matter of habit. It also means forgiving others, since what we are very often most critical of in them is a shadow projection from within ourselves.

To understand the collective unconscious is to know that we all have the capacity to think and do anything—from the highest spiritual attainment to the lowest, most degraded or barbaric act. We may have enough character to hold our less desirable behaviors in check, but the impulses are nevertheless present. Being able to empathize with and forgive everyone who has ever harmed you or another is a way of affirming the shadow part of your own psyche as well as the cosmic human species shadow. As with the story of "The Beauty and the Beast," the capacity to love the beast (Shadow) in ourselves and others often transforms the beast into a prince or princess. There are two important layers here.

But this does not mean you should go along with beastly behavior! Appropriate Ego strength means that to the best of our abilities we do not allow ourselves or others to act in ways that hurt others. On the Soul level, our task is to learn to respond to it all—not just the parts that seem good and pure, or beautiful and fun, or that we approve of, but to experience the whole interconnected reality with deep feeling. This can result in our responding to the beast with great horror or great love. Either way, authentic and deep feeling transforms.

The greatest love story ever told may be the story of each individual's search for what Jean Houston calls "the Beloved of our Souls." This means that what Seekers yearn to find outside themselves, Lovers initially find in loved ones and eventually learn to find within.

What we adore outside ourselves usually carries with it the positive shadow projection of the deep wisdom of our own Souls.

Jean Houston's *Beloved of the Soul* sees the yearning for the beloved of the Soul as a major force in spiritual or Soul development. Houston goes on to say that the "Beloved is yearning for us just as we are yearning for the Beloved." The essence of what she calls "sacred psychology," or a psychology designed to aid us in developing the transpersonal element of the psyche, rests on the identification with whatever beckons as one's beloved—which can mean a lover, a mentor, a therapist, a religious figure, or an archetype.

What we adore outside ourselves usually carries with it the positive shadow projection of the deep wisdom of our own Souls. In fact, as each archetype in this book emerges into consciousness, we may be drawn to people outside ourselves who demonstrate its attributes before we are able to see it in ourselves. They may be lovers, friends, teachers, co-workers—anyone at all. But most fundamental to each of us is the archetype of the Self, which signifies the completion of the individuation process (at least for a time) and provides a sense of wholeness that unifies Ego and Soul. Often it is experienced as the God or Goddess within.

Most responsible spiritual leaders who understand this phenomenon recognize their followers' adoration of them as projection. Great spiritual teachers, if they embody what they teach, inspire us with a vision of what can be in our lives if we awaken the God or Goddess within.

In *Coming Home: The Experience of Enlightenment in Sacred Traditions*, Lex Hixon, in describing the Jewish Hasidic path, talks about a progression from waiting for the Messiah to come to recognizing that the Messiah has come and is within oneself. He tells a famous Hasidic story about Eizek, a devout but poor man, praying for help and being told to go to a bridge in a faraway city to find a treasure. He gets there, and there is no treasure. Worse, the men who guard the bridge arrest him. So he tells the story, and the captain of the guards tells Eizek he has had a dream to go to a faraway town to find a treasure at a location that turns out to be Eizek's home. The guard releases him; Eizek goes home and finds the treasure beneath his own stove. The journey "redirects us to our original home, to the priceless Divine spark of our intrinsic nature." The treasure, Hixon explains, is always "at home."[5]

The most satisfying love of all comes when we recognize that our Souls are one with all that is numinous, divine in the universe. To unify our conscious minds with our Souls is to find the sacred. Not everyone experiencing this sense of wonder and recognizing the great worth within would be comfortable using religious language; yet for everyone—even someone with no sense of any transcendent reality—there is a birth of a sense of reverence for oneself that is totally at odds with egotism. In the hero's journey, this is what it means to find the treasure.

As a pregnant woman sends messages of love to her as yet unborn child, we need to send messages of love to our great treasure, the Self we are birthing. The more parts of our psyche that participate in supporting this birth and, of course, the more people around us who also support this birth, the easier it is to become one with our own Souls and through doing so to birth a Self.

Often we can only do so after great pain and struggle, as with the young woman in Ntozake Shange's *For Colored Girls who have Considered Suicide When the Rainbow is Enuf,* who has suffered perhaps the greatest pain any parent can suffer—the death of her children by the hands of the man she loved. After great pain and anguish, however, comes rebirth. In her words, "I found god in myself & i loved her/i loved her fiercely."[6]

Staying with the depth of our feelings, with the pain involved in living, and maintaining an attitude of commitment to, and love of, life allows us, in Parker Palmer's words, to live the contradictions, the paradoxes, and the suffering of human life and through a kind of acceptance that means fully receiving and feeling the immensity of the struggle or pain to transform "a force of destruction into an energy of creation."[7] Out of that process, the real Self is born.

The belief that God guides us from the center of our being can completely transform the idea of obedience to God's will. . . . The more completely and spontaneously I follow the direction of this inner guide, the more truly I shall be myself, the more I shall be able to realize and live out my own individual truth. In the phrase of a well-known prayer, God's service is perfect freedom.—Christopher Bryant

Exercises

Give some thought to when, where, how, and how much the Lover expresses itself in your life.

1. How much or how little is the Lover expressed in your life? Has it been expressed more in the past or present? Do you see it emerging more in your future? Is it expressed more at work, at home, with friends, in dreams or fantasies?

2. Who are some friends, relatives, co-workers, and others who seem influenced by the archetype of the Lover?

3. Is there anything you wish were different about the expression of the Lover in your life?

4. Since each archetype expresses itself in many different ways, take some time to describe or otherwise portray (e.g., draw, make a collage, use a picture of yourself in a particular costume or pose) the Lover as it is expressed or could be expressed in your life. What does or would it look like? How does or would it act? In what setting does or would it feel most at home?

Daydreams

Using relaxed, deep breathing to enter a meditative state, allow yourself to focus on your heart, imagining a small gold, glowing light in the center of your chest in the heart area. Imagine the gold, glowing light slowly becoming larger until it is as large as your heart, then your lungs, then the whole chest area, and finally, gradually as large as your whole body. From there imagine that light filling the room and then your community, the country, the world, and finally the solar system.

●

Then become aware of more intense, many-colored threads of light connecting you in particular to everything you love, care about, or feel strongly about. These threads may link you to stars, to the night sky, to a certain landscape, to certain animals or kinds of animals, to places and things, and of course to people in your past or present. Take your time tracing these threads until you feel yourself at the center of a web of loving connection.

●

When you are ready, return your consciousness from the threads to the golden light, and allow that light to shrink from the solar system to the world, from the world to your nation, from your nation to your community, from your community to the room in which you find yourself, and finally to your body, then your chest area, your lungs, and your heart.

13

The Creator

When we discover or give birth to our true Selves, the Creator also comes into our lives. When we become aware of our connection with the creative source of the universe, we also begin to become aware of our part in creation.

James Hillman has called the essence of archetypal psychology "Soul-making." As we create our own individual Souls, we are also contributing to the creation of the world Soul. As we create our own lives, therefore, we are co-creating the universe.

Creativity

However, it is our Souls, not our Egos that create our lives. For instance, our Souls may choose to experience sickness or other kinds of loss or suffering as a way to be initiated into deeper wisdom so that we might grow. Such choices are anathema to the Ego, whose function is to help keep us healthy and well functioning, and consequently the Ego feels victimized when such events occur (just as the Soul feels victimized when the Ego makes security and status its main priorities).

Most modern thinkers stress the ways we are being created by our environments. Many contemporary New Age leaders, however, assert that at the deepest Soul level, we choose everything that happens to us, and in this way we are the authors of our destinies, even their most tragic or difficult parts of them. Shirley Luthman and Hugh Prather, for example, say that each of us has the potential to create our own life—including our physical health—by "making the unconscious conscious," or to use the terminology of this book, to develop a partnership between Ego and Soul so that they work together and not at cross-purposes.[1]

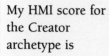

My HMI score for
the Creator
archetype is
_____

(high = 30/low = 0).

It is my _____
highest score
(highest = 12th/lowest = 1st).

The Creator

Goal:
Creation of a life, work, or new reality of any kind

Fear:
Inauthenticity, miscreation, failure of imagination

Response to Dragon/Problem:
Accept that it is part of the Self, part of what one has created; be willing to create another reality

Task:
Self-creation, self-acceptance

Gift:
Creativity, identity, vocation

The more in touch we are able to be with our Souls, and hence with the natural order of the cosmos, the more in touch we can be with this creative, transformative part of ourselves. As Hugh Prather writes in *A Book of Games: A Course in Spiritual Play*, it is not necessary even to believe we have this power to create, transform, and heal. We just need to imagine—to act as if we had it—and we will have it.[2] The secret here is not to make a division between oneself and the great creative spiritual source in the universe. The essence of claiming the Creator within is to recognize that the great spiritual source of the universe is not separate from us. We are part of that source, and hence co-creators of our lives—with God and each other. Claiming our capacity for co-creation can be an incredible, empowering accomplishment.

We can do this by consciously envisioning the future we want. For example, in *Wishcraft: How to Get What You Really Want*, Barbara Sher describes the importance of having a vision of the future that really stretches your sense of the possibilities and that as closely as possible approximates your own ideal life. This vision should be very concrete so that it becomes real to us. We should also try to match our visions with the true nature of our Soul and the reality of at least some of the rules of the external world. Otherwise, our visions may be merely escapist daydreams. For example, it does not help at forty to hold to a vision of someday becoming a professional ballerina if you have never danced before.

A positive but realistic projection of our future frees us to enjoy life in the present and to make our dreams come true. Visions are most powerful when consensually shared. If a group supports your desires for yourself (or for the group) and consciously holds the vision, the results are generally much more powerful.

However, what is most critical is that your vision conforms to who you are at a deep level and what your life, at best, should really be about.

Conditioning and the Shadow Creator

However unified our consciousness becomes, and however true we are to ourselves, most of us are still confined by our conditioning, by the social constraints of society, and by natural laws. If we have not taken our journeys and have not developed a strong Ego and connected with our Souls, we are not yet creating consciously. We experience life as the created, so we feel, and perhaps really are the products of our environment and our conditioning. This is the shadow Creator, creating without any sense of responsibility for what we are making.

Not all powerlessness is a result of the shadow Creator. Sometimes we justifiably feel that we are not in control of what is happening to us—for instance, in the case of an oppressive or discriminatory social system or a dysfunctional family. And although you might have created the experience of going to jail if you broke a law, that does not mean you created the current reality of the prison system! Much of our lives are created collectively, not individually.

Even if most of the basics of one's life are given, there is still the unique way a person puts that life together if one is conscious at all. In the nineteenth century, people talked about the ways our lives seem predefined not so much in terms of conditioning, but in terms of predestination. But either way, they are describing the same thing—the balance between creating and being created.

How much piecin' a quilt is like livin' a life. . . . The Lord sends us the pieces; we can cut 'em out and put 'em together pretty much to suit ourselves.
—Eliza Calvert Hall, Aunt Jane of Kentucky

Beyond Self-Improvement

Whether or not we are the absolute Creators of our lives, we are responsible for the degree to which we maximize the power that we do have. That power undoubtedly differs by social and economic circumstances and by the level of our psychological and spiritual development.

Creativity is the ground of any well-lived life. We all create our lives by the choices that are available to us about the ways we live them, no matter how circumscribed those choices might be. Some of these choices feel like they are freely chosen and within our control, and some feel like they have claimed us, and their processes live and breathe in us. Nevertheless, we do create our lives by the ways that we live.

It is the imagination that helps us find meaning and beauty in our lives. That is why Hillman can say, "We are alive or dead according to the condition of our Souls."[3] The alienation and the ennui so prevalent in modern life are not an inevitable result of some outside reality, but a reflection of the underdevelopment of our imaginative capacity.

It is the imagination's task to interpret the world around us in an artistic way. The contribution of the great visual and literary geniuses is to show us—through the example of their art—how it is possible to look at even the most horrible aspects of human life and find there beauty and significance. Sophocles manages to do this in his plays with incest and patricide!

The contribution of transforming metaphors is often to help us see the beauty or significance in life, whether in our own lives or in those of others. Archetypal psychologists, for instance, may do this by identifying the myth, the archetype, the god, or the goddess that informs an experience—even if the experience is pathological. Often the most empowering friends do this by seeing some significance and worth not only in our achievements but in our very striving (even when we fail). The artist in each of us is the part that sees the underlying "truth" or Self beneath the surface and reveals this truth to us. Such fundamental human truths are always deeply meaningful, beautiful, and moving.

Creating a life means to honor our experience honestly, without denial, but also as worthy and valuable. This means accepting your life as the right life for you, your body and mind as the right ones for you, even your pathologies and bad habits (although in this case, it may be the process of overcoming or dealing with them that will teach you just the lesson you need). It means coming to recognize the form of your own beauty, whether it is the beauty of your body, your mind, or your character.

When the Creator archetype begins to be active in our lives, we often alternate between exultation and potentially paralyzing fear.

Ironically, in our culture it is difficult to feel what you feel, and think what you think, and not worry about what you are "supposed" to feel or think. This is hard in a Warrior/Seeker culture in which we are surrounded by self-improvement schemes, all of which are designed to help us live up to some standard or other. Most of us have learned to judge our every action or thought: Is it good? Is it bad? Is it manly enough? Is it feminine enough? What will others think? Simply being oneself may feel like breaking all the rules and norms, and call forth both a sense of liberation and vague fears of punishment. When the Creator archetype begins to be active in our lives, we often alternate between exultation and potentially paralyzing fear.

When we are in Innocence, it is appropriate to learn to fit in the world as it is, starting with one's family and moving out to include the schools, the workplace, the community. We step into predefined roles and are in large measure defined by those roles.

The rebirth of the Soul puts us on another track altogether, and we begin to allow ourselves to be honest and authentic wherever we are. The process always carries with it some pain, however. As we allow our true Selves to emerge into the light of day after long incubation, the big world out there may scare us—and we might scare it! The rest of the world is used to interacting with the Ego, and may be very disoriented when this new being comes along and declares it has a mind of its own, especially since many of us are not initially very graceful about asserting our desires in the world.

Becoming co-creators of the world we live in takes real courage. This is not the courage of the Warrior, who generally rides out armed to the teeth. This is the courage it takes to be vulnerable, open, unarmed, oneself—not as an Innocent, but with full consciousness of who you are and what you are doing.

Heroes do often end up being able to be both true to themselves and happily loved and in community, but this is only after they have demonstrated the courage and imagination to craft that world a bit to fit themselves. Thoreau spoke in "Civil Disobedience" of our responsibility not just to vote in elections but to cast our whole vote, which means to vote about the world we want to live in by the way we live our own life. This is how the world is made: by the aggregate effect of all the decisions—major and minor—each of us makes as we go about our lives.

Inner Listening

Some of these choices we make consciously, some unconsciously, and some feel more like discoveries than choices. Listening with receptive imagination to discover what to do next is one of the most important life skills we have. Some people do this in prayer and meditation, some by taking a walk or working in the garden. Many people discover what they think and feel through an art form of some kind—perhaps they write in a journal, paint, or make pottery.

People who think they are not creative, or cannot listen in to their own inner intuitive knowing, have not yet learned to listen to their process. Indeed, they may have learned very early how to tune out the imagination's knowledge. Not everyone draws, writes, or sculpts, but everyone dreams, fantasizes, and doodles. The creation of story in dreams and fantasies and the creation of images in doodling are primary activities of the imagination.

When we stop trying to control the imagination and allow it to do what comes naturally—the spinning of words, images, symbols—we discover the depths of our inner wisdom. Similarly, if we are honest, we can note many discrepancies between what we think we are trying to create and what we are actually creating.

For example, in the everyday world of consciousness, I may think I want to be friends with a particular woman and spend time with her. But I never do make

If what we create, in the artworks of our own lives, comes authentically from our Souls, the product will inevitably be beautiful.

that time, and actually do things to offend her. Perhaps unconsciously I really do not want this friendship, at least in its present form, and I am creating a situation that will shatter it so that the friendship can be ended, redefined, or renegotiated.

The Ego often stops what would naturally be an endless and virtually effortless creative flow by its judgment and censorship. The Ego, especially when it's under the sway of the Warrior, is critical and does not want us to create unless we are "good at it." The imagination, however, coming as it does from the Soul, has only two criteria for excellence: that our creations are "true" and "beautiful." For the Soul, though, anything that is authentic and real is also beautiful. If what we create, in the artworks of our own lives, comes authentically from our Souls, the product will inevitably be beautiful.

Stages of Creation

At first we create unconsciously, with no sense that we are in fact creating what is happening to us. When, like the sorcerer's apprentice, we create chaos and difficulty, we generally blame circumstances. If we hear anyone say we are the creators of our lives, it sounds as if they are blaming us. At this point, we simply cannot understand the difference between the Ego's and the Soul's sense of good, and we cannot imagine taking responsibility for our creations without being held accountable for them.

At the next level, we consciously "take control of our lives" with our Egos, and we struggle to do the right things and to make happen what we want. We are often thwarted and have to struggle, but we try to press on. Even though we are often tired, we do create successes and hence begin to feel real pride in our efforts.

However, after our initiatory experiences with the Destroyer and the Lover, we have a greater sense of humility, and we recognize that we cannot control the universe. Indeed, many times we are not even in conscious control. Once we have given up the illusion that we can control our destiny with our wills, we begin learning to trust our imaginations and the ways that our Souls are creating our lives. Though our Souls are notorious for their lack of concern for material success, they are seeking our growth and development at a deeper level. We may recognize at this point that at the Soul level, we do choose every bit of pain and loss and suffering in our lives. Yet still, we might wish that things did not have to be so hard and that our conscious minds would have more voice in this decision making.

Creating neither just with Ego nor just from Soul is satisfactory by itself. For one thing, the Ego's creation has the style of the Warrior. It is about mastery, and it is very hard work, full of conflict and struggle. For another, especially when we first start allowing our deeper Soul reality to create our lives, we do so by consciously repressing the Ego's criticism of and advice about this process. And in suppressing the wisdom of the Ego, we often fail to attend properly to normal human concerns, like making a decent living or noticing how others are responding to us.

After trying to create a life only from the Ego and only from the Soul, we discover the most effective way is to honor and listen to the wisdom of both. Perhaps this is what Jesus meant when he said, "Render unto Caesar the things that are Caesar's and unto God the things that are God's." At the highest level, we experience a "sacred marriage" of Ego consciousness and Soul that allows for the creation of a life that satisfies both Ego and Soul, so it becomes possible to have spiritual depth and to be successful in life, work, and love.

Levels of the Creator

Shadow	Creation of negative circumstances, limited opportunities; obsessive creation, workaholism
Call	Daydreams, fantasies, images, or flashes of inspiration
Level One	Opening to receive visions, images, hunches, inspiration
Level Two	Allowing yoursef to know what you really want to have, do, or create
Level Three	Experiments with creating what you imagine—allowing yourself to let your dreams come true

---

We need to be true to our own deepest Soul reality in shaping our lives, and to allow that reality to emerge and be the treasure that revitalizes the kingdom. But we also need the Ego to be the guard of that treasure, to be certain that it is not vandalized, desecrated, or otherwise dishonored or mistreated.

The highest level of mastery—the level Luthman talks about, with people who literally can choose what happens to them from their conscious minds—requires a level of consciousness that is truly unusual. That is, it requires little or no barrier between the Ego and Soul so that they actively choose everything that happens together. At this time in history, this is relatively rare. Most of us settle for maximizing the more limited power we do have for consciousness to influence the direction of our lives.

Creation and Consciousness

The process of co-creating our world is, in one way, something we share with every other human being, plus plants, animals, trees, stars, galaxies. Every living thing helps the process of cosmic evolution simply by being. We are all creating our world all the time; the important task is to do so consciously.

James Lovelock's *The Ages of Gaia: A Biography of Our Living Earth* rocked the scientific world with its carefully developed premise that the earth is a living, self-regulating system.[4] However, Lovelock stopped short of saying the earth has consciousness. Yes, it is alive. Yes, it regulates temperature and other conditions to insure its survival, which means it is busy co-creating the world, just as we are, but that does not mean it has consciousness.

Although many other cultures—native American, for instance—readily attribute consciousness to Mother Earth, European and American thinking consistently attribute consciousness only to humankind. Jean Houston combines these views by seeing humanity as Mother Earth's sensory system, the organ of Mother Earth that has consciousness.

Cultures differ in their beliefs about whether the earth, the stars, or the galaxies have consciousness, but they all agree that people have consciousness, and with consciousness, the ability to create in very special ways. In the most basic way, we create by "naming," by the power of language to predetermine thought.

The way we order experience—by sound, by words, by images—creates meaning in our worlds. Psychologists have long understood that people's growth is often stuck because all they can see in life is the original way they saw it. If they were battered as children, for instance, they see others as potential batterers and themselves always as victims. They may not notice anything that doesn't fit into this basic pattern. Their actions, moreover, tend to perpetuate this plot structure, and over and over they find themselves to be abused.

Transactional Analysts call this a script and try to help people become liberated from confining scripts. Therapists from all traditions work to help people increase their ability to see the world from various perspectives.

The power of naming is profound. When I was a college professor, I once asked three students to redo an important paper. One of them immediately became a victim, feeling sorry for herself and complaining that this always happened to her. Another went immediately into a Warrior mode, planning the campaign to overcome the obstacle. The third (Innocent) student seemed totally oblivious to her writing problem, but redid the paper just to please me. All three women seemed driven by their archetypal stories.

This experience puzzled me and in large measure motivated my work on archetypes, because I realized that to a very great extent our perceptions of our lives are not so simply the result of what has happened to us. They are the result of how we interpret what happens to us, and therefore what we do. Ironically, both the woman who moved into denial and the one who mobilized the troops fared better than the woman who saw herself as a victim.

Consciousness can help us escape from having our stories written for us in these ways so that, at least in part, we can write our own stories. Educated by initiation into longing, pain, and love, our imaginations can create visions of what our real tasks are in the world. If our Egos are also strong, we can utilize skill and control to channel a higher level of each archetype and help make our visions a reality. With the aid of the Ego, we can fill out the vision, imagine how we can realize our potential in the particular time and place in which we live. If the Soul is underdeveloped, there will be no vision. If the Ego is underdeveloped, the vision will not be realized—unless by extraordinary synchronistic events.

The Awakened Creator

When the archetype of the Creator is active in our lives, we are conscious of a sense of destiny and a responsibility to develop a vision for our lives and to carry through on that vision. We may feel that if we do not do so, we will lose our Souls. It certainly feels like a do-or-die situation—only the death threatened is not physical death but Soul death.

The Creator pushes us out of inauthentic roles to claim our identities. When this archetype is active, people are as consumed with the need to create a life as artists are with the need to paint, or poets with the need to write. Just as great painters and poets will be willing to give up money and power and status to create their art, when the Creator is active in our lives, we are pushed at least to decide to be ourselves, even if it means that we will die unknown, poor, and alone. Usually, of course, people who begin to act out of their authentic selves do not pay this price—indeed many are well known, wealthy, and surrounded with friends and loved ones. However, the only way to be able to be true to oneself is to know that one will do so whatever it costs.

It is also essential to the Creator archetype to have the sense that there is something encoded in your cells that you must do, something that is your basic reason for being on the planet. It may be a particular vocation, a contribution to society, a person or people you must love, becoming healed in some way, learning a powerful lesson; but it is also, simultaneously, about your evolution.

The Creator pushes us out of inauthentic roles to claim our identities.

Each of us has a piece of the puzzle of solving the great world problems of our time and creating a more just, humane, and beautiful world. We know what our part is by what feels not just familiar, but deeply true and right when we do

The seed of God is in us. . . . Now the seed of a pear tree grows into a pear tree, a hazel seed into a hazel tree, the seed of God into God.—Meister Eckhart

it. We know it by what we love and what makes us feel fulfilled. We know it by what we cling to when everything around us and sometimes in us is falling apart.

If everyone who loved to create beauty did so, we would live in a beautiful world. If everyone who loved cleanliness and order, cleaned up, we would live in a clean and orderly world. If everyone who yearned to heal the sick did so, we would live in a healthier world. If everyone who cared about world hunger shared his or her creative ideas and acted to alleviate the problem, people would all be fed.

If we could learn that the wisdom of the Self coded within each of us is never wrong, that what we yearn to do is what we are to do, we would co-create a better world. But that does not mean that your conscious mind knows the answer. Certainly few of us are given a map. To the degree that we trust our own process on a moment-to-moment basis, doing what seems right and authentic, we will grow into what we are meant to be.

Gods, Goddesses, and the Creative Process

The world's religious traditions are full of images of gods and goddesses as Creators. The first image of the Creator was the ancient Goddess, who was seen as giving birth to the universe. In all parts of the world, the most ancient sacred art celebrates the female power to give birth—not only to children, but to art, literature, inventions, indeed to the universe. In these ancient civilizations, femaleness was venerated not only for the power to give birth, but also because of the capacity to create milk to nourish the baby child and, with menstruation, to bleed and not die.

The Goddess's son and lover was also worshiped as divine, providing an additional image of the procreative divine couple. The image of the divine couple creating life through their ecstatic coupling emphasizes the ecstatic, joyful, and pleasurable nature of life and of creation. That is, creation is like sex at its best—full of joy, love, and mutual pleasure. Imagine living in a culture in which such an image was at the root of the understanding of the nature of life!

Later, the creation of the universe was seen not as a natural, physical process of birth from a mother's body or arising from the blissful union of the divine couple, but as a mental process: Yahweh, God the Father of the Hebrew Torah and the Christian Old Testament, created the world through the magic of language, saying, "Let there be light." This is the power of the Word, of Logos, to create through the power of speech and understanding. Similarly, Athena was envisioned as springing full-grown from Zeus's head.

If each of us has a god within, then what god? If the god within creates through a process like birth, then it begins with love and pleasure, but yields control of the process once conception occurs and until the child is born. This view provides the potential for intense experience and feeling, but little control. If the god within is crucified or dismembered, as with Christ or Dionysus, creation will consist primarily of suffering until the moment of rebirth and liberation, when the new reality is completed. If the god within is a King and a Father, creating by command, out of his head, then it is all control, but little passion.

If there is a god or goddess within each of us, then it is useful to image that god or goddess, to find an equivalent in the world outside for your own inner sacred self. We can also gain clarity about our own process of creating or birthing a life by learning from artists and their understanding of the process of creation.

Life as an Art Form

In *A Portrait of the Artist as a Young Man,* for instance, James Joyce imagines the artist as a God, sitting above the action, totally in control, disinterested, objective, "paring his fingernails." Alice Walker, on the other hand, describes how Celie and Shug, the major characters of *The Color Purple,* appeared and asked her to write their story. Her account is replete with emotion as she strives to birth a novel adequate to their stories.

In creating our lives, we can learn equally from both the classical and the romantic views of art, one emphasizing skill and control, the other inspiration and passion. As with creation, the experience of the Muse is an act of receptive imagination. Without her, creativity does not happen. There are dry periods when no matter how intelligent and creative we might be (or have been), we can create nothing of worth.

On the other hand, the Muse's visitation may provide inspiration, but the execution may be sloppy and undisciplined. The skill and control, the distance emphasized by the classical tradition are essential to the execution. The creation of great art is almost always a marriage of hard work and a moment of visitation. Ideally, we begin creative projects with the receptive imagination, but complete them using the creative skills that focus on the achievement of formal control.

So, too, with a life. It is the Ego that works hard to learn the craft of living. Entering the mysteries of the Soul by striving and loving and losing opens us up to grace, to the Muse, to inspiration. The result of the integration of inspiration and skill can be a life lived at the level of great art.

Both artists and mystics learn to think like children—to have what Buddhists call "beginner's mind." This means limiting or eliminating preconceptions about reality that block creativity. Children are naturally and spontaneously creative. When we as adults are not creative, it is only because our creativity has been blocked. We are too focused on the past or the future to be fully open and spontaneous in the now. We only need to regain what is natural to each of us as children.

Some people create their lives spontaneously—as children create art—and this childlike spontaneity and openness to experience has a place in all creation. How alive we would all be if we could respond creatively and anew to each new experience. Yet the greatest art also requires maturity, skill, and wisdom.

The ability to see and name that potential in oneself or another is the primary creative act of liberation.

For others, the process combines control and spontaneity. They have some general idea of the direction in which they are headed, but many of the details emerge as an unconscious creative process that fills out the more conscious one. It is not uncommon for sculptors to speak of their art as liberating a figure they see as trapped inside the wood or stone. Psychologists, therapists, teachers, and clergy also often see their work as uncovering the buried Self or potential in an individual, with the first glimpse of what that potential might be serving as the key to future interventions.

The ability to see and name that potential in oneself or another is the primary creative act of liberation. It is only when we begin to uncover who we are—beneath insecurity and grandiosity, beneath ingrained habit and social conditioning, beyond our outer appearance and our persona—that we can have some confidence that our actions are helping to expand rather than shrink our individual, collective, and world Soul. Then secondarily, we learn techniques of living and working with style and grace that allow us to contribute to the greater good in an effective way.

Some creative people focus on the process of scientific invention. For them the third, empirical stage (which should be a part of all creative endeavors) is most critical. They have a vision, and begin to experiment with what happens when they act on it. Then they analyze the data that they receive back, and alter their vision accordingly. This empirical feedback loop is as important to individual human lives as it is to scientists, inventors, and mathematicians, because if you act and what happens is very different than what you expected, you may want to reexamine your hypotheses and reshape your vision.

Although the skill of the Ego cannot be left behind if we aspire to create and live beautiful lives, its arrogance and superficiality must be. The artistic process itself can be a mode of discovery. Such a process leaves behind the issues of the Ego—even the striving for eternity and immortality, because the Self lives in connection with the cosmos. Our creations are not separate from us. We create as the expression of who we are, and as a way to discover who we are and what we think and know. We do so out of an enjoyment and love of the objects around us and of the act of creativity itself.

Creating a life, then, is not about creating a product, but about enjoyment of a process. One does not have to be at the end state—to have created a wonderful life that contributes to the greater good—to have that sense of great joy. The joy comes from the process itself.

The Dance of Ego and Soul

The highest kinds of art teach us what it can be like when we create our lives out of the truth of our Souls, but through a process in which Soul and Ego are so completely in harmony that we are like two people dancing in perfect accord, or like different energies within a single dancer's body integrated into a beautiful, artistic performance. Efforts at creation do not have to feel like work or struggle or labor; they can feel like "dancing."

It is dangerous to create only from the Soul, because the Soul is notoriously insensitive to the needs of the body and will keep us creating, working, or dancing until the body collapses. The Ego needs to be activated to care for the health of the organism. Anyone who has seen the film *Amadeus* will remember the vivid and painful scene of Mozart's deathbed: he pushes through to finish a great *Requiem* and then dies. Mozart, at least as presented in this film, created from the Soul some of the most beautiful music ever written. But he lacked the Ego wisdom to learn how to manage his health and finances, and the Ego strength to counter pressures to keep composing even long enough to recover from a serious illness. And thus he died young, depriving himself of a long and full life and the world of the music he would yet have created.

Similarly, many of us today have so many great ideas about things to create, or do, or buy that we end up burnt out and overwhelmed by the sheer complexity of our lives. Instead of coming up with yet another activity to try, we need to use our common sense to pare down and do less.

If we think of the creative metaphor as a dance, it is easiest to see how the creation of a life as art depends upon our ability to take care of our bodies, minds, and hearts. Without a strong healthy body, a dancer cannot dance well. The dancing is always the best when the dancer feels not like he or she is dancing, but being danced. The dance or the music or the Soul takes over, but the body or the Ego is so trained, so skilled, that it is adequate to being danced without losing a step or burning out. With a well-integrated Ego and Soul, creativity is experienced not as the suffering that results when the body's needs are ignored in favor of the Soul-call to create a life or a piece of art, but as, in the words of William Butler Yeats, a "blossoming" of the organism.[5]

O body swayed to music, O brightening glance,
How can we know the dancer from the dance?
—William Butler Yeats

In experiencing such joy of mastery, we are prepared to return from our journeys, to bring back our treasures, and to contribute to the transformation of the kingdom. Doing so requires the understanding that we are the Rulers of our own lives.

Exercises

Give some thought to when, where, how, and how much the Creator expresses itself in your life.

1. How much or how little is the Creator expressed in your life? Has it been expressed more in the past or present? Do you see it emerging more in your future? Is it expressed more at work, at home, with friends, in dreams or fantasies?

2. Who are some friends, relatives, co-workers, and others who seem influenced by the archetype of the Creator?

3. Is there anything you wish were different about the expression of the Creator in your life?

4. Since each archetype expresses itself in many different ways, take some time to describe or otherwise portray (e.g., draw, make a collage, use a picture of yourself in a particular costume or pose) the Creator as it is expressed or could be expressed in your life. What does or would it look like? How does or would it act? In what setting does or would it feel most at home?

Daydreams

Imagine a perfect day or hour or week sometime in the future when you are doing everything you would love to be doing. Imagine the setting, the company, and your activities. Imagine what you look like, how you are dressed, and how you feel. Be as specific as you can, and include as much sensory data as possible (what does it look like, feel like, taste like, smell like, sound like?).

●

Imagine you had a magic wand and could change anything in the world you wanted for yourself and others. Allow yourself to imagine what you would change, and staying in a dreamy state of mind, allow the drama to unfold in your mind so that you witness the effects of your work. Allow yourself some time to process the results—to enjoy your successes and to regret any miscreations.

Part IV

The Return—Becoming Free

14

The Ruler

Many stories, fairy tales, and legends end with the discovery that the main character—seemingly a commoner who has struggled through many obstacles and adventures—is really the long-lost son or daughter of the King. Classical heroes were often orphaned in some way and brought up by commoners. This experience of living like the lowest people in the land was of course critical to their development of the humility, empathy, and knowledge of the challenges of ordinary life necessary to truly great leadership.

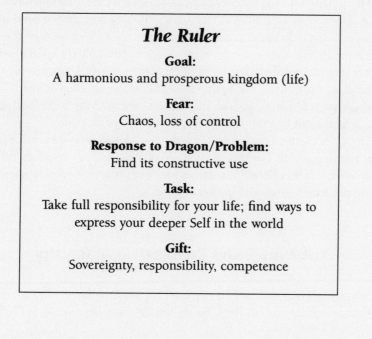

The Ruler

Goal:
A harmonious and prosperous kingdom (life)

Fear:
Chaos, loss of control

Response to Dragon/Problem:
Find its constructive use

Task:
Take full responsibility for your life; find ways to express your deeper Self in the world

Gift:
Sovereignty, responsibility, competence

The hero's journey is often seen as preparation for leadership. As we have seen in the classic Fisher King myths, for example, the kingdom is envisioned as a wasteland because the King is wounded or ailing. The young hero goes on a quest, slays the dragon, and finds a treasure that brings new life to a dying culture. Upon the hero's return, the kingdom is transformed and comes alive once again as the young hero becomes the new Ruler. To the degree that we have forgotten this pattern and see leadership preparation as a mere manner of skill development, the leadership of our kingdom will suffer. No one can become a truly great leader without first taking the journey.

In modern life, we become the Ruler by taking complete responsibility for our lives—not only for our inner reality, but also for the way our outer world mirrors that reality. This includes the ways our individual lives affect our families, our communities, and our societies. When we have very likely become too comfortable and stopped growing, our kingdoms feel like wastelands; we must allow the budding new life—the new hero—within us to take a new journey.

The Ruler is a symbol of wholeness and the achievement of the Self, not just in its formative, tentative stages but as an expression of our selves in the world, an expression powerful enough to transform our lives, inwardly and outwardly. The Ruler is whole because the archetype unifies the wisdom of youth and age, holding them in dynamic tension. When that tension breaks down and imbalance results, a new journey needs to be taken, a new treasure won, that can transform the kingdom once again.

The archetype of the Ruler encompasses not only the extremes of youth and age, but also of male and female. The androgynous sovereign is a symbol of the completion of the alchemical transformational process. As we have seen, the various chemical procedures that separate out the essence of the gold (or spirit) from lesser elements (matter) parallel the stages of the hero's spiritual journey, first out of consensual, ego-dominated reality into the transmutable spiritual domain. The final stage—symbolized by royalty, gold, and the sun—signifies the successful ability to express a Soul truth by manifesting that truth in physical reality.

The Ruler creates a peaceful and harmonious kingdom by becoming peaceful and harmonious inside. The belief system—that inner and outer worlds mirror one another—that informs alchemy is also encoded in the grail myths, especially with regard to the King's relationship to the kingdom.

The Duties and Prerogatives of Royalty

When the Ruler is active in our lives, we are integrated, whole, and ready to take responsibility for our lives. We do not shy away from recognizing that our kingdoms mirror us and we can see ourselves by looking around. For example, if our kingdoms are barren, it reflects some barrenness within ourselves. If our kingdoms are always being attacked and overrun, it means our Warrior is not protecting the boundaries, and the Ruler needs to call forth the troops. If our kingdoms are harsh and unfriendly, our Caregiver is not functioning at a high enough level, and the Ruler needs to attend to this. And so on. Conversely, when our kingdoms are flourishing, this is a sign of a time of relative inner wholeness.

The traditional marriage of the Ruler to the land symbolically demonstrates the erotic union of the Ruler and his or her outer life. Another way of viewing this is the union of Soul with the physical side of life, for the Ruler is the archetype of material prosperity. The Ruler therefore must be ready and able to live with the world the way it is. The Ruler's job is to promote order, peace, prosperity, and abundance. This means a healthy economy, wise laws that are honored and enforced, an environment that promotes the development of each individual, and the wise use of resources, both human and material.

The Ruler is the reigning archetype for this capacity to operate on the physical plane because Rulers cannot be squeamish about the realities of the ordinary material world. When the Ruler archetype is active in our lives, we feel at home in the physical world and in charge of our selves. We enjoy the process of expressing who we are in the physical domain of work, home, money, and possessions. And we have some confidence that we know how to get our needs met.

Responsibility

Rulers are realists who do not have the leisure to have illusions. Indeed, they must understand power politics and, to some degree at least, play them. They can have no illusions about threats from enemies or the reality of evil. Because good Rulers also understand the mirroring of inner and outer, King/Queen and kingdom, they can have no illusions about themselves either. They need to know their own shadow Selves and be willing to take responsibility for them.

So, too, each of us has complete responsibility for our own lives. This does not mean that we are to blame for what happens to us. It simply means that we are sovereign and responsible for taking appropriate actions in every situation we face.

As with nations, some of our kingdoms are poor, some rich; some have great natural resources, some few; some are blessed with peace, some besieged by hostile invaders on every side. Yet if we are the sovereigns of our kingdoms, we take responsibility for it all. Sometimes this means even taking responsibility for seeing that we have become the dogmatic, unmovable ogre tyrants or the wounded Fisher Kings, and that, in fact, our kingdoms have become wastelands because we are in need of renewal or healing. In either case, we need to let go of our stranglehold on the kingdom and our own psyches, and allow a new voice to emerge.

Power and Wisdom

The Ruler as an archetype is about claiming our own power for good and for ill. Many people are fearful of the more powerful archetypes—especially the Ruler and the Magician—because their capacity for harm is as great as their capacity for good. When we begin to own that we create our own realities, we also know that what we create can be no better than the consciousness that inspires our actions.

Inevitably, unless we have reached some state of perfection, our own kingdoms will be imperfect. However, the alternative to acting on the wisdom and insight you do have is to give away your power and allow others to determine your fate for you. In the times when much of the archetypal knowledge about the process of transformation was encoded in various ways for people to learn—in myths such as the grail myths, in tarot cards, in systems such as alchemy and astrology, and in the more mystic versions of our major religions—only a few people were ever expected to walk the hero's path and in that way to become the Rulers of their own lives.

Indeed, care was often taken to be sure that ordinary people, who were unprepared for the mystic journey, would not understand what to do. Alchemical texts, for instance, were purposely written in a way that only those who had been trained in the oral alchemical tradition could ever understand.

Only a few people, it was believed, were capable of taking the journey and becoming Rulers of their own lives. Thus, in the medieval period, people believed in the divine right of Kings. Presumably Kings and Queens had been schooled in the mysteries and could hear and speak for God. Others should simply obey them.

When the Ruler is dominant in our lives, it is our opportunity to see ourselves as sovereign in our kingdoms and to act to make our lives just the way we want them to be.

Of course, Rulers who had no such connection to divine wisdom or whose egotism or arrogance took precedence over that access have been responsible for great abuses of power, but if we govern like the ancient Rulers, who were also graduates of the great mystery schools, we will not make decisions simply on the basis of our Ego needs or whims. We will always be consulting with our Souls. As we learn to live in a way that reflects our deeper, more profound knowing, we live differently, and as we live differently, our lives create ripple effects that influence all the other kingdoms around us.

When the Ruler is dominant in our lives, it is our opportunity to see ourselves as sovereign in our kingdoms and to act to make our lives just the way we want them to be. This differs from the Creator archetype in grandness and scale.

When the Creator is dominant in our lives, we are experimenting with allowing expression to new forces and urges in our lives—usually without much thought (other than occasional panic!) about the impact of our actions on others or on our future lives. It's as though we temporarily have to let go of some of those normal, everyday concerns and responsibilities.

The Ruler does not so much create a life as maintain and govern it. All good monarchs or political leaders identify with the good of the collective, and balance personal desires and aspirations with other people's needs. In deciding what they want for themselves, they also think of the larger social good. Unless we want to be petty tyrants, demagogues, political hacks, or opportunists, we need to enlarge our minds and hearts to encompass a larger sense of our sphere of influence so that as we act to create the life we want, we are also making a better life for our families, friends, co-workers, and even the society as a whole.

Often this means making a real accounting of our lives to date and what kind of kingdom we have been creating. It means taking responsibility for our successes *and* our failures. It means taking some time to create a vision of what we want for our kingdom, and thinking through ways to act to make our vision a reality. (A wise Ruler will always engage the Magician in this task, for Magicians are the quintessential vision people). No good Ruler rules without a plan! And it also often means building coalitions with others—who are recognized as Rulers of their own kingdoms and may have different expectations and desires.

You might also remember to trust synchronicity when the Ruler is dominant in your life. Since our kingdoms really do mirror us, we do not have to make happen every bit of change we want. Often when we hold the vision and begin to act on it, other pieces simply begin to fall into place.

Mastery and Limitations

The emergence of the positive Ruler archetype in the psyche indicates some achievement of mastery in the world. Very often this means some mastery on the physical plane of work, material goods, money, the details of ordinary life. This does not necessarily mean that one is wealthy. It does mean one has reached some kind of satisfactory relationship with money. Whether one lives in extravagant luxury or elegant (or even spartan) simplicity, the choice is one's own. But for the Ruler, it should be a choice.

The Ruler archetype helps us find a mode for generating prosperity to support the full expression of who we are. This could mean great wealth, but just as easily it could mean the ability to feel royal with almost nothing. We've only to think of great figures like Gandhi, for instance, to understand that royal presence and impact and the ability to lead and inspire do not depend on goods owned or money in the bank.

The Ruler archetype typically forces a confrontation with power and with the limits of one's power. Even monarchs do not have absolute power—their power is limited by the financial resources of the kingdom, the state of their army, the degree of support they can wield in the government, army, and the general populace, and by their own ability level. When the Ruler is dominant, and we realize that our kingdoms really do mirror our inner reality and the level of support we have been able to martial from the outside world, we are confronted with our own limitations.

If our coffers are bare, our moats are not well defended, enemies are invading our castles, our courts lack joy, our accounts or our basements are in disorder, or we lack the respect of those around us, we come face-to-face with ourselves. The Ruler archetype helps us see that to spend our time blaming others for our problems takes away our own dignity. We find more dignity in confronting and doing something about our own disabilities, dysfunctions, and blind spots than we ever do by denying them.

Rulers understand duty and what royalty is expected to do, and they do not fight it. In individual psychological terms, this means that we accept our limitations as well as our gifts, and we accept the limitations of mortal human life as well. If the Ruler archetype is active at a relatively high level, we do not waste energy bemoaning what we wish were true. We act as nobly as we can to make the best for all concerned from what we have.

The Ruler within us is also fully aware that we cannot always will problems away. Sometimes the challenges we face are so beyond our present skill level that we are simply defeated by them. Yet while defeated by circumstances, the great Ruler rarely whines. Instead he or she thinks, "What might I have done?" to learn the lesson for another day.

When the Ruler is active in our lives, it is the time to claim responsibility to choose a life, not just have it chosen for us, or to maintain and develop the life you have already chosen. This is the time to act to be certain you are both doing the work you love and making an adequate living; to balance your ideal life-style and your abilities; to balance the way you want to dress and act with what is rewarded and valued by the culture (and in doing so, take responsibility in part for one's impact on others); and to determine what kind of contribution you want to make to the larger societal good.

Good Rulers make choices that balance out their own predilections, hopes, and dreams with their context so that they are realists. Beyond that, they are benevolent. They not only consider the impact on others of their actions because they want to protect themselves from unforeseen or negative results—although this is very important to do—but they also work to balance their own good with that of others. At the higher levels, they also understand that there is no necessary

The Ruler archetype helps us see that to spend our time blaming others for our problems takes away our own dignity.

or inherent conflict between my good and yours, since if I win at your expense and you become either my enemy or a wasted resource and a drain on the kingdom, we all lose. If I hold to my high ideals or my inflated image of what I want in life and refuse to compromise at all with the world as it is, we all lose—because my talents are wasted (just as if I compromise what is essential in my life, we all lose because I cannot give my gift). And it is inevitable that we will all fail at the royal task. That is why the primary myth of the Ruler is the story of the healing of the wounded King (or Queen).

The Shadow Ruler

Anytime we feel a compelling need to control ourselves or others and an inability to trust the process, the shadow Ruler has us in its grip. We want control for its own sake or for power, status, or personal aggrandizement rather than to manifest the kingdom that would gratify us on a deep level. When in the shadow Ruler's grip, we will also inevitably be cut off from our more genuine, humane, and healthy urges. Indeed, we may either feel cut off from any clear sense of inner reality or obsessed with our Soul reality so that we refuse to compromise in any way with the needs of others or the demands of the time and the place in which we live.

Shadow Rulers are ogre tyrants operating out of a scarcity mentality, believing that there is not enough, so my gain must be their loss. They also want to force others to do things their own way, and have tantrums if they are unsuccessful. If they are thwarted, they try to punish someone. The King or Queen who says, "Off with his head!" is a shadow Ruler.

Evil tyrants act out all the traits of the shadow Ruler. They are selfish, narrow-minded, and vindictive—and also usually unimaginative or unintelligent and prone to either indolence and self-indulgence or spartan rigidity and intolerance. Similar traits emerge in any of us when we cannot find a balance between a gracious enjoyment of life and the discipline to get the job done; between our own needs and those of others; or between the demands of our Souls and our real-world responsibilities.

The shadow Ruler may also have "gone over to the dark side," as they say of Darth Vader in the *Star Wars* movies. This, of course, is serious. You begin the journey to find your Soul, but something intervenes, something so traumatic that you find not your own power and potential, but the power of evil.

In most people's lives, and certainly in the lives of people who have grown enough to have the potential to manifest their power in the world, there is the moment of temptation—to use that power for Ego aggrandizement or personal

Shadow Rulers are ogre tyrants operating out of a scarcity mentality, believing that there is not enough, so my gain must be their loss.

pleasure only. The parallel temptations of Christ and the Buddha are examples of this essential moment in the hero's journey.

When each of us has claimed enough power to know we can do real good or real harm in the world, we are typically faced with such a temptation. We know we have made the wrong choice when we begin to feel empty and our lives begin to feel sterile, dead, and maybe even hellish.

When we are using our power in the wrong way for us, or if we have pulled back from our power, the shadow Ruler has us in its grip. Either way, what is called for is repentance. The Destroyer can be invoked to eliminate this harmful new approach, habit, or path, and the Lover to transform that initially harmful experience into a transformative lesson that can guide future action and help keep you on the right life course for you.

It is also important to remember that the shadow Ruler emerges in our lives not because we are manifesting too much power, but too little. Often we are substituting power over others for power from within ourselves. As the Warrior needs to learn to fight for what really matters (not just to win) and the Caregiver to sacrifice only for what is essential (not just to be "good"), the Ruler needs to learn to use his or her power not just to achieve fame and fortune, but to create a bountiful kingdom for us all.

The shadow Ruler emerges in our life not because we are manifesting too much power, but too little.

To settle for being a petty dictator (and bossing around one's kids or employees), for conspicuous consumption, or for creating conspicuous lifestyles instead of full lives is to ask for internal revolution that may begin with possession by one's shadow Ruler. The shadow Ruler will inevitably hurt you or others, and (if you are lucky) in that way get your attention to the need to claim your life and your power.

Bonanza Jellybean in Tom Robbins's *Even Cowgirls Get the Blues* expresses the ways that the concepts of heaven and hell (whatever truth they might contain about the afterlife) accurately reflect our experience on this earth. What we experience reflects who we are and the choices we daily make: "Heaven and hell are right here on earth. Hell is living your fears, heaven is living your dreams."[1] When the shadow Ruler has us in its grip, we are too cynical or fearful to use our power to manifest our highest dreams and aspirations, so we settle for lower order pleasures, or worse, we settle just for consumerism, status, and power. But it is never too late to change direction. Hell may live within us but so does heaven.

Toward a Harmonious Kingdom:
Stages in the Ruler's Journey

The Rulers are at best very ecological. They find the best use for all the resources of the kingdom—human or material. Indeed, this is how the kingdom becomes prosperous and strong, because nothing is really wasted. In one of my favorite children's stories, *Jerome the Frog,* a frog who thinks he is a prince is asked by the townspeople to slay the dragon who continues to scare them and burn their houses. He ends up talking with that dragon, and the dragon explains that it is simply his nature to burn things. The frog proves his princely (and potentially kingly) nature by convincing the dragon to burn the town garbage instead of the peasants' houses. This works out well for all concerned.

Levels of the Ruler

Shadow	Controlling, rigid, tyrannical, and manipulative behaviors; the ogre tyrant
Call	Lack of resources, harmony, support, or order in your life
Level One	Taking responsibility for the state of your life; seeking healing of wounds or areas of powerlessness that are reflected in scarcity in your outer life; concerned primarily with your own life or your own family
Level Two	Developing skills and creating structures for manifesting your own dreams in the real world as it is; concerned with the good of whatever group or community you belong to
Level Three	Fully utilizing all resources—internal as well as external; concerned with the good of society or the planet

---

The Ruler inside each of us is always on the lookout for ways to find the potential in the people we influence so that they can use their gifts in a productive way. The Ruler is also equally concerned with order. The kingdom cannot be fully productive unless some harmony reigns and conflict is not stifled, but handled in a productive way. This requires helping different people to understand and appreciate the gifts of people very different from themselves. The Ruler is also very ecological, understanding that for the highest level of productivity, resources should not be wasted. And the saddest resource to waste is a human life.

However, at the first levels (when the Ego archetypes are dominant in our lives), the Ruler is not this wise. We need to remember that we were really Rulers of our own lives before we became conscious of taking a journey. We only thought other people had all the power.

At the second, more mature Ego level, we may have more sense of being responsible for our lives and those of others, but we claim this responsibility by learning to sacrifice parts of ourselves for the good of the kingdom. In the operetta *The Student Prince,* the young prince falls in love with a peasant girl, but upon accepting the crown, he knows he must leave her and marry appropriate to his rank. As a king, he has a duty to perform. He must act according to who he is—royalty.

The Ruler inside each of us is always on the lookout for ways to find the potential in the people we influence so that they can use their gifts in a productive way.

On a symbolic level, this suggests the requirement that we let go of many of our passions when we take the responsibility of living our true royal paths. The Ruler actually learns to distinguish surface bliss from the greater bliss of living according to one's true royal Self. This requires accepting one's duties along with one's pleasures. Even more, it requires being willing to relinquish many opportunities, which no matter how attractive they might seem are not truly one's own. The issue for each of us as we claim our royal power is to give up some freedom to be true to the necessity demanded by our Souls.

Shakespeare's *King Lear* serves among other things as a cautionary tale about what happens if a Ruler thinks he or she can escape that duty while still living or becomes self-indulgent and self-deceptive. The Ruler's life is rich and privileged, but it also requires fidelity to the task of governing one's own life. This duty may not be relinquished, and it requires a clear mind and a willingness to face reality as it is.

At this second level, although you have integrated the Caregiver and Warrior archetypes, life may seem hard, and doing your duty may feel like a struggle or sacrifice. We are thus likely to blame and exclude others who are weak or selfish or villainous. We are less interested in finding their purpose and gift than, at some level, getting away from or rid of them. There is also little or no sense of a synchronistic relationship with the kingdom, so everything we do to try to make the world better requires great struggle.

At the third level—the level of the journey and Soul initiation—we lose again the sense of power and responsibility in the world, as we either leave a responsible place in that society to "follow our bliss" or find ourselves initiated by love, or suffering, or both and feel temporarily quite out of control. At this point, we may be more interested in simply holding things together than in having any sense of claiming our power in the world. Yet paradoxically, it is this sense of confrontation with our powerlessness, especially in contrast to the greater powers in the cosmos, that prepares us to claim our power in a healthy way through healing our wounds and renewing our Spirits.

At this level, people lose the desire to lord it over others, partly because they recognize their human fallibility and partly because they understand that others are Rulers too, but even more importantly because they have stopped doing life by themselves. Instead they seek to live in alignment with these cosmic forces. For many people, this means they seek always to do the will of God. For others, it means they swear fidelity to their deepest inner wisdom. Whatever they call it, it is surrendering to this inner numinous power that transforms their experience from suffering to joy. Indeed, they are then often so empowered and empowering that things miraculously seem to go right, perhaps simply because they so identify with the good of the cosmos, the world, their community, family, workplace, and so forth that their own desires are no longer narcissistic and self-serving but can be fully lived out.

At best, we know that the good of the larger kingdom comes only when others have claimed their power, so they are not competitive. They trust synchronicity to work for them, recognizing that they do not have to do everything the hard way if they demonstrate harmony within and find the right use for each resource in their kingdom.

The Ruler, the Court, and Continual Renewal

The danger of becoming rigid and locked into old ways and hence harming the kingdom is always present for the Ruler. One way to avoid becoming an evil tyrant is to continue to take our journeys throughout life so that we are constantly renewed. In addition, it is important to complement the Ruler with other archetypal figures that help provide balance. In the traditional court, these characters are known as the Magician, the Sage, and the Fool (or Jester). They are not that different from the key figures in more primitive tribes who balance the Chief: the Shaman, the Wise Old Man or Woman, and the Trickster. We also find them in our dreams and evidenced in our lives. Becoming the Ruler of our life is, in itself, a major triumph, but it is not the end of our journey. To remain vigorous and effective in our life and work, we need to claim and express our inner Magician, Sage, and Fool.

Exercises

Give some thought to when, where, how, and how much the Ruler expresses itself in your life.

1. How much or how little is the Ruler expressed in your life? Has it been expressed more in the past or present? Do you see it emerging more in your future? Is it expressed more at work, at home, with friends, in dreams or fantasies?

2. Who are some friends, relatives, co-workers, and others who seem influenced by the archetype of the Ruler?

3. Is there anything you wish were different about the expression of the Ruler in your life?

4. Since each archetype expresses itself in many different ways, take some time to describe or otherwise portray (e.g., draw, make a collage, use a picture of yourself in a particular costume or pose) the Ruler as it is expressed or could be expressed in your life. What does or would it look like? How does or would it act? In what setting does or would it feel most at home?

Daydream

Imagine that you are literally the King or Queen of the realm (your life). Let yourself imagine that you can change virtually anything you want, since you are totally in charge. There is, of course, a political process to consider; you may need to convince your "subjects" of the wisdom of your dictates, but begin simply by thinking of what you would like to decree. Start with your domain—your home, your private life, the part of your work life that is within your control. Then imagine yourself writing the new laws, or writing a speech explaining the new policies to your "subjects," and negotiating with the Rulers of nearby kingdoms to gain their cooperation.

15

The Magician

The power of the Ruler is to create and maintain a prosperous and peaceful kingdom. The power of the Magician is to transform reality by changing consciousness. Good Rulers take responsibility for their symbiotic relationship with the kingdom, knowing that the state of their life reflects and affects the state of their Souls, but they generally cannot heal themselves. Without the Magician, who heals the wounded Ruler, the kingdom cannot be transformed.

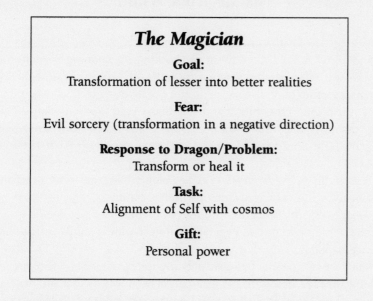

The Magician

Goal:
Transformation of lesser into better realities

Fear:
Evil sorcery (transformation in a negative direction)

Response to Dragon/Problem:
Transform or heal it

Task:
Alignment of Self with cosmos

Gift:
Personal power

Court Magicians often served as advisors to Rulers, as Merlin did to King Arthur, but when the kingdom is inhospitable, they often work alone. People

My HMI score for
the Magician
archetype is

————

(high = 30/low = 0).

It is my ————
highest score

(highest = 12th/lowest = 1st).

who claim the Magician role in society have been known by names as diverse as shaman, witch, sorcerer, healer, fortune-teller, priest, or priestess. In the modern world, they may be known as doctors, psychologists, organizational development consultants, or even marketing wizards.[1]

Starhawk, writing about the tradition of Wicca—the native, goddess-worshiping, feminist, and shamanistic nature religion—defines magic as "the art of changing consciousness at will."[2] She explains that magic can be "prosaic" (as with "a leaflet, lawsuit, or a strike") or esoteric, "encompassing all the ancient techniques of deepening awareness, of psychic development, and of heightened intuition." But in either case, magic has the impact of changing reality—often more quickly than might be expected if we had to do it all with hard work and struggle.

The idea of magic seems esoteric to many people in the modern world. Yet it is important to remember that Jesus, Moses, and Buddha—indeed, all the founders of great religions— performed miracles regularly. If we are to walk in their paths, we can too. Basic in such traditions is the injunction, "Ask and ye shall receive, seek and ye shall find, knock and the door will open." We need to ask for what we want and need.

The Magician Within

The Magician as an archetype can be expressed in any of our lives in very simple and everyday ways. Claremont de Castillejo, in *Knowing Woman: A Feminine Psychology,* talks of the practice in India of calling a rainmaker when experiencing a drought. Rainmakers do not do anything to make the rain happen; they just come to the village and stay there—and the rain comes. They do not make the rain come; they allow it or, more exactly, their inner atmosphere of allowing and affirming what is creates a climate in which what needs to be happens.[3]

Similarly, Shug, in Alice Walker's *The Color Purple,* transforms everyone she meets, simply because she is a woman who has claimed her power; that simple decision makes ripple effects out into the world. She does not decide to change people; she does not set out on Pygmalion projects; she is simply true to herself, and change happens.

Often everyday people unknowingly use the basic principles of magic and never think they are doing magic. The parent who knows that the best way to calm down an overly excited child is to become very calm inside is being a rainmaker and a healer. Peacefulness is contagious, just as hysteria is. Probably all of us have known people who emanate peace and caring, and sometimes we can feel better just by standing next to them. Conversely, we all know people whose inner world is chaotic and desperate, and that inner state affects everyone around them. We are all Magicians in this sense.

Those who claim their gifts tend to create win/win solutions for the people around them. This is most clear, of course, in the case of people who have become famous for their contributions to the world. Claiming our personal power and our vocations results in the most basic kind of magic: we change and grow and in the process enrich the world around us. In a democratic society, it is not just the famous "great people" who do this. We all need to.

We can also influence the world in many other ways as we consciously explore the symbiotic relationship of our inner and outer worlds. When we establish order in our inner world, it becomes simple to have order in the external world. (Conversely, sometimes cleaning our refrigerator, closet, or desk clears the mind.) Similarly, if we want a peaceful world, we must start with becoming peaceful ourselves. (Conversely, acting more peacefully may help us feel more peaceful). If we want love, we start with becoming loving. (Conversely, receiving love helps us become more loving.)

This mirroring of inner and outer does not work by a simple cause-and-effect relationship. It works by synchronicity, what Carl Jung called "meaningful coincidences." It is like a magnetic field, drawing to us experiences that match our inner realities.

To the Magician, the sacred is not seen as above us, judging us (as it is from an Ego perspective), but as immanent in ourselves, nature, society, the earth, the cosmos. Thus the Magician in each of us provides a sense of connectedness with the whole and an understanding that what is within us contains all that is outside ourselves. Or to put it in more esoteric magical terms, the macrocosm and the microcosm mirror one another. We are all connected at some level, perhaps at the level Jung called the collective unconscious. The Magician's role is to learn to make that level conscious.

In the Hawaiian tradition, as Serge King explains, shamans see themselves as spiders in a large web, "stretching out in all directions to every part of the universe. . . . Like a spider he can move along the web without getting caught in it. Unlike a spider but like a shaman, he can also send out vibrations along the web and consciously affect anything in the universe, according to the strength of his *manna*."[4] It is these vibrations that can effect healing. As we ourselves become more healthy and alive, each of us sets in motion a ripple that affects others. Conversely, if we shut down and become less alive, that too has a ripple effect.

Trusting this interconnectedness can also give us powerful feedback on our journeys. For example, when we seem to be going with the flow, and what we want comes easily—so easily that it seems as if the waters part before us—it is

To take responsibility for our power to affect our world by who we are requires great Ego strength and a sense of Self that originates in our Souls.

To the Magician, the sacred is not seen as above us, judging us, but as immanent in ourselves, nature, society, the earth, the cosmos.

often a sign that we are integrated with our Soul purpose. Conversely, when we are going in the wrong direction, obstacles often appear in our paths.[5]

When the Magician is active in our lives, moreover, we begin to notice synchronistic events—that is, meaningful coincidences, such as when we need to know something and a book containing what we needs practically falls into our lap or we run into just the person we needed to see.

Journeying Between the Worlds

All shamanism involves a journey to another world, which means that we move out of normal, everyday beta brain wave consciousness into other brain patterns (alpha, theta, and so on) or just into fantasy or sleep. Techniques for moving into this altered state include drumming, meditation, hypnotic action, trance dancing, and deep breathing.[6]

Magicians move into altered states, and then explore these realities, whether they are exploring their own daydreams, their dreams, an imaginary reality in a guided fantasy, the wisdom and perspective gained through meditation, or "another world" experienced in a shamanistic trance. We all enter these altered states, but most of us choose not to become very conscious of them.

One way we awaken the Magician within is simply to become conscious as we enter these other planes of reality. We can choose to learn their geography, their physical and psychological laws, the people and animals who live there. Many people do this with "lucid" dreams, in which they consciously interact with dream figures, or in waking, active imagination exercises, during which they move into fantasy or even consciously into trancelike states. Anyone who has experienced a guided fantasy that provided insight into his or her life knows something about what Magicians do. So does any habitual meditator who has learned that opening up to a deeper wisdom and a connection with the transpersonal greatly improves the quality of the rest of one's life. So does anyone of strong religious faith who prays daily and knows it is possible to talk with God.

Experiences such as regular meditation, prayer, or guided fantasies help people who might never think of themselves as Magicians to open up to knowing things they did not know they could know—and indeed things they could not know in their regular left-brain beta consciousness. In modern terms, traveling to, or communicating with, such other worlds throws people into their subconscious material and into their right-brain knowledge, and into what Jung called the "collective unconscious." For many, it also connects them to spiritual realities beyond themselves.

In the other world of active imagination—in a guided fantasy perhaps—we might have the experience of confronting a dragon and slaying it. In normal conscious life, this experience may give us the confidence to overcome a great challenge. We can use the experience in the fantasy to avoid living through the experience in our inner life, working with the fantasy image until we find a more effective way of relating to that dragon than slaying, or being slain by it![7]

When the Magician is dominant in our consciousness, we often experience foreshadowings of future events in our lives—in dreams, in fantasies, in moments of intuitive insight. Some people find out their subconscious knows of realities of which they are not consciously aware in surprising and dramatic ways. One woman told me how she was driving down a highway and suddenly heard a voice out of nowhere telling her to get off the road. She did, and several seconds later a major accident occurred that she would have been unable to avoid had she not listened to this inner voice. She had no explanation for the event, but it affected her profoundly. If time is really relative, as Einstein said it was, and if we are all connected, it is not surprising that we might be able to directly intuit past or future realities.

Some people consciously develop both their intuitive or psychic abilities and their capacity for discernment and become known for their uncanny knack of "guessing right." Such a person might be known to be a psychic and seen as spiritual, but could just as well be a person in business whose hunches consistently pay off. All you need to do is pay attention to which voices in your head seem to be trustworthy. Keep track of what kinds of thoughts, images, or feelings you have that seem to be borne out by future experience.

When the Magician is dominant in our consciousness, we often experience fore-shadowings of future events in our lives—in dreams, in fantasies, in moments of intuitive insight.

The Magician as Namer

The Magician in us also has the power of naming. If we do not accurately and objectively name ourselves and our own stories, we are at the mercy of how others see us and of every off-the-wall voice in our head. We first claim our power to name when the Creator is active in our lives and we begin to tell our story in our own voice. However, this is an ongoing process. If we internalize others' voices and listen to the abusive voices (which everyone has) in our own heads, we are "unnamed" by their (inadvertent) evil sorcery.

Magicians have traditionally told the history of the tribe in story form, and such stories help the community—and individuals in it—know who they are. The Magician in each one of us helps find the story that both honestly represents and genuinely ennobles both our individual and collective lives. Such stories have the capacity to heal, and they also help us pass on the knowledge of who we are to the next generation so that they might build upon our mistakes and our triumphs.

Naming reality from the perspective of the Soul can empower ourselves and others. How we name something determines our experience of life. It is negative and demeaning to call a child "dumb" for doing something. If you tell him what he might do instead, you empower him. It is destructive to call someone "crazy" who is hallucinating. If you tell her she has the opportunity to develop enough Ego strength to contain these images, she can learn to differentiate empowering from destructive ways and claim her potential as a Magician.

Every time we name a reality in such a way that we diminish people or possibilities, we are, however inadvertently, acting out a bit of evil sorcery. We are naming people in a way that lessens their sense of possibilities, their self-esteem, their capacity to see hope for the future. At best, Magicians learn to use the power of naming to empower others and transform limiting, dispiriting situations into opportunities.

To refuse to be an evil sorceror to oneself does not mean we have to be dishonest or refuse moral or any other kind of responsibility. For example, when you make a mistake, you can rephrase the criticism coming from yourself or others, reminding yourself, "We all make mistakes. Because I learn from my mistakes, I am always growing and changing." Or you could even tell yourself there are no real mistakes, and begin to wonder why you did what you did and what you were trying to learn.

One powerful way to transform your life is by changing the way you name your experience.

Shirley Luthman, in *Energy and Personal Power,* is particularly articulate at explaining how this works. She talks of a woman who stayed with a particularly difficult man and felt critical of herself for doing so. Luthman asked her if there was anything she was gaining by being in that relationship. On thinking it through, she recognized that dealing with the unpleasantness of the relationship had motivated her to go out in the world more, to go back to school, and to get involved doing things. Paradoxically, it was only when she could respect her underlying motivation and stop beating up on herself that she was able to let go of that relationship and find a healthier way to encourage the new behaviors she so valued.

One powerful way to transform your life is by changing the way you name your experience. The impulse to accuse ourselves is heavily ingrained in this culture. Instead of seeing yourself as sick, inept, or clumsy, or dwelling on past or future mistakes, it is possible simply to trust yourself absolutely, and to know that you choose and will choose everything that happens to you for your own growth and development. Doing so restores dignity and adventure to life and transforms even the most seemingly negative circumstances into opportunities for growth. Acting on the belief that we choose our own realities—and that we do so for good, trustworthy reasons—empowers us because it renames our experience in a way that allows us to receive its gift, whatever that gift may be.[8]

There are currently many books of affirmations available that suggest substituting positive phrases for negative ones in our internal and external dialogue. All of them tell us that our words program our unconscious and that our unconscious affects our actions—conscious and unconscious. We can enter "the other world" of our own internal dialogue and by changing that, change our outer life. For readers who wish to try it, the key is to use only present tense and positive expressions: "I am intelligent," not "I am working on not being so dumb." Experts on this matter say that the subconscious is very literal. If you assert that you are working on something, the subconscious will keep working on it for a very long time, and you will never actually reach your goal! And the subconscious will not hear the "not." It *will* hear the "dumb."

But it is critical that such affirmations not be used to move into denial about real problems. Affirmations affect the mind level and operate by a process of mind over matter. If the emotional level is not also addressed, it can get blocked and cause the development of a monstrous Shadow. So we need to feel, express, and allow our emotions to flow freely through us. Often we cannot just will our negativity all away; sometimes it needs to be exorcised and transformed.

Positive thinking should never be used to avoid responsibility for the harm you do yourself or others. When we do harm, we need to ask forgiveness from ourselves, God, and, when appropriate, the person harmed. When we can do so honestly, we should also atone or make amends in some way. As transformative as affirmations might be, forgiveness is even more powerful, and lessens the danger of denial.

Exorcism and Transformation

Ancient shamans regularly exorcised "demons" and negative presences within people. Today, modern psychology tells us that much, if not all, of our inner negativity really results from repression. The issue is not to get rid of the negativity, but to transform it by allowing it some safe expression.

Such transformations can also happen when we express seemingly negative emotions. For instance, if we sob or beat on pillows until the emotion is spent, we will inevitably break through to a new emotional field. Tears may give way to anger, anger to laughter, and laughter to mystic experience.

One woman who fully expressed her anger in this way began to laugh for just a moment, and then began to sing a hauntingly beautiful song. When she finished the process, she said she had never heard the song before, but as it swelled within her, she felt as though she were singing with the stars. Fully expressing her pain and anger transmuted that pain into mystical acceptance and joy.[9]

It is possible to learn to transmute emotional energy without active catharsis once we learn to feel our feelings fully. They can simply ripple through us one by one until we move fully through suffering into joy. We can also see this in our personal relationships when we talk through our anger and hurt and come out the other side feeling more intimate and loving than before.

Some people can also transmute others' energies, taking in others' negative energy and sending back loving healing energy. One Buddhist meditation tells us to breathe in the world's pain and breathe out love. The idea is not to hold on to that pain or keep it for ourselves, but through compassion to transform it and send it back in a new form. Others do this naturally just by flowing with a situation. They naturally open empathically to feel with another person's pain, and as they move through it with the other person, both feel better.

Just as our pain can be trapped in our bodies, causing blockages that limit our aliveness and eventually make us ill, wisdom that we have not honored gets trapped there as well. When we unleash that buried wisdom—through movement, massage, catharsis, dance, or any other form of physical release—we need to express it in some way. But nothing helps the body and the Soul more than action on our own inner knowledge. Most often our bodies are blocked because we do not allow our process to be manifested in our lives. Acting on what we know and want in a direct way in the world is the most powerful healing action available.

Magician as Healer

To claim responsibility for being Rulers of our own lives and to see that the state of our kingdoms reflects our inner reality can be very painful when we feel totally incapable of healing ourselves. So we suffer. We know the problems in our outer life reflect our inner state, but we are powerless to do anything about the situation without the help of a healer. For most of us, this requires finding healers outside ourselves and eventually awakening the healer within.

When our lives are less than magical, one element is often out of balance.

Healing *can* begin in any of the four centers of power and energy—body, heart, mind, and spirit—but in the modern world most healers work in only one area. However, our affect on the world is most magical when all four are in alignment.[10] The great American Indian shaman Sun Bear emphasizes the need to strengthen our bodies by good nutrition and exercise; our emotions by being open and honoring our feelings; our minds by being tough-minded and rigorous in our thinking; and our spirits by connecting with our spiritual source. We can only connect with that spiritual source by finding the spiritual path that is our own.

A classic image of the Magician in the tarot deck shows a Magician channeling energy from the earth and the sky. The sky—inspiration, dreaming, vision—is balanced by the earthy grounding in the facts of everyday existence; both are equally important. In this way, the Magician is able to transform reality.

In practice, most of us do not heal our wounded Rulers alone. We seek out sources from a variety of places—people who specialize in healing the body, the emotions, the mind, and the spirit. Somewhere along the way our inner Magician is awakened, and we take more responsibility for our own healing as we learn the basics of healthy eating and exercise; ways of being clear, open, and intimate in our personal relationships; increased rigor and clarity of thought; and strategies for staying true to our own spiritual source.

Invoking the Aid of a Mentor, Guru, or God/dess

It is also possible to "borrow" or invoke another's aid in the healing process, as Catholics sometimes pray for the blessing or power of a saint. One is able to aid in the healing process because of the power of one's guru or teacher, a powerful and spiritually evolved being from the past, or a god or goddess. In this situation, it is not one's personal power but one's relationship with a more powerful being that makes possible the healing. Such a relationship is inherent in Christian prayers that end with, "in the name of Jesus Christ our Lord," or in any practice of invoking God's grace, the power of Christ, Mary, a saint, a guru, or a teacher.

In many native traditions, the shaman has spirit guides in the form of animals. Finding one's token animal is essential to gaining the power necessary to transform or heal. Shamans regularly perform the dance of their sacred animal—or rather they let the animal's spirit dance through them—so that it will have a motive to stay with them (the chance for expression on the physical plane).[11]

Maintaining a respectful relationship with the source of your power is very important for keeping the Magician within alive and active. Of course, it is also critical to be certain that that source is identified with positive energies so that you are not inviting harm to yourself or another.

Magicians also need to find their own healing circle, coven, or group—the people with whom they have a special connection. For the Magician, this is part of discovering the net of connectedness that links each of us with very special people, objects, and animals and to one's own spiritual path.

No amount of trying will make you really connected (beyond the cosmic oneness that is always there as well) to someone, some thing, or some institution you are not really connected to, and no one can really break a connection that is real. It is more like taking off the skin of an onion. Eventually we may experience our deeper connection to the entire cosmos, but we need not push that. At first it is enough to take off a few layers and just recognize those special connections—people, places, times, objects, work, a spiritual path—that give us our power (and make us happy).

To be an effective Magician, it is important to be spiritually, emotionally, and physically linked in to the great web of life. Real power comes paradoxically from recognizing our dependence—on the earth, on other people, and on our spiritual source. Thus many traditional shamans begin their work by consciously connecting with and thanking the earth, the four directions, the people they love most (including their teacher), and finally the spiritual power they serve.

Often magic is as simple as prayer. Many Magicians simply ask for what is needed—health, forgiveness, transformation, resources—and then accept the answer to that prayer, whether yes or no, as coming from the wisdom of a power greater than their own.

Transformation Through Ritual Action

Magicians often use rituals to change consciousness or transmute realities. Traditionally, it is the Magician who creates ceremonies to hold the tribe together and to reinforce their connection with spirit. Rituals can be used in healing or transformation as well, as a way of focusing attention on the transformation desired and focusing the consciousness of all concerned on letting go of the former reality and welcoming in the desired new reality.

Rituals help focus the power of the mind to, in Starhawk's words, "change consciousness at will." Ritual actions can be very elaborate or very simple, but they always express a change in commitment. Graduation from high school or college can be a marker event, if the ritual works, that changes the consciousness of the graduates from students to adults. Marriage ceremonies, if they work, help everyone involved begin to see the couple as a unit, not simply as individual adults. Funerals help us grieve and let go of the person who has passed on, so that after an appropriate interval, we can go on with the business of living.

There are few defined, collective rituals in our culture, but there is a positive trend for people to create their own. Not an inconsiderable number of people in the past decades have had renaming ceremonies for themselves, taking on a new name to signify a new identity. Some women are hosting "croning" ceremonies as they grow older (usually somewhere between ages fifty and sixty-five) to celebrate becoming wise women. Such a ceremony announces an important transition and counters the debilitating ageism of a culture with few positive images for older women.

There is also an increasing tendency in organized religions to create an opening for more spontaneous and egalitarian services and rituals arising from the current needs of the participants rather than simply from tradition. The best managers recognize that an effective meeting needs to have elements of ritual, bonding people to a shared vision and shared goals.

Ritual is also being used for healing. One therapist, for instance, occasionally has clients visualize putting their problems on the table. She hands them a magic wand and asks them to imagine their problems magically disappearing. Others arrange simple rituals of exorcism to let go of a relationship, a bad habit, or a mental problem. Such a ritual symbolic action does not "magically" remove the client's problems, but if it is done well and with preparation, it can allow the client to align body, mind, and heart around a commitment to really let go of a pattern of psychological attachment and consequently to accomplish the therapeutic work with less resistance and more optimism and ease.

Even Western physicians are now widely recognizing the power of the mind to make the body sick or to make it well. Treatment for cancer in many environments includes visualizations in which the patient imagines the cancer cells either being killed or leaving the body. Rituals that focus the mind on a desired outcome—particularly if they also harness group energy toward that end—can trigger this placebo effect. This is one factor operative when healing ceremonies succeed in working miracles.

Rituals help group members experience a sense of intimacy and connectedness. If the same ritual actions are repeated over time, they provide a sense of connectedness with history. If they change to meet the needs of the time, they help people live in the now and bond in a more spontaneous, creative way. Rituals are also used to align individuals and groups with cosmic energies/the will of God/ the flow/the force. When a number of people are unified in their support of a goal, a transition, or a healing, their collective energy can be transformative. Rituals help bond people together in this way and lend group support to individual and group goals and transformations.

Private rituals are often essential for keeping the Magician connected and in touch with the deeper aspects of his or her nature and hence with the cosmos. Ritual prayer, meditation, and centering meditations help unify consciousness so that work can be done without internal static. Individuals and traditions differ on the details of such centering practices, but the goal is to center so that your conscious will is in alignment with your unconscious, with your body and emotions, and with your soul connection and fidelity to a deeper spiritual power. If the consciousness is aligned with the time, with the work to be done, and with positive forces in the universe, usually the work to be done will then flow. If it does not, it is usually a sign to change course and go another way.

Stages in the Magician's Journey

The Magical always begins with some kind of wounding. Many times this is an actual illness of some kind. It is only through healing the Self that the Magician learns to heal others. In the modern world, it is the illness—physical illness, mental or emotional illness, or addiction—which often initially opens the Magician to spiritual realities.

All Magicians are not healers. But all learn to listen to their intuition, whether it comes as a feeling, a desire to move in some way, an inner sense of voice, or a vision or an oracular voice. In the movie *Field of Dreams,* the main character hears a voice saying, "If you build it, he will come." He builds a baseball diamond, and great baseball players of the past come—but most importantly, his own father (long-dead) shows up in a way that allows for a healing of their relationship.

The Magical always begins with some kind of wounding.

When we begin to act on our intuitive sense of rightness—despite our awareness that others might think what we are doing is crazy—we awaken the inner Magician. Many Magicians report that early on in life they had psychic or mystic experiences but felt confused that others do not share these realities, and hence they either repressed the experiences or simply kept quiet about them. It frequently takes a traumatic illness, or some kind of inner desperation, to allow those experiences and perspectives to be manifested again in the life.

Often we avoid or deny the Magician within for a long period of time. Some may feel that being a Magician seems too grand and wish to avoid it out of a fear of grandiosity. Others may fear countering the biases of a culture that fears or denies the miraculous. Still others may fear isolation, seeing the Magician's path as necessarily a lonely one. Still others may appropriately fear their inability to tell a positive intuition from a self-defeating or crazy thought. In many cases, we are moved out of denial by meeting or hearing of a Magician who was humble, who was accepted, who worked in community with others, and who knew how to discern true from false direction. Sometimes we actively seek teachers and read anything helpful we can find.

This waiting period also serves as an incubation period while the budding Magician grows strong and wise enough to begin. Since becoming a Magician involves great Ego strength, Magicians are prone to both the positive and negative aspects of Ego. They need the Ego strength to work their magic—on themselves and others. But they may also fall prey to arrogance or egotism of some kind early in the work. Ursula Le Guin's Sparrowhawk in *A Wizard of Earthsea* is a case in point. Showing off one day, this apprentice wizard called forth a demon from the underworld when he was trying to call back the dead. It was then his responsibility to free the world from this evil presence. When he finally caught up with it, he recognized it as his own Shadow.

When Sparrowhawk acknowledges that the demon is his Shadow, the Shadow is integrated with his personality and thus becomes a positive source of energy. As Le Guin explains, he "had neither lost nor won but, naming the shadow of his death with his own name, had made himself whole: a man who, knowing his whole true self, cannot be used or possessed by any power other than himself, and whose life therefore is lived for life's sake and never in the service of ruin, or pain, or hatred, or the dark."[12]

Levels of the Magician

Shadow	Evil sorcerer or wicked witch, synchronistic negative occurrences, calling negativity to oneself, or turning positive into negative occurrences
Call	Physical or emotional illness, or extrasensory or synchronistic experiences
Level One	Experiencing healing or choosing to notice extrasensory or synchronistic experiences
Level Two	Grounding inspiration by acting on your visions and making them real; making your dreams come true
Level Three	Consciously using the knowledge that everything is connected to everything else; developing mastery of the art of changing physical realities by first changing mental, emotional, and spiritual ones

---

To awaken the inner Magician safely, it is important to have taken your journey. The Ego is developed, but is not running the show. It needs to provide a strong container, but the Self—with a strong connection to Soul and Spirit—must be in control.

Because the power of the Magician in each of us is so potentially great, integrating the Shadow is essential so that we do not inadvertently (or consciously) use our power for evil purposes. The Shadow, of course, is composed of parts of our psyche that have been repressed and thus possess us in monstrous form. Integrating our Shadows allows the psyche to be more whole and also decreases the degree to which our lives are ruled by unconscious forces. Recognizing the Shadow, and one's own propensity to betrayal of self and others, is often a big blow to the Magician's Ego, but the resulting greater humility allows in more love. From this point, the Magician's healing of others is less likely to be motivated by personal aggrandizement or other Ego concerns and more likely to come from pure and clear caring and love.

The greatest Shadow that Magicians must face is the reality of their own deaths. When that reality is faced fully, the result is a kind of miraculous freedom that allows for an ability to live and respond in the moment without great fear about tomorrow. Indeed, at best death becomes the Magician's ally and advisor on all major decisions. This is what makes it possible for the Magician to say no to the temptations of using power for wealth, fame, more power, or earthy pleasures. This, of course, does not mean that the Magician cannot be wealthy, famous, and powerful and enjoy life, but it does mean that the powers cannot be prostituted to these ends.

Growth is also facilitated when the Magician finds like-minded people who understand the miraculous aspect of life and can help each other stay grounded, humble, and loving. When this circle is discovered, the Magician's path becomes less lonely and difficult. Where before the Magician was being healed or healing, now the pattern becomes reciprocal, so the Magician heals and is healed continually by this empowering fellowship or sisterhood, and development can speed up exponentially. The most powerful Magicians know their own place in the great web of life, and also understand that with all the power of this archetype, they are as interdependent as any of us. When they are willing to be guided by their peers, their own deepest wisdom, and their spiritual source, they are most likely to be able to claim their power in a way that avoids grandiosity or the misuse of their power.

The Shadow Magician

Magicians in negative guise are evil sorcerers who use their power to harm rather than heal. Actually, all of us who have denied the power from within that allows us to transform ourselves and others have an inner evil sorcerer.

A shadow Magician tends to possess us: with all the best intentions to do good, we may find ourselves acting out in hostile and harmful ways. Instead of helpful naming, we engage in "unnaming," which makes people feel like less than they are. When good energy comes our way, we take it in and transform it to negative energy. (Someone gives us a gift, and we imply that they had ulterior motives for doing so or act guilty because we did not think to give one to them.)

In our fantasy life, we fantasize bad things happening to ourselves and others. We are secretly delighted when something bad happens to others, and we tend toward self-destructive actions, turning what might be a positive opportunity into a dreadful event.

Healthy Magicians know how to use charisma to help their children, students, or clients. The evil sorcerer or wicked witch, however, seeks only to control others. In the most extreme form, instead of using that energy either to transform another and help them grow they use it to increase their own power.

The power of the Magician to *name,* is also the power to *misname.* In education, when students come to us in their wandering stage and ask us, "Who am I?" and we give them only the answer, "You are an A/B/C/D," we are inadvertently engaged in evil sorcery, helping them to see themselves only in terms of better than and worse than. In medicine, when patients come to us for healing and we see them as the kidney in Room 3, we dehumanize them and decrease their chances for healing. When clients come to us for therapy, and we say, "You are schizophrenic," as if that defined their whole identity, we are engaged in unnaming in a profound and harmful way.

In marketing and advertising, it is common to use powerful symbolic imagery and suggestions to manipulate people to buy products that they do not need or (as in the case of alcohol, cigarettes, and sugar) that might actually be harmful to them. Through advertising, people are taught to be insecure and worried (Do I have dandruff? Bad breath?) and to buy addictively to try to become OK. Indeed, the use of advertising to divert people from their journeys to mindless consumerism is a major force of evil sorcery in our time.

To the degree that we do not fully claim our own power to transform, we are more likely to be possessed by this energy in its shadow form and to use it, unconsciously, for no good ends. Power will not be denied. This power is never neutral; it either heals or harms, although to various degrees.

Although many of us are afraid to acknowledge and awaken the magical power we all have because of the power we have to harm, the answer is generally more Magician, not less. The Magician (as with the other archetypes associated with the return) provides a link with the numinous—especially the power of the divine to save, redeem, or forgive. Perhaps the most transformative power of the Magician is the power to transform through forgiveness of ourselves and others. Doing so transforms negative situations into possibilities for more growth and intimacy.

To the degree that we do not fully claim our own power to transform, we are more likely to be possessed by this energy in its shadow form.

Whether we use our powers for good or ill depends most of all on the level of our wisdom and honesty—how able we are to see and deal with the truth of the matter before us and in us. To fully develop the capacity to know when and if the transformation we seek is advisable, we need to develop the wisdom and disinterested quality of the Sage.

Exercises

Give some thought to when, where, how, and how much the Magician expresses itself in your life.

1. How much or how little is the Magician expressed in your life? Has it been expressed more in the past or present? Do you see it emerging more in your future? Is it expressed more at work, at home, with friends, in dreams or fantasies?

2. Who are some friends, relatives, co-workers, and others who seem influenced by the archetype of the Magician?

3. Is there anything you wish were different about the expression of the Magician in your life?

4. Since each archetype expresses itself in many different ways, take some time to describe or otherwise portray (e.g., draw, make a collage, use a picture of yourself in a particular costume or pose) the Magician as it is expressed or could be expressed in your life. What does or would it look like? How does or would it act? In what setting does or would it feel most at home?

Daydreams

Be aware of someone with whom you have difficulty. In your daydream, contact your higher or deeper, wiser Self. Then in your imagination, talk to that person's higher or deeper, wiser Self. Work the issue through on that level. When you return to your ordinary level of consciousness, simply observe whether there is any change in your relationship with that other person the next time you meet him or her.

●

Begin listening to your internal conversation. If you note yourself making a negative comment about yourself, others, or events, stop and turn the statement into a positive one. For example, if you find yourself thinking, "I'll never attract the kind of person I want to love; I'm short, fat, and not bright," turn the statement into, "I'm attractive in mind and body, and I attract to me people equally as attractive." Allow yourself to feel the positive emotions that surround the second statement. If at first you are too skeptical to have good feelings about your positive statement, play around with it until you find a form that does make you feel good. For example, if you are not ready to see yourself as attractive yet, you might say, "I eat small amounts of healthy food and I study good books, so I am attracting love from people who also care about health and intelligence." Notice how changes in your thinking change your life.

The Sage

Both Rulers and Magicians want to control reality and to change negative circumstances into positive ones. Sages have little or no need to control or change the world; they just want to understand it. The Sage's path is the journey to find out the truth—about ourselves, our world, and the universe. At its highest levels, it is not simply about finding knowledge, but about becoming wise. It is the Sage within that resonates to the adage, "That ye shall know the truth, and the truth shall set you free."

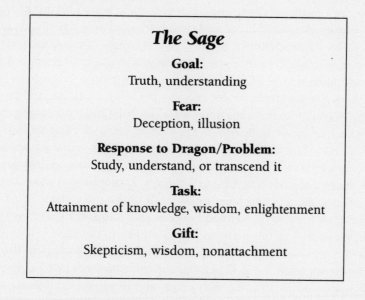

The Sage

Goal:
Truth, understanding

Fear:
Deception, illusion

Response to Dragon/Problem:
Study, understand, or transcend it

Task:
Attainment of knowledge, wisdom, enlightenment

Gift:
Skepticism, wisdom, nonattachment

In day-to-day matters, the most essential question for the Sage is "What is the truth here?" In that way, all Sages are sleuths, searching for the reality behind appearances. Doctors, psychologists, and all true healers need the advice of an inner or outer Sage so that the diagnosis and treatment are appropriate to the patient's true condition. Consultants and managers act as Sages when they struggle to discern the true cause of difficulties in organizations or to clarify an organization's genuine opportunities and strengths. Scholars are classic Sages in that their lives are devoted to furthering the search for knowledge.

Perhaps the most liberating and freeing moment in life is the "moment of truth" that illuminates our lives, disperses confusion, and clarifies what must be done. This is the moment, for example, when the alcoholic "hits bottom" and knows she needs help to recover or when a man realizes that his self-involvement has kept him from experiencing love and intimacy.

Often these deep insights reveal to us our own egotism and the way it has limited our lives and our freedom. The Sage helps us let go of our Ego concerns to open us to a deeper truth about life. Facing such essential truths is ennobling and humbling.

Sage as Sleuth

The challenge of the Sage, as in any mystery story, is to decode the clues and solve the underlying riddle of existence, whether that is our own existence, someone else's, or that of the cosmos. However, if our conscious minds and Egos are overly rationalistic and literal and can understand only a few kinds of clues, our inner Sage or Oracle is put in the classic dilemma of many such wise men and women, who like Cassandra can prophesy the truth, but are not believed or understood. Most often the Sage speaks oracularly in riddles (as with the Sphinx, Sufi teachers like Nasrudin, or Zen masters presenting their disciplines with a seemingly insoluble koan); in parables (as with Christ and most other great spiritual teaches); or in symbolic images (as with artists, poets, and visionaries).

There are many ways to express truth, and the Sage learns the appropriate response to each form. That is why in school we learn how to distinguish the different modes of understanding and inquiry appropriate to the natural and social sciences, the arts and humanities, philosophy and religion. That is also why, at best, we learn to understand how our own minds work and how we can use different aspects of our being to learn in different modes.

Every Sage knows the importance of matching methodology to the task at hand. We do not learn about God by quantitative methods. We do not understand demographic patterns through prayer and introspection. Science teaches us about physical realities in the world outside and within us, but is less than useful in exploring the truths of the human heart.

Every Sage also knows that the mode of inquiry very often preordains the results: the answers we find depend on the questions we ask and our methods of investigation. It is very difficult to filter out our own subjectivity. Often, the more we try to deny it or filter it out, the more it possesses us.

It is generally only when the Sage begins to be dominant in our lives that we recognize that we rarely, if ever, see things as they really are. We are to some degree always locked in our projections. Indeed, a major contribution of psychotherapy is to increase the probability that we might break through such projections long enough to have a genuine experience of any kind.

The discipline of the Sage is to cultivate a desire for truth strong enough to counter the Ego's need to be proven right.

Spiritual seekers labor endlessly to cultivate an attitude of dispassionate reflection and to move beyond Ego so they can have some experience of real truth. Whether we are engaged in learning, in a spiritual quest, or in making decisions about what to do next in our lives or work, the Sage in us wants to achieve some kind of objective truth beyond our limited personal truth.

When we are engaged in spiritual questing, the part of us that wants to experience absolute truth directly is frequently discouraged. Various spiritual practices associated with the spiritual paths of the Kabbala, Siddha Yoga, and Sufism, to name only a few, encourage people to progress slowly. Indeed, in all these paths, care is taken so that unprepared minds do not crack when experiencing the ecstasy associated with experiencing eternal truth.

In meditation, the Sage is that part of us that stands beyond our thoughts, feelings, and desires, merely watching the action. Meditative practices strengthen the part of ourselves that is truly dispassionate, objective, capable of watching without being caught up even in our most pressing needs and issues. They also allow us to know that we are not our thoughts and not our feelings, so we are no longer prisoners, at the beck and call of each fear or desire. Sometimes this inner observer can free us from feeling or thinking at all for seconds at a time and in this way sink into some more primary reality beyond that of the human mind and heart.

Such practices help people be in touch with more reality—whether external, internal, or cosmic—by first recognizing and accepting the radical subjectivity of human life. We cannot move to see truth beyond ourselves until we first become acquainted with our own biases. That is one reason why it is difficult, if not impossible, to be a Sage in any true way without taking one's journey; for it is through the journey that we find our identity and consciously know who we are.

Up until this point in the journey, the issue has been finding one's subjective truth and expressing it in the world. The Sage now must connect with truths beyond oneself.

In meditation, the Sage is that part of us that stands beyond our thoughts, feelings, and desires, merely watching the action.

On a recent radio talk show, I was describing the hero's responsibility to take the journey and find his or her own truth, and a man called to say he did not want to find "his truth." He wanted to find "The Truth." This is exactly what the

Sage in each of us wants. Youthful and naive Sages always believe that this is a simple matter: find the right teacher, the right sacred tradition, and believe what they tell you. This is the sentiment expressed in the bumper sticker, "God said it. I believe it. And that is the end of it."

As the Sage's journey progresses, however, the business of finding truth begins to get more complicated. Thus Sages tend to develop a sense of humility that comes from recognizing their radical subjectivity. Each of us is but a small part of a larger reality; although we may aspire to understand the whole, we will never truly achieve that ambition, for none of us alone can see enough to do so.

Stages of the Journey

William Perry's nine-stage model of cognitive development in college students describes the development of the Sage. The first two stages are variations on what he called "dualism." We want to find truth with a capital *T,* and we believe it is possible to do so. Assuming a dualistic universe, in which some answers are right and others are wrong, we believe truth resides in authorities and judge them harshly if they do not have it or share it with us.

Levels of the Sage

Shadow	Cut off, unfeeling, "ivory tower," "above it all"; critical, judging, or pompous behaviors and attitudes
Call	Confusion, doubt, deep desire to find the truth
Level One	Search for "the Truth" and for objectivity
Level Two	Skepticism, awareness of multiplicity and complexity of truth, all truth seen as relative; acceptance of subjectivity as part of the human condition
Level Three	Experience of ultimate truth or truths; wisdom

If we keep searching for truth, this confidence is eventually undercut when we begin to discover that the experts do not always agree with one another. We may learn this in school, from the media, or from the times Mother and Dad fought, but sooner or later most of us get this message. Then we want authorities to teach us the right process for finding truth so that we can sort out for ourselves whose truth is right.

Before long, disillusionment begins to set in. Indeed, this is the Sage's version of the fall from grace. We begin to realize that if the experts do not agree, then maybe there is no absolute truth. At Perry's stages three and four (versions of "multiplicity"), we may decide that anyone's truth is as good as anyone else's, or we may simply try to figure out how to give authorities the answers they want.

If our anxiety is great enough, we may find some "new truth" and hold on to it dogmatically for a time until our faith in that truth is also undermined. For example, young people who have lost their religious faith as a result of a confrontation with multiplicity of truth may discover a political philosophy and cling to that as dogmatically as they once did their religious convictions. Sooner or later, however, that faith is shattered as well.

If we keep growing, at some point we experience a true revolution in our thinking, when we really understand that there are no absolutes. How difficult this is, is measured by how few people are able to let go of their belief that there is a Truth to find. If we really abandon the search for ultimate truth, we come to accept that all knowledge is contextually relative. Although there are no absolute right answers or even right processes at Perry's stage five we begin to see that some are better than others. And there are ways of evaluating how some might be better than others with reference not to truth with a capital *T* but to context itself.

At this point, we understand that someone from a different culture has an equal right to see the world from a different vantage point than ours. We learn to evaluate a piece of literature in reference to the author's intent, its genre, its cultural context and purpose, and so on, rather than to some "eternal standards" of "great literature." We realize that many religions may offer spiritual truths, and we devise means of deciding what seems more or less true in them.

In Perry's final stages, six, seven, eight, and nine, we struggle with the problem of commitment in the context of relativism. At level six, we understand we can orient ourselves in a relativistic context by making some kind of personal commitment. At this point we see the necessity of choosing a course of study or work, a mate, or even a spiritual path without having to believe that our field of study or work is the "best" one to be in, that our mate is our "cosmic" perfect mate, or that our spiritual path is "right" while others are "wrong." Committing in a context of relativity means that one makes choices because they are right for you, without presuming that they would be right for another, and thus one can also support someone else making a different commitment.

At stage seven, we make an initial commitment; in stage eight, we begin to experience what that commitment means. That is, we find out what it is like to be in this field, going with that person, or exploring this spiritual path. Of course, at this point we may reconsider and try some other choices for a time. Eventually, we make a firmer set of commitments (stage nine), but beyond that realize that it is the act of committing itself that, in a context of relativity, allows us to express ourselves in the world.[1]

A Final Stage

There is, I believe, a final stage that did not emerge in Perry's studies, partly because it is beyond the learning task of the college years, and that is a return to the search for the absolute—but in a spiritual or mystic context. As Jung reminded us, this is a post-mid-life task, not a task for youth. Again there are levels of truth. Here the search for eternal verities differs from a naive search for "Truth" because the seeker has such a powerful understanding of the difficulty of ever knowing anything outside one's own limited experience. This stage we learn best from the great Sages and gurus of various traditions.

The spiritual path of Sufism, for instance, is almost entirely based upon helping individuals understand that ultimate truth is not necessarily "far off or complicated." It only seems so because people are blind about their preconceptions about reality.

Sufis teach us that understanding the relativity of knowledge is the highest task of the rational intellect. But there is one step beyond that. Such an understanding requires us to detach from, or to observe in an unattached way, both our thoughts and our feelings. Such an attitude of nonattachment enables us to know that we are not our preconceived thoughts (however profound they might be) and we are not our emotions (however beautiful they might be). This attitude of nonattachment, in which we do not need the universe to be any particular way, allows us to experience ultimate truth, but it should also be noted that they are talking about a "truth" that can only be experienced, not measured or codified.

Idries Shah explains that intellect "is really a series of ideas that alternatively take possession of your consciousness." Thus intellect can never be sufficient, any more than our feelings can be—for our feelings are inevitably attached to certain outcomes and attitudes. In Sufi tradition, he explains, there is a level beyond intellect or emotion that he calls the "true intellect . . . the organ of comprehension, existing in every human being."[2] This true intellect is responsible for mystic or transcendent experiences that allow us a glimpse of "Oneness" in the cosmos—a oneness that as all spiritual paths teach is also the love that connects us with the All.

However, the Sage teaches that we do not reach this mystic sense of oneness or the higher virtue of love through rejection of thinking or rationality. Indeed, we first must develop both the mind and the heart to their highest possible levels— to learn to understand the relativity of truth both rationally with our intellects and empathically with our hearts—so that we can both let go and just be still inside ourselves, open to experiencing a new reality. Paradoxically, it is not until we have fully come to understand the impossibility of knowing anything for sure because each of us is so fully stuck in our own subjectivity in a universe of contextual relativism that we can let go, stop working at knowing, and allow truth to come into our lives as a gift.

At some point, the Sage stops seeking knowledge and gains wisdom, which, of course, is what the Sage's path is about. Further, the Sage teaches us that we can never be free until we are willing to completely let go of our illusions and attachments and seek to align our own wills with truth itself. The Sage never struggles against what is, but seeks to deepen his or her understanding of what that truth might be.

This is the wisdom illustrated in books like John Heider's *The Tao of Leadership,* which de-emphasize struggle, action, or even transformation in favor of simply coming to understand and live in keeping with the truth about any situation. It is also illustrated in modern teachings about mental and emotional health that emphasize the importance of letting go of pretense and being totally honest about what is true in any given moment—about our hopes, our fears, our vulnerabilities and woundedness. As long as we are wearing masks, and trying to seem to be more than we are, we will never become wise.

The Sage teaches us that we can never be free until we are willing to completely let go of our illusions and attachments and seek to align our own wills with truth itself.

The issue for the Sage is not so much the availability of ultimate truth, but our capacity to take it in. Unless a camera is of good quality, it cannot make a good image of even the most perfect sunset. So, too, unless we develop our minds and our hearts and open our souls, we will never know ultimate reality, even if it is at our fingertips. Indeed, that is why Socrates enjoined us to "know thyself." If we do not understand the filter through which truth comes, we will never have a clue about how we are distorting that truth by our own subjective but unexamined vision.

We need each other because alone we can only experience our own subjective perceptions of the universe. When the archetype of the Warrior is active in our lives, we can debate, argue, or even go to war about our differing truths. When the Sage is dominant in our lives, however, we will recognize that we need to listen to one another, and only then can we piece together some relative truth.

Beyond that, we know that experiencing any truth in addition to those offered by our five senses is a gift. We cannot make ourselves gain such truths; we can only refine the instruments of our mind, heart, and Soul, and then await a miracle. The great Sages know that it is only through miracles that we have any experience of ultimate reality—or even ever experience a new idea!

The Negative Sage

When we are caught in the shadow side of the Sage, we are not so much unattached as cut off from reality. Things happening around us or even within us feel like they are miles away. We can register what is happening, but we have no feelings about it. We feel pretty numb.

We are obsessed by nonattachment, so cannot commit to people, projects, or ideas. Sometimes we delude ourselves that this provides us with freedom, but we are not really free at all. We are simply too terrified of commitment to really attach to anyone or anything.

The negative Sage, moreover, is often addicted to being perfect and truthful and right, and has no tolerance for normal human feelings or vulnerabilities. Such a Sage often tends toward ascetic practices and constantly derides the self or others for any sign of not being perfect. Nothing is ever really good enough.

Or the negative Sage is so overwhelmed by relativity that it is impossible to ever really act. How can one act, such a negative Sage says, when it is impossible to know what is true? Such a person cannot commit to a lover, because he does not know how to know if this is the right person for him. Such a person cannot commit to a work because she does not know if it is the right thing to do. Such persons tend toward cynicism because of a heightened awareness of their inability of knowing anything for sure and of the imperfection of all life.

The negative Sage, moreover, is often addicted to being perfect and truthful and right, and has no tolerance for normal human feelings or vulnerabilities.

When the negative Sage is active in our lives, we often get caught in obsessive thinking, attempting to figure everything out by rational processes. If we cannot figure it out in this way, we are paralyzed. Since most major decisions in life cannot be decided in a rational, scientific way, when we keep trying, the negative Sage may grab us, and out thinking becomes circular.

Shadow Sages also tend to try to make the world seem less mysterious by limiting the number of acceptable ways of perceiving that reality. In the academic world, for instance, people dominated by a shadow Sage become irate at the thought of using any mode of perception but the scientific method. Such individuals are usually also totally incapable of acknowledging the ways that their own subjective biases color their supposedly scientific and rational findings. Shadow Sages in spiritual movements and emotionally-based therapies may become anti-intellectual and strive for mystic emotional experience at the price of turning off their brains.

Shadow Sages typically want to control knowledge in such a way that it is not threatening. Generally, they will only acknowledge the way that corresponds to their own learning style, and hence the one in which they excel. Knowledge then (whether subtly or blatantly) becomes a way of showing superiority to others.

Their primary focus becomes not the attainment of wisdom itself, but evaluation of others. Whatever relative truth they have discovered is identified with absolute truth, and their primary focus, then, is in guarding this truth from assaults by the barbarians. This results in a guild mentality that guards against competing demands of other truths, and also judges anyone who offers such a competing truth as naive, incompetent, or dangerous. The goal moves away from the search for truth to the protection of one's own privileged position.

When this Shadow has us in thrall, we feel cold, empty, defensive, and threatened by others. We often also feel defensive and misunderstood by others, who for some unknown reason see us as dogmatic and traditional. Many times we feel superior to these others, and do not understand why others do not see us in the same way. We may even feel sorry for ourselves when we have so sacrificed to uphold standards. We feel as though we are protecting the sacred flame of truth against those who would stamp it out.

The Sage and Freedom from Attachment

The highest achievement of the Sage is freedom from attachment and illusion. To the degree that we are attached or even addicted to certain things, our judgment will be distorted because we are not free to see clearly. If I feel I need a certain person to be happy, then I only see that person through the lens of my neediness. What I notice about him is whether he seems committed to me or not—and I may totally miss other parts of his life. If we are so attached, moreover, and he leaves, I experience great pain.

The same is true of any work, idea, event, habit, or self-image to which we are attached. If anything happens to take it away from us, we are plunged into great despair and pain. The Buddhist path of the Sage clearly shows us that attachment and desire are the root of all pain and suffering. We suffer because we believe we need certain things to be, or be true. If they are not, we fall apart.

The path of the highest level of the Sage is to learning nonattachment—as Ken Keyes puts it in *The Handbook of Higher Consciousness,* to learn to upgrade our addictions or attachments into preferences. This does not mean that you do not want anything. It means you identify what you want merely as preferences, not needs. You would like to marry that woman or man. You would like to have that job. You would like to be healthy. You would like to have a reasonable amount of money and status.

But if something happened and your lover left you, you lost that job, you got seriously ill, or you found yourself poor, that would be OK too—maybe not your first preference, but acceptable. In *Addiction and Grace,* Gerald May notes that we can never fully free ourselves from addictions, obsessions, or attachments on our own; any time we recognize that we are not free, that we think we have to have something to be happy, it gives us an opportunity to open to "grace" to heal us. Ken Keyes emphasizes the importance of the "observing self" for healing, for it is only when we notice what suffering our attachments cause that we can become free of them.

To the degree that we are attached to approval of others, to accomplishment, indeed to any result at all, we are not free, and in the normal course of life, we will suffer. The only sure path to real freedom and joy, then, is to turn over control of one's life to a more transcendent and wiser power than oneself. To people in many religious traditions, this is turning control over to God. In Twelve-Step programs, it is called turning control over to a higher power. In a more secular, psychological context, it may be trusting one's deeper wisdom.

This does not require us to give up wanting things. Indeed, it is always destructive for someone to choose the Sage's nonattachment who has not already learned to attach—to love their work and other people, to be committed to values and ideas, to fully feel disappointments and loss. To attempt nonattachment before one has learned the Lover's task of attaching and committing will only breed numbness and despair.

But having learned to attach, learning to love and commit without attachment brings freedom. This means that we can love people without being addicted to them or their approval, so we do not need to hold them with us if it is not where they need to be. It means we can totally commit to our work without being attached to the outcome of that work. It means finding our voice and being able to share our vision and understanding, knowing that tomorrow we might confront a deeper truth and have to acknowledge our prior truth as naive or outmoded.

Ultimately, we learn to "let go" of even our attachment to suffering. Suffering teaches us to open up, to trust, and to let go. But most people, and the culture in general, then get the idea that there is something intrinsically good in suffering—that it is virtuous to suffer, that it is best not to feel too good about yourself, that achievement must come out of struggle, and that all joy requires pain.

When we have learned to stop fighting life and to trust its processes, we no longer need suffering. Indeed, in Shirley Luthman's words, when we allow ourselves "to love, to be loved, and to be creative in our lives" and hence when we give up trying to fit ourselves into lives that do not fit, and allow ourselves lives that really make us happy, freedom and joy can be our normal experience of life.[3]

It is this radical letting go into joy and ease that prepares us for the wisdom of the Fool.

Exercises

Give some thought to when, where, how, and how much the Sage expresses itself in your life.

1. How much or how little is the Sage expressed in your life? Has it been expressed more in the past or present? Do you see it emerging more in your future? Is it expressed more at work, at home, with friends, in dreams or fantasies?

2. Who are some friends, relatives, co-workers, and others who seem influenced by the archetype of the Sage?

3. Is there anything you wish were different about the expression of the Sage in your life?

4. Since each archetype expresses itself in many different ways, take some time to describe or otherwise portray (e.g., draw, make a collage, use a picture of yourself in a particular costume or pose) the Sage as it is expressed or could be expressed in your life. What does or would it look like? How does or would it act? In what setting does or would it feel most at home?

Daydream

Imagine you are with a younger person who thinks you are very wise. Let yourself imagine how you meet this person and what makes this person look up to you. In fantasy, let yourself experience spending time with this person as you tell or show him or her what he or she wants and needs to know about life. Be aware of how it feels to you to take on the role of the wiser, older guide.

The Fool

Wise Kings and Queens would not think of ruling without a Court Fool or Jester to express the joy of life and to entertain them and the court. However, this is not the only function of the Court Fool. Fools have a license to say what other people would be hanged for, to puncture the Ruler's Ego when the Ruler is in danger of hubris, and to generally provide balance to the kingdom by breaking the rules and thereby allowing an outlet for forbidden insights, behaviors, and feelings.

The Fool

Goal:
Enjoyment, pleasure, aliveness

Fear:
Nonaliveness

Response to Dragon/Problem:
Play with it or play tricks on it

Task:
Trust in the process; enjoyment of the journey
for its own sake

Gift:
Joy, freedom, liberation

William Willeford, in *The Fool and His Scepter: A Study in Clowns and Jesters and Their Audience,* describes the way the Fool and the King form a pair, and we are not at all shocked when the Fool makes the King the butt of a joke. Willeford notes that the function of the King is to create order, but doing so necessarily requires exclusion of some forces. The Fool "as jester provides an institutionalized link" with the excluded forces and energies, and in so doing, embodies "the principle of wholeness . . . reinstating in measured form the primeval condition before the separation of the kingdom from that with which it excludes."[1]

If the Ruler represents the Ego providing an orderly expression of the Soul, the Fool suggests a principle of wholeness that is beyond the Ego entirely, and speaks of a kind of psychological wholeness that is not built upon exclusion. As such, the Fool both precedes the creation of the Ego, and supersedes it. The Fool is thus the beginning and the end of the journey.

> My HMI score for the Fool archetype is
>
> ———
> (high = 30/low = 0).
>
> It is my ———
> highest score
> (highest = 12th/lowest = 1st).

The Inner Fool

The inner Fool is never far away from us. Indeed, it is the archetype that precedes even the Innocent. The Fool is the aspect of the inner child that knows how to play, to be sensual and in the body. It is at the root of our basic sense of vitality and aliveness, which expresses itself as a primitive, childlike, spontaneous, playful creativity.

It is also very amoral, anarchistic, irreverent energy, exploding categories and boundaries. The Innocent's goodness and obedience and the Orphan's vulnerability are only a part of what it means to be a child. The Fool is responsible for children's desire to try everything and do everything, even when forbidden, and their uncanny ability to know just what lie to tell their parents to save their skins. We tend not to see such behavior as bad or evil. In children we call it "naughty," and in adults, "irresponsible." We have reason to worry as much about overly compliant children (and adults) who never break such rules as about the ones who are always in trouble.

Stories abound about Krishna as a child. He was always playing tricks on his mother and getting into mischief, and sometimes would take pity on her. Once she tried to tie him up, but every time she tried, no matter how much rope she used, it would be too short. Finally he saw how frustrated she was becoming, and he allowed her to tie him. We do not have such stories about Christ, but one does remember that at age twelve he ran away from his parents and they found him in the temple, proclaiming wisdom to the teachers of the time!

When the Fool is dominant in our lives, we explore the world out of innate curiosity, creating for the simple joy of creation, and living life for its own sake

The Fool is the beginning and the end of the journey.

without thought of tomorrow and with little or no concern with convention, traditional morality, or what the neighbors will say. Of the twelve archetypes discussed in this book, only the Fool knows how to "be here now."

When the Fool is active in our lives, we are motivated by curiosity and want to explore and experiment with life. It is a time when we have little or no interest in being responsible—at least not for others—for we want most of all to be free. This means free from duties, responsibilities, deadlines, even relationships that might demand things from us that are not fun, and from possessions (which, after all, just need to be cared for.)

It is a time of being perfectly happy to appear ridiculous, to try a completely unconventional hairstyle or manner of dressing, to develop a relationship with someone others would see as totally inappropriate, to be outrageous. As one might imagine, it is the archetype of bizarre adolescent attire, but it may also reemerge in the mid-life crisis, and of course is part of the adolescent side of us that has a continuing and ongoing role in an adult's life. Like the joker in a deck of playing cards, it can turn up anywhere.

During the years of adult responsibilities, the Fool is primary only in recreation; but it can give spice to our work and private lives if we allow it expression there. In old age, it is the Fool who allows us to give up living life in terms of achievement, goals, and "making a difference," and enjoy living life for its own sake, day by day. At all stages of life, the Fool saves us from boredom, for it is infinitely inventive and entertaining, and from existential despair, because it is too busy enjoying the reality of life in the moment to waste any energy grieving for order or meaning. When the Fool is active in our lives, we are enlivened and invigorated, although we may get ourselves into trouble. When there is too little Fool in our lives, we may become priggish, repressed, uptight, anorexic, tired, bored, depressed, or lacking in curiosity.

The Fool often emerges in our lives at the moments that seem most painful. Someone we love dies, we lose a lover or a job we so wanted, we lose faith in ourselves and suddenly we find ourselves laughing; this is the Fool reminding us that life is sweet, even at its worst moments.

Fools make decisions—whether choosing friends, work, lovers, beliefs, or even spiritual practices—almost exclusively based upon the pleasure principle. If it feels good, it is good. If it feels bad, it is bad. The Fool has a zest for life, for sensual pleasures, ideas, experiences, even spiritual bliss. Often it is the Fool's hunger for experience and adventure that motivates the hero's journey.

The Fool and the Modern World

The Fool is the archetype most helpful in dealing with the absurdities of the modern world and with faceless, amorphous modern bureaucracies—places where no one takes personal responsibility, rules are expected to be followed no matter how absurd they might be, and the tables are incredibly stacked against individual effectiveness.

The Fool as Trickster delights in breaking rules, and except in its shadow form, is well meaning and genial. Mae West's humor, for example, was a scandalous violation of the sex role conventions of her time, but she was accepted and even rewarded with fame and wealth precisely because of her outrageousness. The Fool tradition often provides a means to violate social norms in humorous ways and hence to avoid provoking undue hostility. Bette Midler's humor incorporates the flamboyant sexuality associated with the Trickster with its practical joking side and provides a nice model for a contemporary female Trickster figure.

The Fool's politics are anarchistic, as illustrated by the revolutionary thinking of a woman like Emma Goldman, whose politics were never separated from a desire for freedom and fun. The slogan often attributed to her, "If I can't dance, I don't want to be part of your revolution," speaks for the Fool energy in American anarchist politics, from the Boston Tea Party down to the Beats of the 1950s and the Yippies of the 1960s.

The Fool as Trickster delights in breaking rules.

The Fool, the Hero, the Comic Perspective

Fools succeed sometimes simply because they do not know any better. William Willeford notes that the hero often begins as a Fool. In the Grimm story, "The Golden Bird," and so many other fairy tales like it, the two older of three brothers fail on a quest because they do things the conventional, "wise" way, while the youngest, naive and inexperienced and hence more open to imaginative new ideas, succeeds and wins the princess's hand.[2]

The contribution of the Fool to our lives is resilience, the capacity to get up and try again. Cartoon characters are Fool figures. They shoot each other out of cannons and run over each other with bulldozers, all for the joy of the chase. But no one is ever really hurt.

The contribution of the Fool to our lives is resilience, the capacity to get up and try again.

Without the Fool in each one of us, there is no capacity to enjoy life for its own sake. It knows how to play the moment for all it's worth in joy and experience, and even to enjoy the more negative parts of life if only for their drama. It is the part of us that allows for hope when there is no positive sign on the horizon. Who would want to be without it?

Many would, for in our society, we seem oppressively attached to high seriousness and hence to a tragic or (worse) an ironic view of life. Enid Welsford concludes her classic work on the Fool, *The Fool: His Social and Literary History,* with this observation: "Romantic comedy is serious literature because it is a foretaste of the truth; the Fool is wiser than the Humanist, and clownage is less frivolous than the deification of humanity."[3]

The Fool as Game Player

Fools, whether divine or human, are our link with childhood spontaneity. Especially in their guise as Trickster, they are rule breakers and game players, and almost always have an element of the con artist. As Jesters, they are highly creative and can always think of something new to do to avoid boredom.

Wakdjunkaga, the Trickster hero of the Winnebago cycle, convinces some ducks that he will sing for them if they will only dance with their eyes closed. Then while they are dancing, he strangles each in turn and puts them into a bag, until a few catch on and fly away. His actions, although fatal to the ducks, are not presented as evil. He simply uses his infinite cleverness to get the best of the ducks and give himself a nice dinner.

The Fool enjoys the contest of wits even in the most dangerous of circumstances. Perhaps as a by-product of the Trickster's delight in practical jokes, conning, and getting one's own way through trickery, the Fool is also very difficult to con. While they often see through the manipulations of others, and hence are not duped as often as Innocents, Fools can get hooked because they get caught in liking to play the "game." Many times, they play the part of the Innocent or dupe to outsmart a person who is trying to con them, for example, pretending to be a novice at pool or cards in order to win a big stake.

At the lowest level, the game is played only for personal gratification or the fun of it. Children delight in playing games, and they hate being bored. If there are not enough positive fun games around, they will play negative ones, like "uproar," showing an uncanny ability to know just what will hook their parents or teachers and really get them going.

Children naturally cut up most of the time, and their doing so is related to developing their sense of creativity. Mother Nature is not wrong in this, as we see when we make little children stay in their seats in school to work in boring, repetitive workbooks and then wonder why this generation is not very creative! Later on, of course, major corporations have to spend big bucks teaching executives to play so they can think creatively.

Most adults do play games much of the time, and not just cards, or tennis, or charades. They play political games—at work, at home, and in community or political organizations. And they too play "uproar" when things get dull, creating "drama" and crises to keep them occupied. Transactional Analysis, in books such as Eric Berne's *Games People Play*, has cataloged such adult games, making the point that as long as we are playing games, we are not being real and cannot be intimate. What is dangerous in such games is not that they are played, but that people are fooled by their own Trickster and do not even know they are playing. What this usually means is that their Fool is repressed and is possessing them in negative form. The genius of Transactional Analysis is the way it can alert people to the games they play, and in that way, make those games conscious so that people may choose whether or not they want to play them.

Levels of the Fool

Shadow	Self-indulgence, sloth, gluttony, irresponsibility
Call	Boredom, ennui, desire to have more enjoyment in life
Level One	Life is a game to be played for the fun of it (Fool)
Level Two	Cleverness used to trick others, to get out of trouble, to find ways around obstacles, to tell the truth without impunity (Trickster)
Level Three	Life is experienced fully in the moment; life is celebrated for its own sake and lived in the moment, one day at a time (Wise Fool or Jester)

When we learn to be conscious of the games we play, they may be used for much higher purposes than keeping us entertained or gaining an advantage or revenge. Don Juan, the great shaman of Carlos Castaneda's initiation novels, literally tricks Castaneda into seeing the world from a different, altered perspective. Most great teachers have learned to trick their students into wanting to learn. Even the games people play to make certain good things get done in rule-bound bureaucratic structures are positive channels for Fool energy.

Because the Fool is a shape shifter, it can see the world from many perspectives, and hence can move in and out of traditionally accepted ways of seeing reality. The Trickster can help us see unconventional approaches to problems or entertain an entirely different world view. For this reason it is an archetype that is activated in times of massive societal change, when the capacity to change course in midstream is vital and immensely socially useful.

The Negative Fool

When Fool energy is not allowed, it simply goes underground, and in doing so becomes a negative, undermining force to the society of the individual psyche. To the degree that our Fool has not been befriended by our Ego, it will emerge not so much in exuberance, playfulness, and creativity, as in manipulation, conning, and self-defeating behaviors.

The negative Fool may be expressed in unbridled and undisciplined sensuality—sloth, irresponsibility, gluttony, lechery, drunkenness. The shadow Trickster comes out when presumable pillars of the community—businesspeople, preachers, or members of Congress—are suddenly found with their hands in the till, afflicted with alcohol or drug addiction, or having an affair. Often there is almost a total split between a person's otherwise conventional life and this obsessive and seemingly self-destructive eruption of greed, lust, or gluttony.

Two classic images of the Fool—as naif and as the madman or madwoman—are early shadow images. The shadow Fool keeps us "foolish" and "unconscious." When it has us in its grasp, we are unable to let ourselves reflect on what we are doing. We can then be possessed by a stricter way of behaving and not even see it at all. We are simply stupid.

The shadow Fool is also expressed in madness when the Ego cracks and the unconscious erupts chaotically into consciousness. The Fool tricks us into moving out of a continuing psychological space, but we are then flooded with too much unsorted psyche material. The challenge is either to reconstruct an Ego or to go under.

All Tricksters are also shape shifters and wear disguises. One never knows when or where they will pop up. This phenomenon is most clearly seen when people's Ego identification is strongly with the Innocent or the Orphan to the exclusion of the Trickster. Their Trickster gets them into all kinds of trouble, but is disguised from even themselves. Sometimes the Trickster's disguises are so clever that no one suspects its identity. Other times, anyone else can see how the apparent Innocents bring on the difficulties that recur in their lives; yet they themselves are completely mystified, seeing themselves as victims of circumstances or other people.

The Western Christian tradition has had a tendency to identify appetite and the pleasures of the flesh with the devil, and hence encouraged great repression. Trickster qualities were particularly taboo for women. For example, the serpent in the garden of Eden tempting Eve to disobey God for knowledge has Trickster qualities (the devil is a shadow Trickster figure), as does Eve. It is Eve's Trickster-like curiosity that is seen as responsible for humankind's Fall from paradise.

Of course, it is the inner Trickster that inevitably will disobey the rules, even God's rules, and so it is appropriate that our "fortunate falls" from grace are the responsibility of the Trickster. Perhaps it is for this reason that the Trickster is also associated by some theorists (Jung, for example) with the Savior. If we do not disobey, we cannot begin our own journeys, and therefore we cannot find salvation, whether that salvation is defined in religious terms (as in conventional religious institutions) or psychological terms (as in this book).

Whereas the well-developed Trickster helps us know how to do what we want, the shadow Trickster tells us lies about what is required for survival. It tells us our feelings will be too much to bear if we do not numb out on drink or drugs. It tells us intimate relationships are a threat to our identity, and convinces us to break up the best relationship we have ever had. It tells us that in order to succeed, we have to work all the time and never take off any time for ourselves. This shadow Fool has fun at our expense.

We are also held hostage by a shadow Fool anytime the joy goes out of our lives.

It may also create what Transactional Analysts call a "script"—a plot or story that informs your life and without which you are lead to believe you would die. The shadow Fool can, for example, tell you that you must act out any one of the archetypes in this book or any of the various "scripts" outlined in Berne's book—or you will never survive. If you try another, it may feel like your very survival is at stake.

Usually it stops with being self-destructive, but it is perfectly capable of also counseling actions that are immoral, unethical, and/or illegal. It may even suggest robbing a bank, embezzling money from one's employer, or sleeping with your best friend's spouse, and defend the suggestions as needed for survival, as appropriate retaliation for supposed slights, or as the only means to get our needs met. Besides, the Trickster says, no one will ever find out!

The best way to free oneself from a shadow Trickster is to befriend it, and in doing so, value not only spiritual development but instinctive, earthly life. When we starve our shadow Fool by ignoring it, it will get "lean and mean" and turn on us. Better to fatten the beast a bit with good food, good company, and pleasant experiences so that it will be good-natured.

Becoming a Wise Fool

The Fool generally begins the journey having fun by denying or avoiding life's difficulties. The Fool wants to play all the time and tries to avoid anything hard—study, thinking, work, or committed relationships. Its wandering is aimless and disconnected.

The transition from clown or Trickster to Wise Fool comes when the Fool experiences initiation by Love. The Fool is not that scared of death or loss but tends to fear commitments. When Fools encounter Eros and learn to bond with others, to commit to relationships, work, ideas and values, and God, they can express their transcendent selves in the world. At the highest level, the Fool becomes the Wise and Holy Fool who experiences the joy in all life and becomes almost translucent. There is no longer any need to hide or deny anything because nothing is bad or wrong that is simply natural and human; at this level, the Fool merely is.

The transition from clown or Trickster to Wise Fool comes when the Fool experiences initiation by Love.

At the journey's beginning, the Fool is evidenced in the undifferentiated quality of little children, who are alive, spontaneous, wholly themselves, and in the moment, and at its end in the great "holy fools" of many spiritual traditions. Willeford talks of "fool-saints in the Christian Church" such as Jocopone Da Todi (1230–1306), who having "abandoned the legal profession to pursue a life of religious devotion, once appeared at a village festival on all fours, naked except for a loincloth and the saddle of an ass on his back; he was bridled, with a bit in his mouth. On another occasion he smeared his body with something sticky, rolled in colored feathers, and then burst into a wedding feast."

Zen Buddhism is the path of the holy fool. Shunryu Suzuki's *Zen Mind, Beginner's Mind* actually advocates burning the house, or the Ego, living entirely in the moment: "When you do something, you should burn yourself completely, like a good bonfire, leaving no trace of yourself."[4] Burning out the Ego allows one to stop acting to fit in and please others, and allows one's innate wisdom—that wisdom that is one with the transcendent—to emerge and be revealed. Therefore, Suzuki advises, "Without any intentional, fancy way of adjusting yourself, to express yourself as you are is the most important thing."

The discipline of Zen, then, is about living in the moment, utterly one with oneself and the cosmos, and without sophistication, guile, or premeditation. It is about being unself-consciously who one is, and about fully trusting one's own process and that of the universe. As such, it is the way of joy.

Humor, therefore, has an important part in the process of enlightenment. Lex Hixon, in *Coming Home: The Experience of Enlightenment in Sacred Traditions*, tells of a Zen practitioner who described the experience of enlightenment this way:

At midnight I abruptly awakened. At first my mind was foggy, then suddenly that quotation flashed into my consciousness: "I came to realize clearly that mind is no other than mountains, rivers, and the great wide earth, the sun and the moon and the stars. . . . " Instantaneously, like surging waves, a tremendous delight welled up in me, a veritable hurricane of delight, as I laughed loudly and wildly: Ha, ha, ha, ha, ha, ha! There's no reasoning here, no reasoning at all! Ha, ha, ha! The empty sky split into two, then opened its enormous mouth and began to laugh uproariously: Ha, ha, ha![5]

Such a revelation comes when Ego boundaries have become so translucent that we experience almost no separation between ourselves and the cosmos.

Similarly in the Tantric path, the great guru, Ramakrishna is a classic Wise and Holy Fool. Lex Hixon explains that Ramakrishna considered himself to be nothing but the child of Goddess Kali, the Divine Mother of the Universe.

As a child who knew nothing and decided nothing, he would speak and act spontaneously as She spoke and acted through him. He did not even regard himself as a guru, or teacher. When holy scholars proclaimed him to be an avatar, or special emanation of the Divine, Ramakrishna sat among them unselfconsciously, intoxicated by the bliss of Divine Presence, half-naked, chewing spices, and repeating, If you say I am, you must be right, but I know nothing about it. (pp. 25–26)

By the end of his life, Ramakrishna looked around him and could see nothing but the Great Mother. All life, including his own, was the Goddess. This state, which for him was ecstatic, is also a state beyond judgment and dualism, and it (almost) goes entirely beyond Ego boundaries. They had simply disappeared, and all was one and all was sacred.

This sort of Holy Fool, or Wise Fool, exemplifies the wisdom found at the end of the journey, which allows us to get the great cosmic joke: the great treasure we have sought outside ourselves on the quest and within ourselves through initiation was never scarce or faraway. Indeed, it is all that exists. The Fool helps us create the Ego, and then it helps us let it go so that we can be one with the All, and discover in that Oneness, great joy.

This cosmic perspective on life is frequently hard to tell from madness, because it is so different from the Ego's concerns with safety, propriety, and consensual reality. Indeed, one form of the Fool has always been the madman or madwoman. In Jane Wagner's and Lily Tomlin's *The Search for Signs of Intelligent Life in the Universe*, Trudy, the bag lady, tells how she experienced the "kind of madness Socrates talked about, a divine release of the soul from the yoke of custom and convention." Trudy is a modern-day Wise Fool, whose loss of sanity opened her mind to the cosmos.

Trudy explains that "reality" is nothing more than a "collective hunch" and that it is "the leading cause of stress among those in touch with it." She decides to let it go. Thinking of the great jokes she plays now, she says, "I never could've done stuff like that when I was in my *right* mind. I'd be worried people would think I was crazy. When I think of the fun I missed I try not to be bitter."[6]

The lowest level comics use humor to degrade. The highest, most ennobling comics help us to test the Fool's perspective by causing us to chuckle in sympathetic enjoyment and celebration of life's most difficult moments and to enjoy the common bond of our fallible humanity, even with people who are ordinarily seen as "others"—like bag ladies. The Fool allows us to enjoy life, the moment, and each other without judgment but also without illusions. The kind of enlightenment Trudy illustrates—the ability to celebrate one's life as a bag lady without needing money, status, a home, or even sanity—returns us perfect freedom, and to innocence.

So the circle is complete, and we are ready to experience the cycle again—but this time beginning at a new level. Because we have learned to enjoy life for its own sake, we need not protect our innocence with denial or hold on to conventionality to protect our "social places." We know it is safe to trust, not so much because bad things do not happen in life but because we have learned about our great resilience. We are not just our bodies. Our Souls and Spirits will not only survive whatever comes but find some way to enjoy life's drama—even when the Wise Innocent knows that whatever the details of our lives might be, life itself is a gift and our task is to accept and enjoy that gift fully. As Annie Dillard writes in *Pilgrim at Tinker Creek,* "the dying pray at the last not 'please' but 'thank you' as a guest thanks his host at the door."[7] It is this sense of radical thankfulness and celebration for the whole of life that encapsulates the wisdom of the Fool and, as such, opens each of us to joy.

Exercises

Give some thought to when, where, how, and how much the Fool expresses itself in your life.

1. How much or how little is the Fool expressed in your life? Has it been expressed more in the past or present? Do you see it emerging more in your future? Is it expressed more at work, at home, with friends, in dreams or fantasies?

2. Who are some friends, relatives, co-workers, and others who seem influenced by the archetype of the Fool?

3. Is there anything you wish were different about the expression of the Fool in your life?

4. Since each archetype expresses itself in many different ways, take some time to describe or otherwise portray (e.g., draw, make a collage, use a picture of yourself in a particular costume or pose) the Fool as it is expressed or could be expressed in your life. What does or would it look like? How does or would it act? In what setting does or would it feel most at home?

Daydream

Meditate on the funniest and most enjoyable moments in your life thus far. Think of one fun or funny moment after another. Imagine yourself telling humorous stories about these events. Continue at least until you find yourself laughing out loud.

Part V

**Honoring Diversity—
Transforming Your World**

From Duality to Wholeness—A Life Stage Model

Recognizing the ways our own lives connect with the twelve archetypal stages of the hero's journey helps ennoble and give meaning to the everyday experiences of our lives. However, it is equally important to honor our own uniqueness. Groups and individuals spiral through these stages in different orders and ways. Part V is designed to help you explore how your journey and those of others are *affected* (but not necessarily *determined*) by life stage, gender, culture, and personal uniqueness.

This chapter considers the human life span—from childhood to old age—as a distinct journey of its own and provides an opportunity for you to chart your own journey from childhood to realizing who you are today. Each stage of life affects the archetypes that emerge in your life. Typically, each major chronological stage of life calls forth two archetypes that seem to be in opposition and that press for resolution.[1] At first, we may relate to that stage using only one of the archetypes to the exclusion of the other, a strategy that usually gets us through the transition, but not necessarily in a very fulfilling or complete way. We get through, but we feel somewhat incomplete. We feel more whole and are usually more effective in life when we learn to use both. Rather than one approach defeating or repressing the other, one simply leads in a mutually respecting dance. These archetypes are initially experienced dualistically as opposites, but at best they have something more equivalent to a yin/yang relationship—being two sides of the same phenomenon. When they are experienced in this way rather than as two opposing, dualistic choices, the life issue is resolved. However, even when the dichotomy becomes a partnership, most people still continue to lead habitually with one of each of the six pairs.

If you have taken the Heroic Myth Index (HMI) in the Appendix, it is a good idea to complete the analysis exercises included in this chapter. Then you will be aware of which archetype in each pairing leads in your life, at least at this time.

Each major chronological stage of life calls forth two archetypes that seem to be in opposition and that press for resolution.

Although it is ideal eventually to integrate the pairs, it is equally important in the process of getting there to specialize—and to develop one at the expense of the other. This allows you to reach a high level of development in that archetype and makes it easier, at a later time, to complement it by also reaching a high level of development in the other as the pair becomes integrated in your life. There is no need to push to integration. That will come in time.

You cannot tell from your HMI scores whether relative balance in the pairs means that they are undifferentiated or integrated. You need to think about it. Do you use both parts of the pairs easily and well? If so, you are integrated. If you have low scores in both and/or find it difficult to do either well, then you are undifferentiated in this area of your life. Remember, if you are young, it is quite normal that you might not have high-level development in the pairs associated with life passages you have not yet experienced.

Before looking at the six major stages of life—childhood, adolescence and early adulthood, adulthood, the mid-life transition, maturity, and old age—remember that the archetypes do not *belong* to that chronological moment in life. Although archetypes do contribute to our growth and development, they also have their own separate existences as psychic entities. They can emerge at any time of life, and in many ways. They are the basis of great art and literature and music, and make many contributions to our lives other than helping us through the major transitions of life.

Each of these chronological passages presses us to learn certain developmental tasks, and thereby calls forth the archetypal energies related to these tasks. We can learn the lessons of any of these archetypes at any time. But at a particular life passage or stage, if we have not learned or do not learn certain tasks, we will experience psychological discomfort. For instance, we can learn the ability of the Fool to enjoy life in the moment, without needing to have goals to energize us, anytime in life. But if we have not developed this capacity by old age, when we are unlikely to be able to be as goal-oriented as we were in the years of taking responsibility in the world, we will be unhappy.

Similarly, we can become Caregivers at any point in our development, but if we have not done so by the time we are responsible for others (children, employees, aging parents), we will feel at a loss as to how to respond to this challenge, and our charges will feel abandoned, let down, and undernurtured.

It is never too late to learn the lesson of an archetype.

It is also never too late. Many people today do not resolve their childhood issues until well into adulthood, or even into old age. Although ideally we would move to a relatively high level of Innocent and Orphan by adolescence, few people really do so. If their childhoods were too traumatic for them to deal with their own issues, perhaps they have not received the help they need to do so.

Recognizing what issues are incomplete, by itself, can have a powerful effect on our lives, allowing us to open up to the archetypal energy that can complete that process for us. It can also help us see what kind of help we might need. People whose issues are around the Orphan archetype might want therapy that focuses on healing early childhood traumas or want to join a group or go to workshops for Adult Children of Alcoholics, since anyone having an unhappy childhood can benefit from these workshops and groups whether or not their parents were alcoholic or drug-addicted. Similarly, people who have Warrior issues might benefit more from assertiveness training, and so on.

Finally, although most healthy, well-functioning adults succeed in fully developing at least one half of each pair and develop some functioning in the other half, and hence find some way to move relatively successfully through each life passage, it is relatively rare to completely integrate the pairs. Indeed, the numinosity of the symbols for doing so at each stage—images of the Divine Child, god or goddess, Promised Land—suggest that this integration is more characteristic of the gods than of mere mortals. To fully integrate the pairs in even one category is a big accomplishment. To do so in all categories would practically mean you had become an enlightened being. The virtues associated with each pairing, however, indicate more ordinary mortal integration of the pairs. One archetype may still lead, but both work enough for you to successfully transverse that life stage.

Archetypal Pairings by Life Issue

Security

Innocent	The Innocent is the prefallen person who lives—or tries to live—in Eden. The Innocent's gift to the world is trust, optimism, and belief in things as they are. At the lowest level, belief is preserved by denial; at the highest level, by transcendence.
Orphan	The Orphan has the same wish as the Innocent—to live in a safe world—but the Orphan feels betrayed, abandoned, victimized. At the lowest level, the Orphan is a confirmed victim and cynic. At a higher level, the Orphan simply reminds us of his or her vulnerability and interdependence.

Identity

Seeker	The Seeker explores internal and external realities and is willing to give up security, community, and intimacy for autonomy. Seekers find out who they are by differentiating themselves from others. At worst, they are just outsiders. At best, they find their unique identities and vocations.

Lover	Lovers find out who they are by discovering who and what they love. At a lower level, the Lover may love only a few people, activities, or things. At a higher level, Lovers expand that love to enjoy and respect all of life's diversity.

Responsibility

Warrior	The Warrior defeats the villain and rescues the victim. Warriors are courageous and disciplined, imposing high standards on themselves. At worst, they run roughshod over others. At best, they assert themselves appropriately to make the world a better place.
Caregiver	Caregivers take care of others even when doing so requires sacrifice. They give to make the world a better place for others. At worst, the Caregiver's sacrifice is maiming or manipulative. At best, the Caregiver's giving is compassionate, genuine, and of great help to others.

Authenticity

Destroyer	When the Destroyer is active within a person, what we see are the effects of tragedy and loss. At best, this initiatory loss leads to a greater receptivity to new ideas, empathy and compassion for others, and a deeper knowledge of their own identity and strength. At worst, it simply disseminates a personality, and we see before us simply a ruin of what was.
Creator	When the Creator is active within a person, that person is in the process of discovering or creating a more adequate sense of Self. At best, this new identity is transformative and leads to a more fulfilling and effective life. At worst, it is simply an experiment, and the person retreats or goes back to the drawing board to start over.

Power

Magician	Magicians create new realities, transform old ones, serve as catalysts for change, and "name" and thereby create reality. At worst, their efforts can be "evil sorcery." At best, they discover empowering, win/win solutions.
Ruler	The Ruler in each of us understands that we are responsible for our inner and outer lives: the buck stops here. At worst, the Ruler is a despot. At best, the Ruler's order is inclusive, creating inner wholeness and outer community.

Freedom

Sage   Sages find freedom through understanding the big picture (global or cosmic) and a capacity for detachment. At the lowest level, the Sage may have little interest in the ordinary, mundane pleasures of life. At the highest level, however, the Sage combines detachment with love, wisdom, and joy in life.

Fool   The Fool finds freedom through unconventionality and a capacity to enjoy every moment. The Fool lightens us up, finds clever, innovative, and fun ways around obstacles—intellectual or physical. At worst, Fools are irresponsible. At best, Fools live lives of joy because they live fully every moment.

An Archetypal Timeline

Fill in this timeline by indicating the archetypes that are active for you at different stages of the life cycle. For example, if the Orphan dominated your childhood, circle "Orphan." If there was little or no Innocent in your childhood, cross out "Innocent." Also fill in the blanks with the names of archetypes other than the pairs that might have been active during a particular period. (If as a child you were expected to take care of your parents and your siblings, you might add "Caregiver" to your list. If you also had to fight all the time to protect yourself, you might add "Warrior.") Stop at your current stage of life. (The marked example is for a person at mid-life.) To construct the timeline, connect the names of the dominant archetypes branches.

Example:

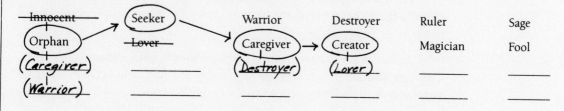

CHILDHOOD	ADOLESCENT/ YOUNG ADULT	ADULT	MID-LIFE	MATURITY	OLD AGE
Innocent	Seeker	Warrior	Destroyer	Ruler	Sage
Orphan	Lover	Caregiver	Creator	Magician	Fool
_____	_____	_____	_____	_____	_____
_____	_____	_____	_____	_____	_____

Scoring the Archetypal Pairs

Add up your scores for each of the pairs, using the results of your HMI:

Innocent _____ + Orphan _____ = _____ (Security)

Seeker _____ + Lover _____ = _____ (Identity)

Warrior _____ + Caregiver _____ = _____ (Responsibility)

Creator _____ + Destroyer _____ = _____ (Authenticity)

Magician _____ + Ruler _____ = _____ (Power)

Sage _____ + Fool _____ = _____ (Freedom)

Follow the instructions given, and consider these questions:

1. Circle any totals of forty-four points or more, or your top total score. Is the issue related to this pair (or these pairs) important in your life right now? (For example, if your highest total score is the Ruler/Magician pairing, is claiming your power in the world a current emphasis for you?)

2. In each pair, circle the archetype that leads in most situations (usually the archetype with the highest score). Do you also have some access to the other paired archetype?

3. Notice if you have relatively equal scores in both archetypes in a pair. Consider whether the archetypes work independently (and perhaps at cross-purposes) or in an integrated way. (For example, if you have equal scores for both Warrior and Caregiver, you might alternately exhibit the qualities of one or the other: that is, you will fight or sacrifice. If the archetypes are integrated, you might exemplify the archetypal good parent, who can protect and nurture the child within and without.)

Childhood

In childhood, the major issue is security, and our task is to grow from dependence to interdependence. We are aided in this work by the inner Innocent and Orphan. Successful resolution of these two archetypal energies is demonstrated when we can assess situations accurately and know when we can trust and when it is not safe to do so. When we lead with our Innocent, we tend toward optimism and may be overly trusting of others and inattentive to potential dangers in the environment. When we lead with the Orphan, we tend to be more aware of dangers and threats, more pessimistic, and somewhat less able to trust, even when trust may be warranted.

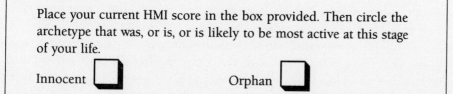

Place your current HMI score in the box provided. Then circle the archetype that was, or is, or is likely to be most active at this stage of your life.

Innocent ☐   Orphan ☐

If your inner child is an Innocent, you tend to be sunny and to overlook potential dangers. You may also be very annoyed by people who are negative or self-pitying and fail to look for silver linings. Even when terrible things happen to you, you know it is all for a purpose—and it will all become clear soon.

If your inner child is an Orphan, you tend to overemphasize life's problems. You often feel powerless, or victimized by life. You wish others would help you more, but even when they do, that help never seems like enough. Or you may always give others the help you yourself would like to have, but it never seems to stem the tide of suffering. If you have also developed your Warrior and Caregiver, you may not acknowledge this underlying feeling to anyone—often not even to yourself. The fact is, when you are really honest with yourself, you feel generally victimized by life and see few possibilities for getting what you really want. You may even have given up asking yourself what you want because getting it seems so out of the question. You may feel both envious of and annoyed by the sunnier Innocent types, whom you see as lost in a dream world, but happier than you in their self-deception.

When we lead with our Innocent, we tend toward optimism and may be overly trusting of others. When we lead with the Orphan, we tend to be more aware of dangers and threats, more pessimistic, and somewhat less able to trust, even when trust may be warranted.

Resolution

The resolution of the dualities is expressed mythically in the image of the Divine Child, who embodies perfect innocence while also seeing and understanding the world as it is, and who is full of empathy and understanding for others and their pain. The Divine Child has appeared in many mythological systems, but is most present in our culture in the celebration of Christmas.

The image of the Christ child integrates aspects of both Innocent and Orphan. The baby Jesus is Innocent in the sense of being totally pure and blameless. He is an Orphan in being illegitimate, born in a stable, and destined for sacrifice ("My God, my God, Why hast thou forsaken me?").

When we can see the pain and suffering both in ourselves and around us and yet have hope and faith that inspire us to give to one another, we have integrated our inner Innocent and Orphan. Doing so also yields clarity of perception. On the hero's journey, the integration of the Innocent and Orphan is evidenced when the hero can see without distortion by either undue sunniness or undue pessimism. Therefore, he or she can correctly assess whom to trust and whom to distrust, and then evidence discretion in the world. The virtue associated with successful integration of this pair is discernment.

As children, we would initially trust anyone, and our parents needed to tell us not to accept candy from strangers! Because children are concrete and dualistic in their thinking, moreover, they tend to lump people into two categories. There are heroes, and there are villains; good mothers and bad ones; witches and fairy godmothers; friends and enemies. If we continue in this vein into adolescence, we see two kinds of women: virgins and whores (or more recently, those who sleep only with those they love and those who "play around"); we see two kinds of men: the bad ones (who are predators or seducers) and the good ones (who are rescuers and make good husbands). Mentors and other authorities are either perfectly good and wise or no good at all.

Until we experience the integration of Innocent and Orphan, our inner children will always be unsettled.

The ultimate resolution of the Innocent/Orphan dualism comes not only when we can tell the difference between the good one and the bad one, but when the dualisms themselves start to break down and we recognize and thoroughly accept the mixture of good and bad within any human being, including ourselves. We learn then that it is more complicated than we had at first thought. The issue is not so much whom to trust, but when and in what circumstances they can be trusted. Your father might be trusted to bail you out if you need money, but not to give moral support. You might be able to trust yourself not to overspend your budget, but not be able to trust yourself not to eat chocolates if you keep them in the house. Further, following whichever part of the duality leads, we tend to go back and forth between them in a seesaw fashion until they are integrated. We move into Innocent and trust indiscriminately, then experience the inevitable disappointment when someone does not live up to our expectations. We move to Orphan and feel very despondent. However someone reaches out to help us, and we immediately idolize that person—only to be disappointed later. And so it goes. Developing a more balanced set of expectations about life that recognizes that all people and experiences will bring both joy and pain helps integrate the Innocent and Orphan, so we stop teetering between them.

Until we experience this integration, our inner children will always be unsettled. We will either live in partial denial or experience constant disappointment. The acceptance of life in its multiplicity is what gives the Divine Child such an expression of satisfaction and peace. There is never a time in life when we do not have a child within. But when the Innocent and Orphan are integrated, that child feels like a Divine Child and is neither afraid to see difficulties and suffering in life nor disappointed by them. We have an underlying sense of safety even when acknowledging and confronting difficult external realities. Then our inner child can become a source of peace and equanimity rather than of vulnerability.

Adolescence and Early Twenties

From adolescence through the early twenties, the Seeker and the Lover come to the fore, each helping us to find our identities, but in different ways. Seekers are most concerned with autonomy and independence and tend to be fearful of the pull to community and intimacy, fearing their own identities will have to be sacrificed to the relationships. Lovers, however, find identity by discovering what they love. Resolving this duality provides the ability to love and commit while also maintaining one's own separate sense of boundaries.

Throughout life, if our Seeker leads, we tend to find our identity by differentiating ourselves from others. If our Lover leads, we find out who we are by what we love. Generally in adolescence and early adulthood, both of these archetypes are active. The Seeker helps us pull away from our parents and begin to explore the world on our own. We do not want anyone to tell us what to do or think. We explore options and do not want to be tied down. We also explore provisional identities by wearing what parents see as outlandish costumes or hairstyles. We may even enjoy shocking the older generation, and we see ourselves as expressing our individuality, even when we are doing so primarily in the same way all our friends do.

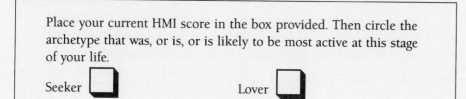

Place your current HMI score in the box provided. Then circle the archetype that was, or is, or is likely to be most active at this stage of your life.

Seeker ☐   Lover ☐

This is also a time when we are very interested in romance, love, and sex. By early adulthood, moreover, we begin to be pressed to make commitments—to commit to a major, a job, a career, a marriage partner. However, this activation of the Lover energy is often at odds with our continuing questing focus. We often marry or join in a committed relationship of some sort, but then get into a push-pull situation because we feel the other person is tying us down. We may commit to a job or career, but will feel a similar ambivalence about it, for we are still trying to find out who we are. We feel tied down, restricted.

Conversely, if our Seeker leads, we may resist commitment to a partner or work, continuing to explore options. Perhaps we work at a number of jobs, just trying them out. We go with a number of people, or with no one. We may then feel free, but also somewhat lonely and adrift.

If our Seeker leads, we tend to find our identity by differentiating ourselves from others. If our Lover leads, we find out who we are by what we love.

We may choose one mode for a while and then switch to the other. For example, early on you may settle on a spouse, a career, and so forth, and then the Seeker emerges and you leave it all. Perhaps you have been wandering all your life, and suddenly you have this desire to commit and settle down. The worst cases, however, are people who never did either. They may have married and taken a job, but just because it was expected, not out of love. They may do iconoclastic things, but they have never really searched for their own identity. Both Seeker and Lover may emerge suddenly in later life as they leave an unauthentic existence to find what and who they might truly love. At this point, like adolescents, they may experiment with life and act in an unaccustomed disregard for the opinions of others: buy a sports car, get involved with a younger person, or follow a guru and adopt exotic spiritual practices.

Resolution

In the hero's journey, we find the Seeker/Lover duality inherent in the heroic call to follow one's bliss. That is, one is questing, but in search of and in the service of love. We also find symbolic resolution in the treasures heroes find. Such treasures—the grail or sacred fish of the wasteland myths, for instance—symbolize the attainment of true identity and connectedness with transcendent love. Heroes often embark upon the quest to find their true families, that is, the places they would feel genuinely themselves and at home. Initially, they feel they are somehow in the wrong family and wrong place: they can fit in and have love, or be true to themselves. The successful completion of the journey allows them to find, or form, a family unit in which they can both be who they are and have love. The virtue associated with this pairing then is "identity"—a sense of autonomy that is manifested in real commitments to people, a work, a place, and a belief system.

The resolution of the duality is symbolically represented by the image of the Promised Land, which is the larger archetype for the true family. If we think of the Exodus story, Moses and the Hebrews needed to leave Egypt for two reasons. First, they were slaves in Egypt, and they needed to be free. This is the Seeker's motivation: to be free from confining, constraining structures. Second, they needed to be able to be true to themselves by serving the God they loved. This is the Lover's motivation.

In our everyday lives, the Promised Land is that place where we could be free—which means we could express our true Selves and not have to be limited by a set role or set expectations—*and* love and be loved. As long as we have an internal conflict between the Seeker and the Lover, we cannot reach the Promised Land. Freedom will always feel hollow, and love will feel confining. That's why the Israelites had to spend forty years in the desert. First, they had to have time to outgrow the habits of slavery so they could be really free. Second, they had to stop going back to other gods. They had to learn to be true to their commitment to their chosen path. When they learned to be free and to commit, they entered the Promised Land—just as each of us can do. We find the Promised land only when we are able both to be true to ourselves and to commit to the things and people we love. Finding our Promised Land can be evidenced in settling down in a place with people you love, or it can be an inner state that goes with you wherever you go.

We find the Promised Land, which is the larger archetype for the true family, only when we are able both to be true ourselves and to commit to the things and people we love.

Early Adult Life

The years between becoming an adult and the mid-life transition provide the challenge of learning to be strong enough to take on life's challenges and responsibilities so that we can make a difference in the world. The Warrior and the Caregiver provide us with two modes for doing so. Both the Warrior and the Caregiver are responsible, work hard, and are concerned with protecting the kingdom. This means protecting particularly the child within and without. The Warrior does so through assertion and struggle and the Caregiver by nurturance and self-sacrifice.

Together they teach us the virtue of responsibility. Throughout life, however, one will inevitably lead. If your Warrior leads, you will prefer to act in the world through competition, assertion, and achievement. If your Caregiver leads, your preferred mode will be giving, caring, and empowering others. If your Warrior leads too strongly, you may "win" at the expense of others. If your Caregiver leads overmuch, you may help others at your own expense. The virtue of responsibility—for others and to oneself—therefore requires a careful balance.

The archetype that leads at this point in life, in relatively traditional societies, is heavily influenced by sex roles. The Caregiver is often the mother's

If your Warrior leads too strongly, you may "win" at the expense of others. If your Caregiver leads over-much, you may help others at your own expense.

nurturing role, and the Warrior is the father's protecting role. Today most of us are expected to fulfill both roles. Increasingly, both men and women are expected to be Warriors in the work world, and Caregivers at home and with their friends.

Place your current HMI score in the box provided. Then circle the archetype that was, or is, or is likely to be most active at this stage of your life.

Warrior ☐   Caregiver ☐

We develop these archetypes by having to be responsible for other people. Indeed, the best parents, teachers, therapists, and managers integrate elements of both. They can both nurture individual development and set limits. When we lead too strongly with either, it is not just that the people in our charge are short-changed; we also feel one-sided. If we focus overly much on the Caregiver, we may feel lots of love and compassion, but we often cannot adequately protect ourselves or those we love. We get overrun. If we focus overly much on the Warrior, to the detriment of the Caregiver, we may protect our boundaries and also achieve a great deal, but at the cost to the human side of our life. Often we are so tough, we hurt other people. Because we do not know about nurturing ourselves either, we brutalize ourselves in the service of achieving our goals: we work so hard and unrelentingly that we develop heart trouble, or we lose the relationships most dear to us because we are always competing, struggling, and achieving and cannot seem to make space for nurturance and intimacy.

Resolution

On the hero's journey, the resolution of this dilemma occurs when the hero slays the dragon not for personal gain, but to rescue the damsel in distress or some other victim. Actually, resolving this dilemma so that we are willing to fight for others at some sacrifice to ourselves is what our culture generally means by heroism.

The resolution of this dichotomy is seen in the archetypal images of God the Father, which emphasize God's gentle and nurturing side as well as his power, and of the Mother Goddess, who gives birth to all life, nurtures that life, but also brings it to an end. Such Goddesses are Caregivers, but they are also enormously powerful. They are the origin of all life, and also of all death and destruction. In each of our lives, the resolution of these two archetypal energies allows us to be ideal parents—to our children, our own inner child, and anyone else in our care. Early in life, we trust our parents to care for us. Then we internalize the parental role and care for and protect ourselves as they would have done. Finally, we are able to access archetypal energies beyond the parent that help us learn to protect and care for ourselves and others in ways that may go far beyond these skills.

Mid-life Transition

The mid-life transition is aided by the archetypes of the Destroyer and the Creator. Together they help us to let go of the identities we spent half our lives creating (our Ego identity), and to open up to a deeper, more authentic sense of Self. In the process, we find we must let go of much of what we thought we were and recreate our lives. This transformation or rebirth, which leads to the virtue of authenticity, requires finding and expressing one's true Self at a deeper level than the provisional identity found by the Seeker and the Lover. Whereas the identity the Seeker and Lover define tells us what and whom we commit to, the Creator and Destroyer help us discover how those commitments will be manifested in daily life, and hence provide an opportunity to evidence our identity in commitments in a way that is unique to us, not predetermined by the culture.

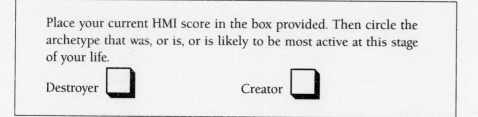

Place your current HMI score in the box provided. Then circle the archetype that was, or is, or is likely to be most active at this stage of your life.

Destroyer   Creator

For example, earlier in life you may have discovered your identity and vocation as a teacher, found a suitable partner whom you really loved, married, and settled down. In mid-life, you may find another, less traditional expression of your vocation as a teacher, perhaps as a consultant or trainer, or perhaps developing your own content to teach. You might also work out a slightly or very different way of being with your spouse or family that is less determined by how you think it should be, and more determined by what really fits for you (and, of course, those in relationship with you).

You may suddenly find that none of it fits anymore. Maybe you need to find a new vocation. Maybe you need to leave your spouse or negotiate a radically altered relationship. Maybe it is time to change your habits and life-style in a marked way.

Together the Destroyer and the Creator help us to let go of the identity we spent half our lives creating (our Ego identity), and to open up to a deeper, more authentic sense of Self.

If your Destroyer strongly leads, you will find it relatively easy to give up what no longer serves your growth, but you may have problems recreating yourself and finding a new sense of identity. By facing a void in your life, you may become dispirited. If your Creator strongly leads, you may be very good at spinning out possible new identities, but without the ability to differentiate what to let go, you may become overwhelmed by the possibilities.

For example, when the Destroyer strongly leads and the mid-life crisis hits, you may quit your job, leave your marriage, leave behind your possessions, let go of the system of beliefs that has informed your life up to this point, and find yourself with almost nothing. (And this can be appropriate if your life to that point has been inauthentic and does not fit you at all.) If the Creator strongly leads, you will not let go of anything. You will just keep adding things in the hope that you will feel better. So you end up with what Buckminster Fuller called the "extravagant complexity." (This can also be positive for a time if what you need to leave is still very attractive to you. You keep it while exploring new options, but life will be very complicated.)

Resolution

The result of finding a satisfactory partnership between the Destroyer and Creator within is the capacity for "elegant simplicity," the creation of a life that has everything you need, but no more. You let go of what no longer fits for you, and add things—not indiscriminately, but only those things that really fit who you now are. It also means redefining relationships to people, work, and institutions so that they are more fulfilling to you in this new stage of your life.

This integration is embodied in the myths of the fertility gods—Christ, Osiris, Inanna, Dionysus, Kore—who embodied the process of death and rebirth, and in all other forms of the archetype of rebirth. Too much Destroyer brings us death and loss, but no resurrection. Too much Creator keeps giving us more options without any way to let go of the inessential. It is continuous birthing, with no deaths.

We live in a culture that reverences life, but not death. The denial of death is rampant everywhere. Yet if nothing died, all new life would be strangled. It is like families who keep having babies but do not have the resources to care for them, so each one goes out into the world ill-nourished and ill-prepared, or like people who cannot let go of a job, a friend, a belief system, and so can never go beyond. In all these cases, the denial of death causes a kind of living death.

The wisdom of the fertility religions is to understand the importance of both birth and death, and to honor both elements of our lives. If we do so, we can balance out those energies, and experience renewal as we let go of what no longer serves us to allow room for new growth.

In the hero's journey, the Destroyer and the Creator are evidenced in the journey to the underworld, where the hero encounters death, and the return to the land of the living. The virtue of authenticity requires us all to confront our mortality because until we really acknowledge that we are going to die, we will not feel the pull to be fully who we are. For most people, the decision to allow oneself to be oneself and to let oneself have what one truly wants—not what society or a religious institution, or one's family or friends says one should want—comes with the dawning recognition that half one's life is over. There is not much time left.

The integration of Destroyer and Creator is embodied in the myths of the fertility gods, who embodied the process of death and rebirth.

Maturity

The archetypes of the post-mid-life transition years help to claim our power and to express that power in the world. The Ruler does so by taking charge, setting directions, and maintaining order in a way that takes into consideration the best use of all resources in the kingdom (inner resources, people, money, things). The Magician's power combines vision, creativity, and the will to transform existing reality or to create something that has never existed before, also with the good of the whole in mind.

The virtue the Magician and the Ruler teaches us is transformation, the ability to aid in the healing or evolution of the world. If your Ruler leads strongly, you may achieve order but at the expense of innovation. If the Magician leads strongly, you may seek the new at the expense of harmony and balance. Too much Ruler leads to stagnation. Too much Magician gives us chaos. But together they help renew the kingdom.

Maturity is the time of claiming your power. Many people, however, do not do so. In fact, instead of becoming either Magicians or Rulers, they simply start closing down and giving up on life. Many are just marking their time until retirement and then death, or just leading lives as they always have, which is a version of going stale and dead.

But those who made good use of the mid-life metamorphosis will claim their power to create a new life—leading either with the Ruler's emphasis on

The virtue the Magician and the Ruler teaches us is transformation, the ability to aid in the healing or evolution of the world.

control over life and others or with the Magician's emphasis on transformation. Both the Ruler and the Magician learn to understand synchronicity and to understand that the outer world mirrors our inner world: we attract to us what we are.

If your Ruler leads, you will see this primarily in terms of responsibility and will recognize your responsibility for the state of your kingdom. If your kingdom is a wasteland, you will begin dealing with it by taking charge. All Rulers understand, as Harry Truman said, "The buck stops here." When Magician energy leads, however, the mirroring of inner and outer is a tool for transformation. The Magician is less interested in having overt power and responsibility than in healing and transforming.

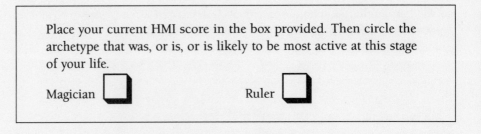

Place your current HMI score in the box provided. Then circle the archetype that was, or is, or is likely to be most active at this stage of your life.

Magician ☐   Ruler ☐

If the Ruler leads too strongly, you will be overly aware that you are totally responsible for your life, but you will lack the capacity to heal yourself or transform your world. You feel responsible, but cannot do anything about it. If the Magician leads too strongly, you may be able to heal and transform yourself and others, but you will lack a sense of responsibility for your actions, and hence may (like the sorcerer's apprentice) create havoc around you.

Resolution

Both the Ruler and the Magician establish healthy, peaceful, and prosperous kingdoms, and together can aid in the healing of the planet. The archetype that best embodies the integration of these qualities is the World Redeemer. Think, for example, of Christ performing miracles at the height of his power, and how he has been seen historically as both "Lord" and "Redeemer." Think also of Buddhist tradition of the Bodhisatva, a totally realized being who could escape coming back to this earth, but returns voluntarily to serve and help others on the path. Think, too, of the Jewish emphasis on "daily acts," the responsibility of each of us to act in ways that help redeem the world.

Of course, upon their return, heroes become "World Redeemers." Having taken their journey, they return to the kingdom to effect its transformation. Any of us become world redeemers when we allow ourselves to truly claim our power to affect the world in which we live, and act consistently out of the core of who we are, knowing that when we do so, there is always a ripple effect that affects the world beyond ourselves.

Too much Ruler leads to stagnation. Too much Magician gives us chaos. But together they help renew the kingdom.

Old Age

Finally, in old age, the Sage and the Fool help us let go of the need to control or change the world so that we might become truly free. Many of the stereotypical images of old age, which on the surface seem so contradictory, come from these archetypes. On the one hand, the aged are portrayed as the wise old man and woman. On the other hand, the elderly are often dismissed and not taken seriously because they are seen as senile or in their second childhood. Actually, in old age we need both the Sage and the Fool in our lives. Indeed, not only do we need them in old age, but anytime after we have "retired" from viewing our work in terms of achievement, whether that achievement is in the world of work or the raising of children or both. We have given our gifts to the world, we have served, we have accepted leadership in our families, communities, and/or workplaces. Suddenly, it is time to learn to be free, and to be free in a context that includes a growing acceptance of death, both in terms of the eventual end of one's life and the more immediate losses of dreams, illusions, and opportunities.

Place your current HMI score in the box provided. Then circle the archetype that was, or is, or is likely to be most active at this stage of your life.

Sage ⬜   Fool ⬜

When the Sage leads, it may be most important to you to have an overview, a context, which gives your life meaning, but you may become detached and disconnected from the everyday, present aspect of life. If your Fool strongly leads, you may be good at staying in the moment and enjoying it for its own sake, but you may become somewhat frivolous and neglect the task of facing the "great questions," especially the issue of finding, in retrospect, the meaning of your own life. Together they allow us to see our life in context and to affirm that life so we may face the transition into death and beyond with optimism and faith.

In old age, we find ourselves remembering less what happened yesterday, than what happened long ago. Our challenge is to think through our lives and sift out its meaning. We also begin to lose our strength and perhaps also our health. Our friends begin to die. Thus we are pushed to let go of attachments—to friends, places, health, even life itself. These tasks require an opening to the wisdom of the Sage.

The Sage finds freedom through serving Truth; the Fool through knowing joy. Together they bring us freedom.

But in old age, we are also challenged to go beyond the need to find meaning through taking care of others, through achievement, through changing the world and making a difference. We need to learn to simply love life for its own sake, day by day. This is also the time when we have the license to be eccentric, irrational, and even a bit childish if we want. Indeed, we may feel foolish because our memories fail, our wits are not so clear as they used to be, and we feel at the mercy of our bodies, which embarrass us by their frailty and incapacity. This is the challenge of the Fool—to love life for life's sake and ourselves just as we are.

Resolution

If we lead too strongly with the Fool, we may act foolishly and neglect the great questions or to seek inner peace and prepare for our dying. If we lead too strongly with the Sage, we may become ponderous and overly serious. If we resolve the duality of Sage and Fool into a partnership, we become Wise Fools. One might not inappropriately think of the stories of Krishna or of Buddha who attained such a state of wisdom and joy that he was often lost for days in blissful ecstasy. The state of reaching enlightenment, essentially goes beyond the hero's journey, indeed beyond heroism into enlightenment. The hero myth finds its completion in the hero's return to transform the kingdom. The achievement of enlightenment moves us beyond heroism, into transcendence and true freedom.

If we resolve the duality of Sage and Fool into a partnership, we become Wise Fools.

Not inappropriately, in such a spiral system, the end of the journey leads us back to innocence, where we began, but this time at a higher level. The cosmic round continues.

A Developmental Spiral

As we recognize the affinity between the archetypes of age and childhood, the idea of the spiral progression is underscored; yet this also illustrates another important reality. By describing this predictable progression, I do not mean to suggest that the archetypes cannot emerge in one's life at any time. For example, anytime we fall in love, the Lover archetype is present. The spontaneous playfulness of the Innocent, and sometimes also the "naughty" acting out of children, certainly reflects the Fool archetype, but it is generally only later in life that the Fool is not just a clown, but the Wise Fool—like the Fools in the classic court who were qualified to advise as well as entertain the King.

Although the issues named here tend to erupt at certain life stages, they keep surfacing until we successfully resolve them. When we do so, we are left with a set of abilities and perspective that support our lives. For instance, although the Innocent and Orphan are archetypes associated with childhood, they will stay active in our lives until we develop the capacity to balance trust with caution. Some people, therefore, who have so lost their innocence that they cannot resolve this duality, still act like Orphans or even victims in mid-life. If they also have not developed the Caregiver's or the Warrior's ability to be disciplined and responsible and they have not learned to commit to themselves (Seeker) or others (Lover), they may have a very difficult time with life indeed. Not having been successful in completing the learning tasks of the first half of life, they are often unable to cope with the mid-life transition on its own terms. The experience of loss at mid-life initially reinforces the sense of Orphaning instead of pushing us into a transformative initiation. Ideally, this intensification of the Orphaning may motivate the individual in question to give up the illusion they can fix it themselves and seriously seek help. Of its very nature, doing so allows for the integration of the Innocent (trust).

When the core, unresolved issue is resolved, people often move very quickly to learn the lessons and gain the gifts of other archetypes associated with prior stages because, of course, they have already done some of the work.

In short, one may go on through the various life tasks without having completely resolved those that preceded. In fact, we almost all do this, since it is only a very healthy person indeed who fully resolves each issue in order at the requisite chronological time period. Indeed, doing so would be a sign of extremely high level of development. However, if the buildup of unresolved issues is great enough, it becomes hard to go forward without addressing earlier issues.

Although there is a progression in these issues and archetypes, none is more important than any other. We can begin developing seemingly higher level archetypes like Magician or Sage, but we are always hampered by any of the earlier ones that have not yet found a way to be reflected in our lives. What is most important is that we fully honor the archetype that is active in our lives at the moment. If we feel like Orphans, we need to stop and fully feel the pain of feeling abandoned and powerless, and reach out and allow others to help. If we do so, we will gain the gift and be able to go on.

And although it may be important at any given moment in life to "specialize" and focus almost exclusively on one part of a duality, if the other remains truly underdeveloped, the result is a life out of balance. For instance, if one has developed one's Caregiver to an extreme, one may have to almost completely stop caretaking in order to develop one's Warrior ability to set the boundaries. Doing one then to the exclusion of the other is healthy. However, if over a lifetime, you developed only Warrior and never Caregiver (or the converse), that would verge on the pathological, and in the modern world at least, it would clearly be dysfunctional. So, too, with the other pairings.

But don't judge yourself against the system. Any person's individual life is unique. If you discover differences between what is going on at a particular stage and what is described here, don't try to conform to the system; honor what is happening in your life and gain its gift.

Despite that caveat, it is important to recognize that generally the hero's journey moves at each stage through duality into union through the process of thesis, antithesis, synthesis. Reaching the higher levels of the archetypes associated with the Self—the Ruler, the Magician, the Sage, and the Fool—depends on a reasonably successful resolution of a prior duality; it is only necessary to integrate the pairs adequately enough to move on.

A successful synthesis of Caregiver and Warrior is a prerequisite for becoming a great Ruler, who can protect the boundaries of the kingdom while also nurturing and empowering everyone within those boundaries. The successful synthesis of the Creator and the Destroyer provides the groundwork for becoming a Magician who can be a transformer or leader for others.

Similarly, it is the successful synthesis of Innocent and Orphan that prepares the way for the Fool to become the Wise Fool, who with complete innocence and no illusions finds joy in life as it is. Finally, it is the synthesis of Seeker and Lover that provides us the highest level Sages—those who completely know and honor who they are and for this reason can accept and affirm everyone else as well.

The major ideas of this chapter are integrated in the illustration that follows. It shows the relationship of these six pairings to the development of Ego, Soul, and Self and the three stages of the hero's journey (preparation, journey, return), using the six-pointed Star of David to represent visually a double integration.

Preparation, Journey, Return

If we integrate the life stages, pairings, and archetypes of their resolutions with the categories of Ego, Soul, and Self, or (on the hero's journey) preparation, journey, and return, we can best see the pattern using the six-pointed Star of David.

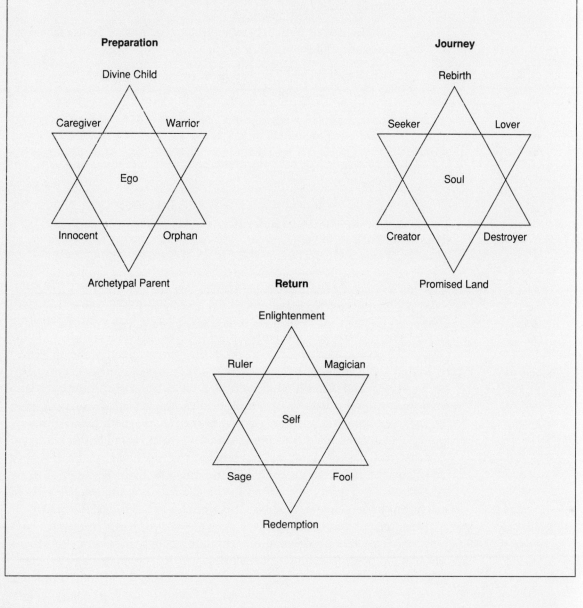

The Archetypes of Completion

Which, if any, of the archetypes of completion are expressed in your own life? What form do they take?

❑ The Divine Child (you have wise innocence without naïveté, denial, or illusions)

❑ The Archetypal Parent (you can protect and nuture the inner and outer child)

❑ The Promised Land (you can be true to yourself in a community that supports who you are)

❑ Rebirth (you have experienced metamorphosis, have given up an old identity and allowed or created a new one)

❑ Redemption (you take responsibility for transforming yourself and your kingdom)

❑ Enlightenment (you can live in the moment freely and joyously, without attachment)

The process of Ego development includes the dialectical processes of Innocent, Orphan, and Divine Child and of the Warrior, Caregiver, and Archetypal Parent (Mother or Father God). The psychological terrain here is the internalized family. When we are able to become the good parent to ourselves, generally the child within is also healed. The process of the journey includes the dialectical resolution of the processes of Seeker, Lover, and Promised Land and of the Creator, Destroyer, and Rebirth. Here, too, the successful completion of a later developmental task allows us to complete an earlier one, for we can only enter the Promised Land and find our true homes after we have been reborn or transformed. Finally, the dialectical processes of the return include the Ruler and Magician, who together bring redemption, and the Sage and Fool, who bring us enlightenment. Again, we can only become truly effective redeemers when we have let go of any need to transform the kingdom and can do it freely without attachment to the outcome. So becoming free also helps us heal the planet.

Finding ourselves and transforming our world involves all these processes and more. To be fully whole, we also must confront our gender, our cultural heritage, and our personal uniqueness—subjects which form the basis of the chapters which follow.

Gender and Human Development over the Life Span

Gender identity is initially established when we are in innocence. Before the age of three, each of us knows what it means to be male or female and usually has learned to act in ways consistent with these traditional sex role messages. The fact that in patriarchy neither sex has a real sense of its gender identity outside of a system of hierarchy and dominance (where male is better and females give up or try harder) is a primary wounding to both; that is a major part of the Orphaning experience (although boys may not *initially* see it as a wounding, since they are taught—explicitly or subtly—that they are better). However, non-culturally derived gender differences also account for the equally important gifts that "femininity" and "masculinity" offer the world.

Differential wounding results, in part, from the variations in the ways men and women experience the journey. Men and boys who fail to live up to a perceived image of masculinity are seen as a sissy, as girlish, and hence lose power and status in the world. One cannot underestimate how difficult it is for little boys to pull away from their relationship with their mothers, especially if this relationship has been the most nurturing and empowering relationship of their early life, and to curtail their more vulnerable emotions—to not cry or be too sensitive, even when they feel totally powerless, vulnerable, and caring.

If their fathers are not around very much (because they are absent or simply involved in work or other activities in the outer world), then they are also trying to live up to a role that they do not really see up close. As a result, a boy may try to live up to a macho image rather than have the opportunity to follow the model of a real warm, loving (and vulnerable) man. Often a whole family will collude in acting as if the father lives up to the idealized masculine image, even when he falls very short, and this, too, is terribly confusing for the son.

Establishing a female identity in a patriarchal society can be deeply wounding to a woman if she comes to believe that to be female is to be, if not

The fact that in patriarchy neither sex has a real sense of its gender identity outside of a system of hierarchy and dominance is a primary wounding to both.

inferior, at least limited in life's options. Everywhere she looks, a woman sees men in positions of power and authority, and when women are there, she learns they are pioneers or special cases. Whether blatantly or subtly, she learns from the culture, if not from her family, that being male is better. In fact, she is encouraged to be feminine, for to act masculine (to have an Ego and think well of oneself) is unnatural (or conceited). While she is allowed to express soft and vulnerable feelings, unless she receives strong messages counter to the prevailing societal ones, she learns to cut off from aggression, anger, and the will to power.

In the modern world, a woman may be taught to develop some stereotypically masculine qualities (like ambition) to complement the feminine ones because without them, her options in the society will be limited and she will have little or no status ("I'm just a housewife"). This can lead to the superwoman syndrome: a woman tries to be both the perfect woman and the perfect man—and usually ends up burned out and exhausted.

But the deep woundedness many men and women feel, which is essentially the result of their societal conditioning, is associated with the genitals. Just as boys fear the loss of the penis (which empowers them with status) and associate the threat of that loss with their continuing love and desire to connect with the mother, the wound to women is the absence of a similar cultural valuing of the power of vulva, vagina, and womb.

Freud had no sense of the numinosity and power women's genitals would have in cultures that venerate the Goddess. He was, of course, a product of his time, so he saw female genitalia only in terms of an absence; women were castrated males.[1] He saw femaleness not as a positive source of strength, wisdom, and power, but only in terms of what it lacked. Therefore he reasoned that female power had to come vicariously through relationship with a man. Such attitudes create a kind of psychological female castration, a patriarchal wounding of women, alienating them from their female identity. This denigration of women, furthermore, cuts individual men from openness to experiencing their own inner feminine, and keeps the culture unbalanced, as male values dominate female ones.

A young girl's wounding comes partly from internalizing messages to repress her urge to autonomy and assertion, and partly from lacking adequate role models. It is more likely that a woman will have her mother present and available in her life than her father. However, to the degree that her mother has internalized a sense of inferiority or limitation and/or to the extent that the mother is trivialized by others (especially by the father), the young girl is unlikely to want to be like her mother. Yet she cannot realistically be like her father.

If at school and on the news she is always learning about the views and works of not only "great men" but also villainous men, and even ordinary men, while power in a woman is presented as unusual, threatening, or destructive (as in the image of the witch), either her aspirations will be stunted or she will try too hard, believing that to succeed she has to be perfect.

Men's and women's journeys often originate from different dilemmas and are informed by different psychological and spiritual problems. The typical male pattern—which we have been taught to see as the classical heroic pattern—begins in arrogance or hubris, and thus requires sacrifice of the Ego to achieve the humility necessary to find the treasure of his true identity. The female pattern usually begins in humility and submission; the problem is not too much pride or Ego, but too little. Without enough Ego and enough faith in herself, a woman cannot find herself or make her contribution to the world.[2]

A young girl's wounding comes partly from internalizing messages to repress her urge to autonomy and assertion.

Sex Role Conditioning

1. What are some of the messages you received as a child about appropriate behavior for your gender? From your father? From your mother? From other relatives? From school, media, religious institutions, peers?

2. Which of these messages have helped or empowered you?

3. Which have limited you?

She tends to overemphasize relationships and to de-emphasize her own value within them. He tends to overemphasize himself and his achievements and to underemphasize the ways he is dependent on others and needs their help and support. Thus, she undervalues herself, while he undervalues relationships. This difference affects what archetypes initially lead in adolescence and adulthood.

However, all gender differences are not necessarily a result of this wounding. There are more typically female and male versions of each archetype, so the issue of gender difference is quite a complex web, consisting of differences not only in sequence, but also in the actual manifestation of each archetype in a single human life. Maleness and femaleness are influenced by the archetypes and by a complicated interweaving of societal conditioning and genetic influences; but they also are more than that, having as much to do with an underlying energy pattern as with the narrative structure of how we put meaning together.

The typical male pattern begins in arrogance or hubris, and thus requires sacrifice of the Ego to achieve the humility necessary to find the treasure of his true identity.

Gender-Related Difference in Journey Patterns

Many men and women today do not conform to the typical pattern for their gender—and that pattern is currently in flux. Nonetheless, it is probably safe to say that gender influences our basic stance in life, whether we see ourselves, as psychologist Nancy Chodorow puts it in *The Reproduction of Mothering,* as primarily "selves-in-connection" or "selves-in-separation," the former being the more typical feminine stance and the latter more typically male.

Gender differences in the progression through the stages of adult life tend to center around four archetypes. Women have traditionally been socialized into Caregiver roles and men into Warrior roles. Female caregiving and male warrioring can feel deeply satisfying when they emerge out of deep, instinctive roots, going back to the ancient divisions of labor by gender in hunting and gathering days. The Seeker and the Lover are associated respectively with the *energies* of the masculine and the feminine. The typical "masculine" stance is to find identity and truth through separation; the "feminine" stance is to find it through identification and connection. Although both men and women have access to both the "masculine" and "feminine" within, the "masculine" energies tend to predominate in men and "feminine energies" in women—at least from early years until mid-life, at which time androgyny becomes the prevailing issue.[3]

We see in the male preferences the influence of Warrior and Seeker and in the female preferences the influence of Caregiver and Lover. Therefore if—and it is a big *if* in the modern world—a woman follows a reasonably traditional female path, she will initially lead with the Caregiver and Lover archetypes, while a similarly traditional male pattern will initially lead with the Warrior and Seeker archetypes. Women have tended to prefer the more affiliating, caring archetypes, and men the more separated and independent archetypes, and this preference has been heavily reinforced (if not absolutely determined) by the culture.

This means that women are more likely initially to seek identity in relationship and to place great value on caring for others. Therefore, the great challenge for women, as Carol Gilligan has demonstrated in *In a Different Voice: Psychological Theory and Women's Development,* is to develop boundaries and to take care of themselves as well as others. Indeed, in early development, women often have problems because they do not adequately assert themselves and they do not differentiate their own needs from those of others; they end up martyred, fearful, or dependent in relationships. (Sometimes this is incorrectly diagnosed as "relationship addiction" when it is really just a fairly typical female way of being in our culture, until, that is, a woman fully develops a sense of separate identity.)

When women eventually develop the Seeker and the Warrior as allies to the more dominant Lover and Caregiver, they know who they are independent of

When women develop the Seeker and the Warrior as allies to the more dominant Lover and Caregiver, they know who they are independent of their relationships and are able to factor their own needs into the network of caring relationships.

their relationships and are able to factor their own needs into the network of caring relationships. They still emphasize affiliation and the networks of caring interrelationship, but now find positive ways to get their own needs met rather than sacrifice their autonomy to relationships.

Conversely, more men lead with their Seeker and their Warrior and therefore early on value autonomy, toughness, and the ability to complete. Their problem areas tend to be relationships, in which they may lack intimacy and empathy skills and hence alienate others. Although they may not acknowledge their need for others, they know they do not show others adequate love or concern, and have an underlying terror that they will be abandoned because they lack depth and the ability to show their love. They may compensate by working harder in the hope that they will be loved for their accomplishments. But they may frequently not even know what they feel or what they want in the feeling realm of life. At worst, even sex becomes a matter of conquest, and relationship one more way to show one's power over another. All that makes men feel more and more empty inside (until they take their inner journeys).

Such gender differences lead to frustration and dissatisfaction in same-sex relationships as well. While women often feel caught in the world of connectedness, men often feel totally cut off from it. Many times men and women have trouble in relationship because they expect different things. Women's relationships can lapse into symbiosis, with the resulting loss of boundaries. Men's relationships can degenerate into contests of power and dominance.

In maturity, men often develop their Lover and Caregiver as allies to their Seeker and Warrior, and when they do so, they become more genuinely interested in generativity, care, and intimacy. At this point, they may want to mentor children and protégés, and to pass on their knowledge in a way that will empower others. They want to act in ways that are good for others as well as themselves. Yet even though men and women become more alike as each develops, at least to some degree, the attributes and virtues associated with the other, there generally remains a difference in emphasis and value. For example, it is still typical for men to see the achievement of autonomy as the desired outcome of the developmental process, even when they see concern and empathy for others as important. Similarly, it is more typical for women to see the achievement of interdependence as the desired outcome of that process, even when they see the achievement of autonomy as a necessary prerequisite for living responsibly in interdependent community.

Carol Gilligan shows how men tend to think in terms of ladders, with the goal being to get to the top of the ladder (think of the Seeker's urge to ascend). Women, on the other hand, tend to think in terms of nets or webs of human interconnection. The goal is the collective good or the good of everyone within that web (think of the Lover's focus on connectedness). Men tend to have

In maturity, men often develop their Lover and Caregiver as allies to their Seeker and Warrior, and when they do so, they become more genuinely interested in generativity, care, and intimacy.

difficulty with intimacy, fearing they will be swallowed up in the web or net. Women tend to have difficulty with self-assertion, fearing isolation at the top of the ladder. The transformative act for a woman, then, can be seeking her own good and advancement and facing her terror of being alone. The transformative act for a man is often putting aside his terror of being swallowed up by feminine connectedness and risking genuine intimacy. In short, the challenge for women is opening to the Seeker. For men, it is opening to the Lover.[4]

Gender and Ego, Soul, and Self

Male and female journeys also differ by their relationship to the three aspects of the psyche: Ego, Soul, and Self. Men classically tend to have so much Ego that it drives out Soul, so strong measures are necessary for them to find the balance necessary for the Soul to emerge. Women, on the contrary, may have more initial engagement with their Souls, but not enough Ego development to express themselves productively in the world.

Women often have an easier time entering the mysteries because they have less resistance, and they may likely be drawn to the Lover archetype not only because of cultural conditioning (or innate predilection) but because sexism has already done much of the work of the Destroyer. Women, however, often need to go back to the Ego archetypes and shore up their Ego strength before they can manifest their true Selves and their gifts in the world. Unless women do so, they may find their true Souls but be unable to bring back the wisdom they gained on their inner journeys to benefit the world.

Men and women at mid-life often show, in their outer life, patterns previously identified with the other sex.

Conversely, a man's success on the journey depends on his willingness to let go of his pride or egotism (which is, of course, also just a product of societal conditioning), and he may linger very long in the Seeker stage—particularly in its aspiring energy—before the Destroyer does its work. For men, this is usually not until mid-life, unless some great catastrophe happens earlier (such as the death of a child, a heart attack, or a major defeat of some kind). Even when such events occur, conditioning and societal pressure often discourage men from exploring the meaning of such events, pushing them to focus simply on stoically making it through. The traditional approach to Soul development emphasizes the taming or demolition of the Ego. Such approaches, I believe, came from the need to subdue the overly dominant Ego, which is often found in men, and they can be extremely destructive to anyone—male or female—who has inadequate Ego strength.

Whether one is male or female, the journey calls for balance. Neither arrogance or obsequiousness will do. Furthermore, these generalizations are not absolutes. Some women tend toward hubris, and some men to underestimating their gifts. Some women tend naturally to be Warriors and Seekers, and some men to be Caregivers and Lovers in spite of their cultural conditioning. The point is for both to take their journeys in such a way as to find their own way to be male or female, and eventually to achieve a positive kind of androgyny, which is not at all about unisex, neutered behavior, but is about gaining the gifts both gender energies and experiences have to offer us.

Sorting It Out in the Contemporary World

In the contemporary world, where sex roles are in transition, the pattern of gender development through the six major stages of life is very complicated, and differs greatly from individual to individual. Sex role prescriptions are simply less rigid than they used to be, and people are more conscious of the effects of sex role conditioning on their lives. Many women, therefore, lead with the Seeker archetype because of the degree of alienation they feel from the culture and from many men in it. Also, this culture tends to overvalue autonomy and competition and undervalue care and relationship. There is, great societal reinforcement for women to act like Seekers and Warriors whether or not these archetypes would organically emerge from within.

Women receive very mixed messages, since to succeed they are told they need to act like men have. If they do so, they are frequently seen as unfeminine, or even unnatural. Therefore, the prescription for career success runs counter to that for personal success. Many times women let the Warrior dominate in their career lives, their Caregiver and/or Lover in their privates lives, and the Seeker inside themselves, as they try to sort it all out and figure out who they are.

There is also, for women, a relatively strong prohibition against claiming the power of the Ruler in any external way—unless that power is strongly diluted and filtered through the Caregiver/Lover lens. This prohibition is reflected in the "glass ceiling" that keeps all but a small number of women out of the highest level leadership posts and in the fear generated in others by women who seem "threatening" to men.

Archetypes and Gender

Traditional Woman's Journey

Traditional Man's Journey

Frequent Pattern for Nontraditional Men and Women

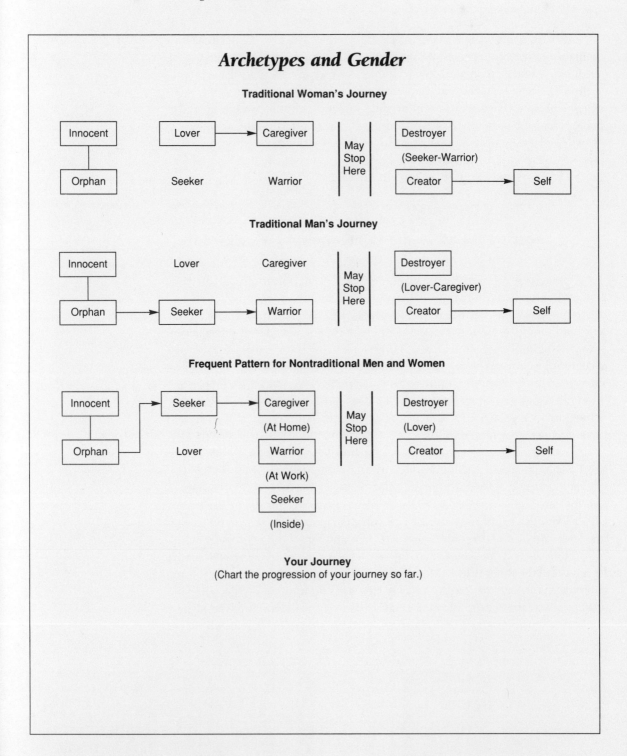

Your Journey
(Chart the progression of your journey so far.)

For men, things are also complicated. Men are strongly pressured into being Warriors, Seekers, and Rulers (but not really androgynous Rulers) to the exclusion of all else. That is the definition of masculinity and of success in the culture. This pressure works against psychological wholeness, and it deprives them and those close to them of genuine intimacy. Thus many men feel really stuck. Some, like women, split and are Warriors at work, Caregivers at home, and Seekers inside themselves or in their free time.

Your Gender Development

1. Beyond sex role socialization, what does it mean to connect with your essential femaleness? With your essential maleness?

2. How has your own developmental progression been influenced by your gender?

Men's lives are also confused by mixed messages from women, who say they want them to be sensitive, vulnerable, and intimate; but if men are, women often find them lacking in masculinity. Conversely, if men act in what they believe to be masculine ways, they are cut off, isolated.

For all the attendant difficulties, the contemporary pattern breeds more chance of psychological health and wholeness than the more traditional one—for a deeper and fuller relationship between the sexes (and between members of the same sex), as we share enough to really be able to understand one another. But it does demand a lot of us. In prior generations, men carried most of the masculine energy for the culture. Women carried the feminine energy. Both were incomplete without the other. Men and women who had the capability to do more suffered a great deal. Others just thought feeling like half a human being was just what life was like.[5]

An Androgyny Inventory

1. What are some androgynous behaviors, traits, feelings, or energy you currently exhibit or experience?

2. How androgynous are you?

False Androgyny: Superwoman/Superman

The current media images of superman and superwoman are not real androgyny. Buying this promise that we can have it all often results in having nothing authentic. As Joanna Russ parodies the superwoman image, we tape Kirk Douglas to the perfect mother to the Playboy dimwit to describe the "perfect woman."[6] Attempting to live up to this new standard of female perfection is a prescription for burnout. However, it is often just this burnout that causes women to begin to search for integration and wholeness—and beyond that, for some more authentic mode of trying to be both true to their womanhood *and* successful in the world. Contemporary women do not want to be confined to traditional roles, and they do not want to be males either.

Similarly, many men are now trying to tape Caregiver onto Warrior—often because they want to be good parents to their children and helpmates to their partners. They are still trying to be every bit a Warrior at work, but in their private lives, they try to be nurturing, caring, and intimate. Their models of nurturance and deep feeling are mainly female. They do not want to be stoic and cut off from their feelings, but they also want to be men, not women.

With all the variations on this basic pattern, the attempt to be Superwoman or Superman can just wear us out or force us to confront ourselves. Lyn—the career woman, gourmet/vegetarian cook, feminist, New Age Seeker, and mother of hyperactive twins in Jane Wagner's *The Search for Signs of Intelligent Life in the Universe*—initially thinks she and her husband can "have it all." But as her marriage with a seemingly perfect New Age man falls apart, she has the wisdom to know it is not personal. While he is presumably still looking for Superwoman, she begins to sell everything—to let go and find herself. She saves only two things: an autographed copy of the first issue of *Ms.* magazine and the "Whales Save Us" T-shirt her husband was wearing the first time they met. The wisdom is profound. She does not give up her dream of a liberated, free, androgynous vision, but she stops looking for it in extravagant complexity and pares down to essentials. She will, and perhaps already does, know the strong woman (represented by her feminist ideals) and the environmentally sensitive man ("Whales Save Us") within herself. Her task now is to find some adequate, human-scale outer expression of this inner reality.[7]

Finding a Deeper Sense of Gender Identity

One step in this process—whether we come to the state of suffering by the traditional or the new burnout pattern—is to find the womanly way to focus on autonomy and achievement or the manly way to experience intimacy and connectedness. The result of this is one level of true androgyny. The birth of the true Self always comes out of a marriage of the inner man and woman.

Before we can be androgynous, we must find out what masculinity and femininity mean separate from sex role prescriptions for behavior—encountering one's inner man or inner woman and finding out what he or she requires from you. Most cultural definitions of masculinity and femininity are mutually exclusive. You prove you are a man partly by not doing feminine things. You prove you are a woman by preferring womanly to manly pursuits. So before we can be androgynous, we need to find a meaning for our gender identities that does not preclude wholeness.

For many men and women today, finding out who they are requires moving beyond prescribed sex roles to find what it means to be a man or a woman at a deeper, more genuine level. In particular, the connection of Caregiving with women and Warrioring with men seems less connected for many men and women with a genuine sense of gender identity than with long-standing cultural roles (descending perhaps as far back as hunting/gathering societies).

The birth of the true Self always comes out of a marriage of the inner man and woman.

Today, men like Mark Gerzon, in *A Choice of Heroes: The Changing Face of American Manhood,* see a need for men in the nuclear age to move away from identification with the Warrior mode of heroism and find a sense of masculine identity at a deeper and more adequate level. Otherwise, men are threatened with a deep crisis as the qualities that have defined their sense of masculinity no longer have social utility. In particular, he says, men need to get beyond defining themselves as Warriors (so that we might have world peace), and also beyond the notion that they prove their masculinity by doing things (battle or achievement) that women cannot do. When women are in the boardroom, as he believes they should be, then men cannot prove their masculinity by being there.

Similarly, Judith Duerk, in *A Circle of Stones: Woman's Journey to Herself,* calls upon women to go beyond caretaking and sacrifice to find a more innate sense of femaleness, which she sees (as did Anne Wilson Schaef in *Women's Reality* before her) as a kind of capacity for living in process. Whether women have traditional life-styles and are defining themselves as Caregivers or are on the fast track with men, the issue, she notes, is ultimately the same: women have learned to disregard their own feeling needs. "What if a woman allowed herself to leave a mode of doing that does not nourish her," she asks. "Perhaps what is asked is that each of us come to her own renewed grounding in the archetypal feminine, come to a . . . conscious awareness, understanding, and embracing of it in her own being and her own life."[8]

For women, the issues are, how can they move into what were traditionally male roles without becoming male clones, and how does one retain the deeper values of the female without living to serve others? The value of women moving from a Caregiver modality to a deeper sense of the feminine is that as long as women's lives are defined by doing for others and responding to the needs of the outside world, they can never find their unique rhythm, their wisdom, or their sense of what is uniquely theirs to give. To do so, Duerk says, women must slow down, take time out, attune themselves to finding their own rhythm, their own process of living and being in the world.

In describing the male heroic journey, Gerzon suggests that as long as men define their relationship with others only in terms of competition or superiority, they never have a sense of genuine relatedness, so they are always lonely. Ultimately, Gerzon sees the "emerging masculinities" as not inherently in opposition to femaleness. They are forms of emerging ways of being human. Although he leaves the subject there, others (such as Robert Bly) go further, searching for a more genuine sense of masculinity—beyond the patriarchal stereotypes.

Dealing with gender is like peeling off the skin of an onion. We do so in layers. At the first and outer layer, the layer most defined by the culture outside ourselves, most of us identify femaleness with Caregiving and maleness with Warrioring. At some point, however, men and women begin to feel possessed and enslaved by these roles. This means we are ready to move on. Often we do so by identifying less with our gender identity and more with being fully human. Doing so opens us up to the whole other side of life. At first it feels really exciting to be exploring ways of behaving one has associated with the other sex. Men find it freeing to discover they can be nurturing and sensitive, and women find it freeing to discover they can be tough and can achieve things just for themselves.

Yet after a while, a new kind of dissatisfaction emerges, a hunger to find out something about one's identity at a deeper level. At this point, more typically, the masculine emerges as the spiritual questing energy of the Seeker. Its tendency is toward judging what is and striving for what could be better. The feminine emerges as the spiritual loving energy of the Lover. Its impulse is receptive; its tendency is to affirm and celebrate life as it is.

Some men and women today, moreover, are also moving still deeper to attempt to connect at an even more primal level with what Robert Bly calls "the wild man" or the "wild" or "natural woman" beyond cultural sex roles. If we imagine the Lover, Seeker, Caregiver, and Warrior as archetypal riverbeds that typically channel the river, primal masculine and feminine energies are the water itself.

Our deep, underlying wound is alienation from the feminine or masculine source within ourselves.

To get to this level, we almost always have to go through the pain of first experiencing the lack of connection to our personal and the collective mother or our father. We may, for instance, feel a sense of orphaning in not having a parent who could provide an adequate gender role model, and beyond that, we may also feel orphaned by the society for its incapacity to provide us adequate sex role models in this age of rapid transition.

Yet as difficult as these wounds may be, the deeper, underlying wound is alienation from our feminine or masculine source within ourselves. When we connect with that source—the archetypal man within a man and the archetypal woman within a woman—that pain about inadequate mothering or fathering goes away or is lessened. It also makes it possible for us to open to the contrasexual energies—the anima in a man and the animus in a woman—so that we become androgynous in an empowering, rather than a reductive, unisex way.

For many, the key to finding an authentic sense of femininity and masculinity comes through exploring the numinous, spiritual meaning coded in our primary and secondary sexual characteristics. For example, early feminist books such as Anne Kent Rush's *Getting Clear* provided meditations for women to relearn to love their breasts and genitals, as well as the rest of their bodies. Marija Gimbutas in *The Language of the Goddess* provides an in-depth analysis of sacred images of vulva and birthing as well as other goddess-related images.

Eugene Monick (in *Phallos: Sacred Image of the Masculine*) explores the phallus as a soul image of male power that is not determined by patriarchal authority. John Rowan in *The Horned God: Feminism and Men as Wounding and Healing* finds a model for manliness without macho in the archetype of the Horned God—consort of the goddess—who is a hunter, but is also gentle, who is a god and hence holy, and also sexual. He is a prototype of the gods who die and are reborn, their sacrifice being always in the service of life. His sexuality is primal, but it is also sacred, deep, and erotically connected.[9]

Similarly, some women find in the archetype of the Goddess an image of what it is to be thoroughly feminine, without being subservient or secondary to men, to be both spiritual and sexual in an embodied female way—with genitalia, womb, and breasts as objects of sacred worship, uniting the Lover and the Ruler. The embracing of the feminine as a source of power, rather than subservience, often frees women to genuinely reverence the masculine in the men around them and in themselves. Indeed, the experience of the goddess within themselves frees women to experience the god within in a different way.

There is a classic story about the god Krishna coming to dance with all the maidens in the village, his masculine presence and love for the feminine being so complete that though he was dancing with every woman there, each woman felt totally danced with and totally loved. She experienced the visitation of the god so completely that it was as if she had him to herself. Until women fully venerate the goddess within, they cannot experience the masculine as loving and nourishing them in this way. Until this point, the masculine is often experienced as a judging voice, telling them they are not good enough.

Conversely, until men open to the more primal masculine within them, a masculinity totally at odds with patterns of dominance and submission, they experience the feminine within and without as dangerous and a snare—certainly dangerous to their illusion of superiority. To them, the feminine always has to be kept enslaved, and controlled. Because they are equally enslaved by not having access to the feminine, they are always trying to control women outside them so the women will continue to provide the feminine nurturance their souls and hearts crave but their minds do not value. When they experience their primal masculine source of energy, they can also open to the feminine nurturing source within, and they do not need to be so controlling of women because they are no longer so dependent on them. Indeed, they are then free to love a woman or to be alone, knowing the goddess within them will nourish them in either case.

In *Body Metaphors: Releasing God-Feminine in Us All*, Genia Pauli Haddon corrects the stereotypical view that women are yin and receptive (as demonstrated by the vagina) and men are yang and active (as demonstrated by the penis). She also uses a biologically based argument that men and women each have a unique kind of yin and yang energy. Male yang energy is thrusting, aggressive energy associated with the penis. Male yin energy, associated with the testicles, provides the virtue of a kind of reassuring steadiness. Similarly, while agreeing that the vagina is yin and receptive, she argues that female yang energy is evidenced in both the clitoris and in the uterus. The latter is evidenced in the female activity of birthing—babies, projects, poems. To make things more complicated, every human being has within them the potential for both the masculine and feminine versions of yin and yang.[10]

Genuine Androgyny

Developing a capacity for androgyny allows for more room and variety and freedom in the ways we express who we are in the world. Initially, androgyny is often defined as a kind of neuter stage—as in unisex clothes and hairstyles—and in adolescence, it is healthy to express it in that way. True androgyny is not simply a matter of successfully doing some conventionally male or female tasks (like combining serious and committed parenting with a career), although the ability to do so contributes to the achievement of more genuine androgyny.

Genuine androgyny is a layered experience. At the outer, most culturally defined layer, it is about integrating (not just taping together) Caregiver and Warrior. At the next layer, it is about integrating Seeker and Lover. At the innermost layer, it is about a union of primal masculine and feminine energies within. Thus, establishing our primary gender identity (beyond Caregiver and Warrior) and achieving androgyny occur as part of our initiation into Soul, that is, finding out who we are as men and women is about our connectedness to our Souls. Caregiver and Warrior can feel deeply satisfying as well, when doing it comes out of deep, instinctual roots, related to the programming of the species to care for and protect the next generation. Warriors protect the boundaries, and Caregivers foster the development of the tribe. When Ego development is complete and successful, we learn to do both.

Before Soul initiation, trying to integrate Warrior and Caregiver is very stressful and difficult. We almost always do it on the tape model. After initiation, when we have a Self to contain the archetypal energy coming through, the integration may be more organic and simple and less forced. This does not mean, however, that it is wasted effort to try to do both first, for going through the motions associated with an archetype provides the ritualistic form to invite in the archetype. This means when we want the Warrior archetype to visit us, we set goals, struggle to meet them, show courage in adversity and in meeting the challenges of life. When we want Caregiver to visit us, we show compassion and care. When the archetype emerges fully in one's life, one can do these things without it seeming so hard or forced.

Remember that the Ruler archetype, which signals the completion of the alchemical process, results from the symbolic union of male and female that gives birth to the true Self. That Self is envisioned as an androgynous monarch, and at best signals some integration of Caregiver and Warrior abilities. Indeed, all the archetypes associated with the Self are androgynous. Magicians and Fools often express this androgyny by the capacity to change sex, or to go back and forth from one gender to the other. Both are very sexy archetypes and actively use erotic energy—in the first case for transformation and in the second for ecstasy and joy. This means that the man and woman within must be activated, but distinct enough for energy to move between them, as with alternating electrical current.

The Sage is often seen as having gone beyond gender identification entirely, and men and women in old age look increasingly alike as secondary sexual characteristics are de-emphasized. The wisdom of the Sage comes in part from true integration of the perspectives of male and female so that there is no separation between them.

Elderly men and women, however, are hampered by having so few positive images in the culture for aging. This situation is worse for women since at least men can be seen as distinguished—although it is certainly difficult for many men to find an identity in retirement, especially if their primary identity has come from their work. To the degree that women are defined by the culture only in relationship to men or children, they may get the message that they have no cultural use in old age. Other cultures—Chinese, for instance—venerate the elderly for their wisdom and experience. In Western culture, the image of the wise woman or crone is currently aiding women in honoring the task of old age—to claim wisdom and freedom and to express an experienced mode of female wisdom in the world. So too, this is the time many men feel freed up from the demands of macho performance to be true to a deeper well of wisdom in their actions and words.

Real androgyny is a kind of psychological integration seen in people who live authentically, out of the truth of who they are; at this level we are both uniquely ourselves and connected with the full human potential of all people—and both genders—in all times and places. This can be a grand release, for we are not expressing a Self in terms of restriction (I'm this, not that), but a complex, often contradictory set of possibilities, adequate for the whole of who we are. But unlike Superwoman/Superman, this does not mean trying to do it all. It especially does not mean trying to fulfill entirely the traditional male and the traditional female roles. It means doing what fits you, and being true to who you are at a deeper level, so that you can express yourself through the masculine or feminine polarities as each is congruent with who you are.

Self-Portrait

Draw or otherwise render yourself (through photo, collage, symbol) in a way that reflects your own wholeness and androgyny and that gives form to both the man and the woman inside you.

Ultimately we learn that masculinity and femininity are part of a continuum, not an either/or choice, and people make different choices on that continuum, balancing these energies in their own unique ways. It has several times been said as a result that there are really more than two sexes, because the ways to combine these energies are so many and so diverse.

June Singer, in her book *Androgyny*, explains that "androgyny is not trying to manage the relationship between the opposites; it is simply flowing between them. One does not need to do anything but flow between the masculine and feminine, touching both, yielding to all obstacles and thereby overcoming them, the energy building upon itself as it follows its natural tendency."[11]

An androgynous culture allows us to be individuals, separate and ourselves, and to live in process with the natural world. The chapter that follows begins with a consideration of the importance of the emergence of the feminine and the development of a more androgynous cultural potential to our time.

Gender, Diversity, and the Transformation of Culture

Too often the hero's journey has been seen as belonging only to some people and not others. As we have seen, it has often been assumed that heroism is male and not female. When we believe this, we see only the heroism that is male, and not that which is female. Women are seen as damsels in distress to be rescued, rewards for the journey, supports along the way, or villains (as with the wicked witch), but not heroes in their own right. In European and American cultures, moreover, the hero is usually assumed to be Caucasian. Darker-skinned males are cast as sidekicks (remember the Lone Ranger and Tonto, or Huck and Jim) if not enemies (as with cowboys and Indians), or victims to be rescued because they are not able to take care of themselves.

If we are all to take our journeys and give our gifts, we must honor the many variations on the journey that result from our diversity. We also must recognize that each of our individual journeys exists in a historical context and is affected by the collective journeys of our gender, our family and other affiliations, our nation, and our race, and by our common human journey. To look at our individual journey without reference to its context and the ways it interacts with others is to miss much of the point. We may feel very alone on the journey, but actually we are all journeying together. We both influence and are influenced by the world in which we live.

At the culmination of the hero's journey, the hero returns to the kingdom with a sacred object, a new life-giving truth, that helps it to be transformed. If only some people are encouraged to take their journeys and find their gifts (or if only some people's gifts are accepted and recognized by the culture), the kingdom can be only partially renewed. Large areas of the kingdom will remain a wasteland, because no one kind of people has access to the new truths we need.

For example, the white male hero has brought us much progress, but has not been able to help us learn to live in harmony with the earth. But there are

If we are all to take our journeys and give our gifts, we must honor the many variations on the journey that result from our diversity.

traditions—American Indian, most conspicuously—in which ecological wisdom evolved to a high level. While the hole in the ozone layer continues to grow and acid rain falls on our crops and cities, the dominant culture, by and large, ignores the wisdom of the many heroic Indian forefathers and mothers who knew what the dominant culture needs to know. Similarly, there is widespread evidence that women are inherently less violent than men, yet in a world where the overriding issue is the need to find a way for lasting peace, men continue to look to one another, not to women, for answers.

Archetypes, Gender, and Cultural Change

Gender identity and androgyny are cultural and political as well as individual issues. Living in a patriarchal culture as we do, we all suffer from the devaluation of the feminine and the way this inhibits women from taking their journeys and giving their true gifts to the culture. It is no wonder that we cannot solve many of the great world problems when we are relying predominantly on only one sex and one sex's perspective in doing so.

Jung believed that the revival of the feminine would save society, and any number of writers have been arguing from different vantage points that we are moving from patriarchy into an androgynous phase of culture. Riane Eisler, in *The Chalice and the Blade,* for instance, defines ancient gynocentric (woman-focused) societies as operating on the partnership model. Without any need for dominance/submission patterns, without war or class structures, such societies, she argues, flourished worldwide and were responsible for most fundamental inventions—from fire to agriculture, to language.

If we want a transformed kingdom, we will need to recognize the potential for heroism and the capacity for wisdom of all people.

Patriarchal culture, she argues, created a dominator social model that brought with it competition, war, sexism, racism, and class structure. Although she seems to see no redeeming value in patriarchy, I would add that it likely brought us the development of the Ego and a sense of individual identity, and an increased ability to differentiate self from others.

Analogous to individual human development, early gynocentric societies were caring, inventive, and peaceful, but they could not defend themselves from invading patriarchal bands, so they were enslaved and disempowered. Patriarchal societies were strong and warlike, but bred conflict internally and externally. People were always grappling for power, so they could not just let down and be loving and caring with one another.[1] Women-centered societies had the virtues of the Innocent, Caregiver, and Lover archetypes. Patriarchal societies demonstrated the virtues of the Orphan, Warrior, and Seeker.

Patriarchy has brought us many gifts, but without the current rise of the female, it was bringing us to the brink of disaster. (Of course we will have to get the Warrior's higher gifts before we fully move on.) It is not just that the patriarchal overemphasis on Warrior values has threatened the world with nuclear war. We are all aware of that. It is also that people have come to justify polluting the environment in the interest of competitiveness. If profits would go down or a company would be in jeopardy, ecological concerns are often forgotten. At the root of this is the overemphasis on Ego, which cuts everyone—male and female alike—off from their Souls, Eros, and the life force. Our Seeker energy is then siphoned off from true questing into obsessive achievement and, of course, causes us to court the Destroyer in a massive way.

Indeed, it is probably not an exaggeration to say that in various ways our culture has been experiencing the work of the Destroyer for most of the century. This initiation began with the great world wars and has continued with the wars in Korea, Vietnam, and Iraq. In many parts of the world, it is evidenced by widespread famine, and virtually everywhere by poverty and homelessness. The Destroyer has also been active in other ways, with the massive erosion of traditional mores and ways of behaving, peaking in the revolutionary 1960s. The drug crisis and attendant decay of family life are part of this initiation, as is declining national economic competitiveness.

We are also suffering from an absence of the Caregiving archetype. In earlier periods of patriarchal history, men's emphasis on Warrioring was balanced by women's Caregiving roles. In part, the contemporary women's movement was motivated because women were assigned most of the caretaking, nurturing functions for the society, but that work was not, and is not now, respected or rewarded. As many women have stopped nurturing and caring for others full-time—seeking roles that would give greater rewards—men have not moved in to fill the void. So we have a crisis. Who will care for the children? Who will maintain our homes? Who will care for the elderly? Who will create community and help people know they matter?

Right now, we are a world of Seekers living in the "in between," as we move from one cultural age to another. Various theorists have said this in different ways, but the most common is to say that we have been moving out of an industrial and into an information age. Many have talked hopefully about moving into the "New Age" of abundance, peace, love, and prosperity. As with all such major cultural transitions, the ground beneath our feet feels shaky.

Some people respond by holding on for dear life to old, anachronistic values, habits, and traditions. They may, for instance, want to go back to former patterns of relationship between the sexes and between parents and children (that is, "reestablish family values"). Others opt for cynicism and just go after money and "making it."

We are a world of Seekers living in the "in between," as we move from one cultural age to another.

But most people at some level know we are experiencing a major societal challenge to rebuild and recreate our society and the world. Most of us, however, must start with ourselves and our own lives, and the great challenge of accepting that the old world is dead or dying and the new world, if left to create itself, may not be worth living in. We need to consciously become part of the transformation.

Doing so requires people all over the world to take their Soul journeys. The women's liberation movement, the civil rights movement, the human potential movement, the New Age movement, and the struggles for liberation in places like eastern Europe, South Africa, and Latin America are part of this massive movement into questing. This is the positive side of the Seeker, but its shadow side is also obvious in the overemphasis on striving, achievement, and self-improvement, even at great cost to the environment and in burnout of human resources. We are questing as the Destroyer is daily eroding everything we have assumed to be stable. Knowledge is expanding at an incredible rate. Technology is evolving very quickly. Cultural mores are in great flux, and we're not aware of what this environmental damage will mean to life on the planet. The dismantling of the Berlin Wall is a powerful cultural symbol that the Destroyer has done its work. We are no longer in the world we knew. The old world is dead, and we are in the process of beginning to create the new. The result can be devastation unless we open to the Lover archetype, determine what we really love and value, and find out who we are. We need to sort out what values and traditions of the past and present need to be cherished and retained. We need to determine individually and collectively what we would love to do or create, what kind of world would make our hearts sing.

The threat of annihilation by nuclear accident, war, environmental disaster, or economic collapse has been an underlying motivator for some time now, pushing all cultures and major powers from a Warrior/Seeker stance to integrate Caregiver/Lover ones. To be called by the Lover is simultaneously to be called by our Souls to learn about a depth of connectedness between and among people previously unknown to humanity. It is the Lover archetype that teaches us that the walls between people and peoples can come down.

On the Soul level, the Destroyer archetype is teaching us, as W. H. Auden wrote, "We must love each other or die."

This means that culturally we need to experience the power of the archetypes that have been both devalued and associated with the feminine journey, but not stop there. As we integrate Warrior with Caregiver and Seeker with Lover, we achieve a new androgynous possibility. As individuals move through their Soul initiation to create a life of androgynous potential—with fulfillment through love and work, personal achievement and Soul connection—so, too, we help create a world where peace and harmony is possible in a context in which diversity is truly valued. As long as we are all operating only at the level of Ego, these challenges are impossible to meet. The moment we say yes to our Souls, and become firm in who we are, we can work things out in a global way.

Right now, the archetype of the Creator is active in helping various people provide visions of what that world might be like. Artists, writers, and futurists provide this function in our cultural life, in our imaginations, in our individual lives.

The Ruler archetype is not yet manifested, for there are few places where true renewal has happened in any macrocosmic way. Each of us individually helps to make that possibility a reality when we create a vision of our ideal world and then act to make that vision a reality. We also do so when we simply take responsibility for what is and stop blaming others. A transformative part of this process for both men and women is to reaffirm femaleness, and the values and archetypes associated with it, in women and in men. Another part is to value and affirm the differing gifts of different cultures and races, rather than simply assuming—or striving to prove—the superiority of one's own.

Collectively, we transform the world by political action, which involves individual effort. It is not enough to follow our own bliss when so many people in the world are disempowered by poverty, ignorance, prejudice, or tyranny. If we believe that adequate solutions to the world's problems will take all our gifts, it makes sense to support and engage in political action to extend access to education, jobs, and beyond these to life, liberty, and the pursuit of happiness to all people. Certainly, engaging in efforts to help others is ennobling, and doing so helps create a peaceful and prosperous world.

It is not enough to follow our own bliss when so many people in the world are disempowered by poverty, ignorance, prejudice, or tyranny.

Culture and Archetype

Various environmental, societal, and cultural factors may lead in any of the pairings. For example, any disempowered or oppressed group—including all women and members of racial minorities, lesbians and gay males, the poor, the disabled—are genuinely Orphaned by their culture. This means that they are likely to lead with the Orphan rather than the Innocent archetype—except if the environmental pressure to deny that unfair inequities exist is strong enough, it may mean leading from an Innocent stuck in denial. As these groups begin to press for their rights, the power of white males feels eroded, and they feel orphaned as well.

Cultures are even more dynamic than individuals, so they include all twelve archetypes in ever-changing patterns. Moreover, all of today's major world cultures are patriarchal, although most are in the process of transformation. That means that the Warrior archetype will be strong in each, simply because that is *the* patriarchal archetype.

Archetypes Expressed in the Culture Today

1. The comments just made are based on conditions in the world when this book was being written. Based on reports in the media and other information you receive about the world, what archetype or archetypes are active in community, national, and world events right now?

2. Remembering that you affect the course of history by how you live your own life, what could you do to contribute to the health and success of the collective enterprise? What are you willing to do?

Although each embodies all the twelve archetypes, many of the major cultures of the world put them together in a unique way, and some also have developed to a high level archetypes de-emphasized in others. Looking at the cultures and what is currently happening to them is both illuminating and alarming. For example, the cultures most aligned with Soul—native American and other native populations (such as the aborigines) and black American ghetto culture—are most in danger of being destroyed. The oppression of Soul cultures mirrors the current repression of Soul in the world. To the degree that environmental factors continue to orphan these cultures, the world is in danger of losing their richness and wisdom.

We can understand something of the uniqueness of various countries and nations by recognizing the archetypes that predominate in their spiritual heritages. Christianity, the religion that dominates in cultures of European extraction, has developed a "World Redeemer," Ruler/Magician religion. However, the emphasis in everyday life is on the Ruler's physical, quantitative values, because the archetype of the Magician is seen as belonging only to the divine. Therefore, magic—if not directly undertaken with the Christ's aid, and hence called miracles, not magic—is often seen as evil and a sign of witchcraft or devil worship.[2] Thus the image of the Magician often inspires fear, except when the miracles invoked are technological.

At worst, the Ruler archetype (combined with the Warrior) has resulted in "manifest destiny." At best, it has resulted in a genuine concern for the good of the whole world (as exemplified, for example, by the Marshall Plan or the Peace Corps). The dominant culture in America is a subset of Western culture that differs by its simultaneous Seeker inclination, making it much more concerned with the freedom of individuals than group cohesion or caring for people.

So too, despite Western influences, Eastern cultures (many of which also are high in Ruler) still retain the emphasis in Buddhism on mind and spirit, aspiring to the nonattachment of the Sage. These are, of course, cultures that developed Buddhism in all its forms and that strive for enlightenment. They are also Warrior cultures, but the Warrior archetypes have served not the individual but the group. As one Japanese businessman put it, "Any nail that stands out is hammered in." As Western cultures have developed the virtues of individualism, Eastern cultures have developed the virtues of group solidarity.

Both African and American Indian cultures have a much greater understanding of, and appreciation for, the Magician and the Fool archetypes than either European or Eastern cultures, as is evidenced by mythology that often emphasizes the roles of the Trickster and shaman. From the Fool we learn joy and the capacity to live in the moment. From the Magician we gain a strong sense of the connection of human and natural life, and thus a respect for the ecological balance that Seeker cultures usually lack.

All major cultures, races, and nations in some way have specialized in developing different kinds of human potential. Together, they supply us with wisdom that can provide wholeness for *human* culture and an adequate understanding of the world in which we live.[3]

Honoring Our Own Cultural Traditions

It is not at all a problem that our life myths are influenced by those of our families and our ethnic heritages because, although we do not want to be totally defined by those traditions (because we want to be ourselves), it is important that we do exist within a cultural tradition and that we take responsibility for the strengths and weaknesses of that tradition.

In any family, both positive and negative attributes are passed on from generation to generation. We know, for example, that children from abusive homes are more likely to abuse their own children. Children who had alcoholic or drug-addicted parents are more likely to succumb to addiction themselves than children with more healthy parents. Children who were treated kindly and well by their parents are more likely to treat their own children well.

One great responsibility we all share is to carry on the best traditions of our families, and not to pass on those that are hurtful. Every person who comes from an abusive background and does not abuse their own children has accomplished a major heroic act—breaking a chain of suffering that may have gone back many generations. You are passing on a new, more positive tradition. Many of us do this in less spectacular ways, simply trying to be a little kinder, a little more wise, a little more effective than our parents were. Not all of us succeed, but if we do, we have helped to make the world a better place.

So, too, each of us is part of other traditions and carries responsibility within them. We are part of a gender group, a racial group, a region, a community, a nation, and if we are of immigrant stock, of our country of origin. We have the same relationship to each of these as we do to our families. Our challenge is to conserve what is best in our gender, our racial, ethnic, or other cultural heritage, and to change, at least in our own lives, what is not so good.

We make that change by taking our journeys and becoming different. In so doing, we not only transform our own lives, but make a contribution—however small—to transforming the groups of which we are a part. An example of this is religion. Perhaps you come from a fundamentalist Christian heritage, but have left it because you disagree with many of its beliefs. You may not believe, for instance, that Buddhists or Hindus are going to hell unless they take Jesus as their personal savior. You may believe that this places you outside the group.

Your Cultural Heritage

1. What of your family, ethnic, racial, political, and/or religious heritage do you honor and want to continue in your own life and pass along to the next generation?

2. What might you wish to change? What do you want to do differently?

But really, you are as much a part of the Christian tradition as Fundamentalists are. You can be in that tradition and believe any number of things. Whether or not you see yourself as remaining in the Christian tradition, the change in your theology ultimately casts a vote for change in the collective theology. If you realize that, you can also feel free to honor and cherish what is still life-giving to you in the tradition.

The same is true for Judaism, Buddhism, Hinduism—whatever your religion of origin might be. The same is true of atheism. The same is true of socialism, capitalism, conservatism, or liberalism. It is also true for our participation in the American tradition, the Russian tradition, the Afro-American tradition, the tradition of our region or neighborhood, or in the place where we work. It is true for heterosexuals, bisexuals, lesbians, and gay males. It is true for men and women.

When we take our journeys and come back to share what we have learned, we help transform much more than our own lives. Inevitably, we find others like ourselves who have found similar truths. We are lonely only when we are conforming or hiding and not sharing what we know with others. When we have the courage to be who we are—to see what we see, know what we know, and act on that knowledge—we can find others like ourselves. And then together we can begin creating new worlds.

Conserving Endangered Values and Wisdom

If we are smart, we will also learn from other traditions and other people's journeys, rather than waste precious time asserting superiority over them or being angry at them for how they see the world. Right now the lack of appreciation of various cultural traditions threatens the annihilation of important human insights. For instance, Anne Wilson Schaef, in *Women's Reality,* writes about how what she calls "white male society" places a great premium on clock time, and being "on time." She notes that the further a group is from subscribing to this (and other such) values, the more punished they are by the dominant culture.

Women, she notes, tend to have more appreciation than men for process time, partly because raising children requires an understanding of process: any working mother who has internalized the value that she has to feed her family by six o'clock will have the experience of trying to make dinner with a two-year-old holding on to her leg, until she learns to attend first to the feeling needs of her child, and then in due time to its feeding.

Schaef goes on to talk about native Americans as the group in America holding the most divergent attitudes toward time and other issues, and also the group most punished by white male authorities. She tells how the Bureau of Indian Affairs would make an agreement to hold a meeting with a particular Indian tribe for a particular day and time and would get there "on time." The Indians, however, might come several days "late." Yet in their view of time, they were completely "on time." They had been praying and dancing for days, waiting for the moment to be right. And when it felt clear and right to hold the meeting, they showed up—on time, not in a clock sense, but in a deeper process sense.

The great danger today, not just about time but about any number of matters, is that the dominant culture in most societies tends to be so convinced of its superiority to all others, and so sublimely oblivious to the effect of its attitudes, that the human virtues that have been cultivated and developed by other cultures or subcultures die out and are being lost (just as certain species are endangered). This happens not directly, but indirectly. The penalties are so great for deviance from the dominant culture (not being taken seriously; being seen as inferior, naive, unsophisticated, and in need of development; unable to even make a living without assimilating the dominant customs and values) that people cannot withstand them. In the United States, for example, living up to the white, male, European ideal is fairly consistently rewarded (whether one is female, Black, Indian), while acting out of another tradition is systematically (although subtly) punished. The process is largely an unconscious one. No one means to wipe out the accomplishments and values of whole cultures; it is just that the assumption of superiority by the dominant culture is so strong, it never occurs to them to do anything else.

We cannot ask people in the traditions that are dying to preserve them because if they do so, they are punished. Individuals need the freedom of opportunity and choice. But in making this possible, we will all lose if we do not find a way to conserve the traditions of cultures that are at present being destroyed.

One way is for each of us to cherish and conserve those values that fit for us in other traditions and our own. As the walls come down between nations and cultures, it no longer makes sense to keep people in reservations, ghettos, and separate schools or spheres. That was the order of another time. That was the time when only Italians ate pasta, Asians ate rice, and WASPS ate steak and potatoes. Just as our palates benefit from being able to enjoy pasta, rice, yogurt, bagels, steak, potatoes, curry, and any number of other great foods from a variety of cultures, we can choose to hold on to the best of each tradition, rather than assuming that pasta is inferior to steak!

I am not an American Indian, but I hold the value of finding the "right time," even if in a clock-oriented society I cannot always stay entirely true to this value. I can continue to learn from an Indian ecological sense of balance with the earth and to open more to loving and valuing that very Mother Earth without whom I would not exist. I am not Black, but I can consciously strive to learn from the relational, playful, improvisational, and soulful elements of Black culture, and I do so for my own benefit. However, I am also aware that doing so helps maintain and conserve elements of Black culture that in my eyes are superior to my own.

I am also a career woman, and in many ways my life is similar to many men's, but I can also hold the value of an ancient kind of feminine wisdom and attempt to stay grounded in my own rhythm as a woman—even if in doing so, what I do seems somewhat unconventional. If tomorrow white male cultural strengths were in danger of being lost, I would strive to hold to them as well, and even without that threat, now hold to many of those values.

To benefit from the smorgasbord of cultural richness available in a world made small and available by the explosion of knowledge and media connections, however, we need to give up the illusion that any of us is superior to anyone else.

Heroism for this age necessarily honors diversity because it recognizes that each individual and each culture has a vital, important piece of the puzzle, but no individual or culture has them all. We need each other. Nature, God, the universe did not make a mistake in making some of us brown and some white, some male and some female, some heterosexual and some gay and lesbian. The goal is not to have one group declare its superiority and shape up the rest.

It is also important that in incorporating elements from cultures other than our own, we do not do so as imperialists. In adopting qualities from any culture, it is important to do so with respect. One of the Ten Commandments tells us to honor our father and our mother, and many native cultures have traditions of honoring the ancestors. All cultures are our ancestors insofar as they have contributed to the riches of the cultures we know. This respect requires collective political action, as well as individual kindness and respect, to move us toward a world in which no people are disregarded or disadvantaged because of their race, gender, or cultural heritage.

When we take our journeys and fully realize our potential as individuals and cultures, and when we humbly open to learn from each other, we will be able to solve the great problems of our times. This is the heroic challenge before humanity today. The old order, indeed, is dead. In fact, we are all experiencing metamorphosis—death and rebirth—so that we can really love and value one another. This begins with holding on to the best of what was generated in the previous age, and allowing cross-fertilization of these many traditions and wisdoms so that their synergy will produce something even greater than what came before.

Archetypes, Culture, and Wholeness

There is a further kind of wholeness, beyond androgyny, for which we do not have an adequate name. The closest I can come is to be cosmopolitan, or a citizen of the world. However, one cannot get there by fleeing from one's own culture—just as one cannot achieve androgyny by rejecting one's own gender identification. This requires the ability to be fully within one's own culture, to appreciate its strengths and values and to take responsibility for its weaknesses. This means really accepting that we each live within a tradition and we are part of that tradition whether we approve of it or not. We had best make peace with that tradition, and if there are parts of it of which we disapprove, we better act to change those aspects by changing our own lives.

When we are willing to be part of our own culture in this honest way, we can then be open to learning from other cultures. This means moving beyond seeing one's own culture as either superior or inferior to another. It is merely where we sit that defines so much of who we are. This does not make it better or worse. From this stance, we do not need to put down another culture or our own, and we can learn from the wisdom other cultures can bring.

In the inner realm of our psyches, this also means we can make a place for the part of us that does know the wisdom that has been better developed by a culture other than our own. For example, a white male of European extraction may find he has within him a number of men and women of different races. One such man told me of the Japanese gardener he had within him who shared his wisdom and peace with him. Another talked of having a Black man within who taught him to loosen up, relax, and enjoy life. Still another talked of the old American Indian woman who taught him to connect with the earth.

Similarly, an Afro-American woman may have within her a white European male who coaches her on how to succeed in a white male world, a Chinese woman who encourages her to stop and meditate and open up to inner wisdom, and a native American Medicine Man who counsels her on how to heal herself and others.

Of course, it is important to recognize that these archetypal figures in our heads (which are powerful presences behind the stereotypes that often so limit us) do not correspond to any actual people around us. We may learn from them to increase our own wholeness, but we cannot assume that the Black (or white) inside our heads speaks for, or is in any way typical of, the Black (or white) people we know. This is equally true of any other grouping. If the figure in our heads is only a stereotype, it will not empower us. If it is an archetype, it will strengthen and teach us, but we must not generalize to other human beings on the basis of it.

Other Cultures

1. What qualities, traditions, or ways of doing or thinking do you admire in cultural, family, and/or religious traditions other than your own?

2. Which of these might you want to incorporate into your own life?

Women often get mad at the men around them because they have a patriarchal male in their heads telling them they are inadequate. It is always important to take a moment to see if the real men around you have those attitudes and act in those ways or if you are projecting. Similarly, men often fear women because of the inner woman seducing them into experiencing Eros. If they project this inner anima figure onto a woman, she may seem immensely powerful—and both attractive and menacing in that power. It is important for men to take a moment to disengage from that projection to see what is actually true about the women around them.

So, too, the images Europeans carry around of Asians can define their experience of them, unless they take pains to differentiate the inner archetypal image from the real person with whom they are interacting—and so Asians with Europeans, blacks with whites, whites with blacks, Hispanics with Anglos, Anglos with Hispanics. This is also true of the French and the English, the Germans and the Italians, the Russians and the Hungarians. Within the United States, it is true of Texans and New Yorkers.

Stereotypes limit. Archetypes are sources of power and wisdom. We need to move beyond limiting stereotypes to experience the empowering archetypes beneath them. Different countries, races, and geographical areas often have archetypes associated with them, and these archetypes all contribute to our greater wholeness and complexity. But these archetypes do not define individuals within those cultures. If we can keep this balance, we can both benefit from the diversity of different archetypal cultural traditions and retain the individual ability of people within them to demonstrate many different attributes, approaches, and gifts.

The great trick to experiencing wholeness is to let go of the illusion that any of us is either superior or inferior and to fully allow ourselves to be who we are—our gender, our culture, our individual selves—without that preventing us from also learning from and incorporating the wisdom of others. It also means not getting bamboozled by other people who think they are superior or inferior to us, because such notions always lead to unauthentic lives. They lead to a mental state in which we are either afraid to be who we are or afraid to deviate from a limited notion of what that means.

To understand how the archetypes operate in your life, it is important to understand your own context—including your life stage, your gender, your family tradition, your racial or cultural tradition, and archetypes constellated by national or global events, or the immediate context in your home, work, or community life. The diagram on page 286 is provided for you to make notes about the various archetypal energies that are currently active either within your own psyche or in cultural context.

The great trick to experiencing wholeness is to let go of the illusion that any of us is either superior or inferior.

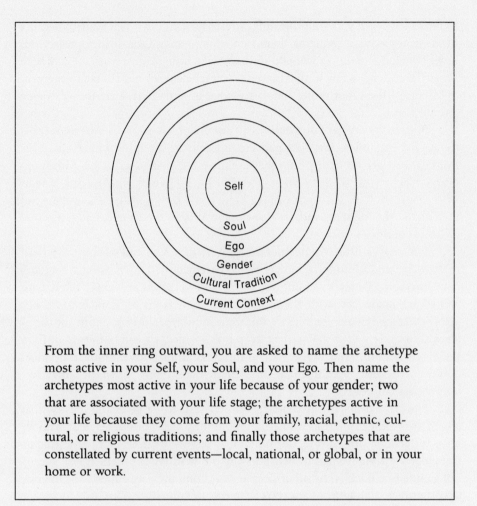

From the inner ring outward, you are asked to name the archetype most active in your Self, your Soul, and your Ego. Then name the archetypes most active in your life because of your gender; two that are associated with your life stage; the archetypes active in your life because they come from your family, racial, ethnic, cultural, or religious traditions; and finally those archetypes that are constellated by current events—local, national, or global, or in your home or work.

Archetypal Qualities of Cultures

You may want to use this chart to identify the archetypal qualities in your own cultural heritages. Note that these are simplifications, and that most cultures provide a mixture of these qualities, or variations on the ones described here. For many cultures—and families—you will be able to identify one archetype each out of the categories Ego, Soul, and Self, just as you can for individuals. You may also find that your cultural heritage has either a masculine or a feminine cast to it.

Archetypal Qualities of Cultures

Innocent
: Authorities honored and responsible for protecting and caring for others. High premium on following rules and traditions, and the value is placed upon the culture or group good, not on individual good. Indeed, individuals are expected to conform and do things right. At worst, deviance or rule breaking is severely punished. At best, deviance and rule breakers are seen as in need of help, and authorities patiently try to enlist more correct behavior.

Orphan
: Very equalitarian, people banding against oppression, or for help in hard times, illness, poverty, or other suffering. People feel very fragile. At best, people feel victimized, but at best help each other. At worst, they victimize each other.

Caregiver
: Everyone is expected to give unselfishly with no thought to their own welfare. At best, this works, and everyone is very well cared for. At worse, everyone gives and gives, and no one gets what they want because no one can ask for what they want—it would seem selfish! Or (as in enabling cultures) no one wants to admit some truth about their situation.

Warrior
: Demanding, disciplined, hardworking, stoic cultures with a high premium on competitiveness. At best, they band together to fight others. At worst, things break down into a brawl.

Seeker
: Very atomistic, individualistic. No one takes much responsibility for each other, but everyone has a right to "life, liberty, and the pursuit of happiness." At best, individuals find themselves. At worst, they are all just very lonely and on their own.

Destroyer
: The culture bands together out of a mutual desire to destroy something or someone. People are motivated to hang together out of a shared belief that something must go. At best, this can be a crusader, rebel group, unified against evil. At worst, if there is no positive outlet for this anger, it turns inward. People destroy themselves with violence, alcohol, drugs.

Lover
: Very egalitarian, passionate, and intense cultures, which place high value on artistic expression, personal relationships, and living well. There is high drama, intensity, concern with quality of life. At best, people feel good and have deep relationships, and life is lovely. At worst, peace is shattered by jealousy, bickering, or gossip, or undermined by submerged, unacknowledged conflict.

Creator
: Highly visionary, innovative cultures in which the primary concern is what we are building together (as with utopian experiments). At best, the vision is

actualized in some way. At worst, the desolation of the moment is excused by the great vision to be realized some very illusive, future day.

Ruler

Emphasis on governing and leading others, setting a good example in all one's deeds. Often these cultures place great value on the attainment of material wealth as a sign of merit. At best, this can be the highest and most responsible form of noblesse oblige, where the haves help the have-nots in a gracious, statesmanlike or stateswomanlike way. At worst, it is smug, snobbish, and imperialistic.

Magician

Emphasis on empowering self and others, in a context of mutuality, between self and other, humankind and nature. At best, transformative action is rooted in connectedness and shared humility. At worst, it becomes manipulative and out of balance, and ego-driven; or it becomes impotent because of a failure to deal adequately with visions different from one's own or to recognize the changing needs of changing times.

Sage

High valuation on high-mindedness, authority earned by the attainment of greater wisdom or expertise, little need for innovation, for the focus is on the eternal verities. At best, these are refined, uplifting cultures, which may even help individuals within them attain great wisdom. At worst, they are precious, disconnected from life, stultifying of individual initiative, and resistant to change.

Fool

Cultures with emphasis on experience, being fully alive for its own sake. These are not highly motivated by achievement or material acquisitions, but rather by enjoyment, play, and the fulfillment in the moment itself. Challenges are undertaken because they would be fun. At best, such cultures may embody the highest level of existence: the experience of ecstasy in life itself, with little need for security or achievement. At worst, they are poor, prone to drug use, and nothing gets done.

Female

Egalitarian, cooperative, receptive, with high emphasis on living in process with each other and the natural world. At best, these are empowering, nurturing, harmonious cultures, which allow for a wide range of behaviors as long as they are open to be talked about and worked through. At worst, conflict is repressed, and conformity is enforced through gossip and a network of shame and abandonment.

Male

Hierarchical, competitive, aggressive, with an emphasis on achievement and mastery. At best, these teach courage, discipline, and the maintenance of high standards in the interest of the common good. At worst, they are unfeeling, exploitative, imperialistic, and destructive to the earth.

Claiming Your Life Myth

Finding the great story that informs your life is a sacred task. To know your story is to know who you are. It is not to be taken lightly, although it does not have to be unduly heavy either. (Indeed, creativity comes more easily with a good dose of Fool!) If you know your own great story, you are much less likely to sell yourself short, to get confused by the inessential, or to let others manipulate you or talk you into being less than you could be.

For most of our lives, many of us feel as if we are traveling without a map. We know we're moving, but we have no real sense of where we have been, where we are, or where we are headed. The model provided in this book provides a general map for the journey, but it is a generic map, not one tailored to your individual life. Your own great story will very likely have one or two dominant archetypes, and very definitely will include many different archetypal elements, but the way you put them together will be unique—and your own.

Jean Houston, in *The Search for the Beloved: Journeys in Sacred Psychology,* stresses the importance of writing one's own great story as a way of participating consciously in the "new story" that "is beginning to emerge in our time." Houston's book includes very helpful exercises for writing one's great story, and it stresses the importance of writing the story mythically. She suggests first writing one's autobiographical story in a normal way and then translating it into mythic language. She includes the following example of the same story written first "existentially" and then as myth:

Well, I was born into an average family. My mother was a schoolteacher and my father worked as a conductor on the railroad. As the youngest child, nobody paid much attention to me. My mom was away working all day and my dad was away for days at a time.

Identifying your own great story (or stories) helps you to find something of your own specialness in a way that helps you understand the significance of your own life. No one but you can tell this story because you are the only one who knows what you are here to do or to learn.

The same story is then translated:

> Once upon a time, there was a very special child, born with a promise and a light within him that was so bright that it blinded all others and they did not dare to look at him. Even his mother, who knew of the Ways Things Work, and his father, who officiated on Caravans to Distant Realms, could not see him.[1]

You do not have to be comfortable with writing in this way to find your great story. Some people may do best writing the story in a more ordinary way, others telling it to friends, and still others painting or drawing it, or expressing it in movement, dance, or drama. Sometimes the form that beckons is as important for telling you something important about yourself as the content of the story itself. More accurately, the process and the content of your great story are not really separable. You find yourself in both.

Your Life Story/Your Life Myth (I)

1. Write your life story in an ordinary narrative way. You might want to employ the insights you have gained in doing the exercises in the preceding chapters. Think, for example, about the archetypes active at different ages; consider the impact of your gender and culture, the balance between what you have been taught to be, what you want to be, and the deepest truth about your life purpose.

2. Then write it in mythic language as a story of your heroic journey. (Alternatively, express your story in mythic and heroic images through art, dance, drama, or music.)

Finding Your Dominant Myth

The best way to determine your dominant myth is to write or otherwise express your life story—as honestly as you know how—and then notice its underlying plot structure. You can do this by comparing the basic plot of your autobiography with the chart of archetypal stories included on the next page.

Archetypes and Their Stories

Innocent	Paradise lost but faith retained; paradise regained.
Orphan	Paradise lost, resulting despair and alienation; gives up hope of paradise; and works with others to create better conditions in world as it is.
Warrior	Goes on journey; confronts and slays dragon; rescues victim.
Caregiver	Sacrifices and does what others ask; feels maimed or is manipulative of others; gains the capacity to choose to live as feels right and life-enriching.
Seeker	Feels alienated in community by perceived pressure to conform; goes off on journey alone; finds treasure of autonomy and vocation; finds real family and home.
Lover	Yearns to love; finds love; separated from love, and (in tragedy) dies or (in comedy) is reunited with loved one.
Destroyer	Experiences great loss and pain; loses illusions and inauthentic patterns; faces death and learns to make death an ally.
Creator	Discovers true self; explores ways of creating a life which facilitates the expression of that self.
Ruler	Is wounded and kingdom is a wasteland; takes responsibility for kingdom and own woundedness; kingdom is restored to fertility, harmony, and peace.
Magician	Overcomes debilitating illness; through healing and transforming self, learns to heal and transform others; experiences destructive effects of hubris or insecurity; learns to align will with that of universe.
Sage	Seeks truth through losing self; recognizes own subjectivity; affirms that subjectivity; experiences transcendent truth.
Fool	Lives for pleasure but without rootedness in self, community, or cosmos; learns to commit and bond with people, nature, universe; is able to trust the process and live in harmony with universe; finds joy.

Perhaps you see that your story is one of constant heartbreak, disappointment, or victimization. It should be obvious to you that your formative myth is a variation on the Orphan plot. If it is the record of challenges overcome or battles fought and won (or lost), it is a variation on the Warrior plot. If you find yourself writing about how you sacrificed for others, it is a variation on the Caregiver plot. If it is a search for love, or truth, or answers, you are in some version of the Seeker plot. And so on. (You may find that your story combines major elements of several archetypes.)

The danger of not knowing one's life myth is that it is possible to be continually judging oneself by the standard of a journey that is not one's own. For example, someone whose compelling myth is that of the Lover may continue to be apologetic about his or her failure to achieve great feats, since most people in our culture measure themselves against the yardstick of the myth of the Warrior and the Ruler. Someone whose informing myth *is* the Ruler, however, may feel inadequate for failing to live simply in the moment, that is, to be a Fool.

People often feel a great sense of relief after they write their story and find their informing myth, since they see that what they have been doing is, in fact, just right for them. However, not everyone feels this way. When people identify the plot they have been living, they may suddenly realize that they are possessed or imprisoned—not liberated—by this story and its informing archetype. One way of talking about this is to see such a myth as one's "script."

Recognizing Your Script

Each of us has a script that has been devised in childhood as a response to what others told you about what your abilities and options were. Transactional Analysis tells us that we can actually have a "script" and a "counterscript"—the result of our unconscious rebellion against our scripting. A great moment of liberation comes when we recognize our scripts and can see if they breed positive results.[2]

Such scripts are heavily determined by outside influences because they are related to our initial accommodation to the world outside ourselves. If, for instance, our parents named us after a famous general or cowboy, or if they always bought us guns and toy soldiers, we are likely to identify with the Warrior; if they bought us dolls and told us what a great mommy we would make, we are likely to identify with the Caregiver.

The script is often a compensation for some early wounding. We try to come up with a plot for our lives that will keep us safer and less vulnerable to pain. As we have seen, the wounding is frequently the negative or limiting messages we get about ourselves or our possibilities. Such messages can refer to our gender, our race, our size or appearance, our energy level and temperament, or anything at all about us. As long as we unconsciously and literally enact the script, we intensify the wounding because most scripts, taken literally, hurt us by interfering with our wholeness. They reflect an underlying fear that unless we act according to this script, we will not survive.

Yet when the script is read as myth or metaphor, the means for healing that wound is also embedded in that script. Thus the psychological function of our script is to heal us of our primary wounding so that we may go on to express our true story. When we recognize that scripts have an archetype embedded in them, we can understand that most of us are better off if we can not so much fight our scripts as simply recognize them and take them to a higher level.

It is often useful to imagine that you chose your parents, your race, your sex, and your general environmental circumstances because of something you needed or wanted to give and/or learn. When looked at in this way, we can take some responsibility for choosing a situation that would provide us with the script we needed in our early life. It's like a puzzle we need to solve before we can go on to express our true selves in the world.

Your Script

1. Who have you been scripted to be?

2. How does this script limit your life?

3. What might be the gift or lesson in your script?

What might initially be a limiting, confining, or even destructive script is transformed when we see the archetype or archetypes embedded in it. Often the transformation requires the ability to interpret scripts metaphorically, not literally. For instance, a woman with the Cinderella script might initially be unable to act on in her own behalf since she is always waiting for her prince to come. When she recognizes her script, she can look for the metaphorical wisdom encoded in this plot. In fact, her script encodes in symbolic form exactly what she needs to do: to let her own animus come and rescue her. In her case, it is her animus that can help her learn to function in the world and to provide for herself.

If your story seems to be a confining myth to you, you may want to reinterpret what the myth *could* mean to you. The woman with Cinderella plot could revise her story so that instead of always waiting for her prince to come, she integrated the prince within and found her own palace. In time, when she acts on this new knowledge, her wound will be healed, and she will be ready to write a new and even more empowering story.

If your story seems to be a confining myth to you, you may want to reinterpret what the myth could mean to you.

Your Life Story (II)

1. What was the most empowering thing anyone ever told you about yourself?

2. Who and what has most inspired you? Has your life been altered because of this person, idea, or experience?

3. What brings you real pleasure and satisfaction? What are you good at? What do you really love to do?

4. Write your life story in the form of an obituary that will describe the essential truth of your life. It is not necessary to write what you think your obituary will say. Write what it would say if you fulfilled your potential in every area of life—personal and spiritual as well as professional. What would it say if you lived your life fully and on your deathbed had no regrets?

5. What archetypes have been active in your life? What archetypes would have to be active in your life for you to fulfill your potential?

Many people find that they have two major stories active at the same time: a script and a deeper, more empowering myth. This was actually the case with the woman who identified with Cinderella. At one level, she had been waiting for her prince to come. At another level, she had been occupying herself by painting, and as she took her "Soul journey," her paintings took on a deeper quality and had a transformative effect on others. At this level, she was a potential Magician, but that potential could not be actualized until she broke the spell that kept her looking for the masculine only outside herself. Then she was able to use her feminine nature to paint well and her masculine nature to sell her work. We see this pattern often in people as they find their deeper myth. The script has kept them busy but has frequently seemed to cripple them. All the time they were getting just the education they needed to be able to act out their deeper story.

Although it would be ideal to know our own myth once and for all, it is unlikely that we will do so, for our understanding of our life tasks and the attendant life story is an evolving one—and one that is usually greatly affected by what is on top for us during the specific chronological period during which we're writing.

As the Ruler who holds on to the liberating "new truth" too long, thereby becoming an ogre tyrant, any of us who gets too attached to any one version of our own story, or is living out an unexamined story, needs the renewal that comes from reconsidering that story in the light of current realities. It is wise, therefore, to update your myth frequently to see that the plot you are living is still a useful and enlivening one.

Finding a New Story—A Dialectical Process

David Feinstein and Stanley Krippner, who have written a whole book on finding your great story (*Personal Mythology: The Psychology of Your Evolving Self*), outline a process for identifying the ways that your current mythology might be limiting you and for expanding your mythology so that it becomes a liberating force in your life. Actually, it is a little like outgrowing old clothes. At one time, they were new and attractive and they fit. But little by little, we grow and outgrow them, as they also become tired, worn, or out of date (and incongruous with the needs and attitudes of the time in which we are living).

In Feinstein and Krippner's five-stage model, we first "recognize when a guiding myth is no longer an ally." We recognize the ways our myth is limiting us and consciously feel the pain engendered by our holding on to a guiding myth that is inadequate for the time in which we find ourselves. The second stage is to bring "the roots of mythic conflict into focus." "Even before you consciously recognize the shortcomings of an old myth, your psyche is usually generating a countermyth to compensate for its limitations." Like dreams, these countermyths have a "wish-fulfillment" quality. "But like dreams, countermyths are often removed from the requirements of the real world."

Thus, the new myth may emerge in fantasies or daydreams that seem escapist. Feinstein and Krippner provide a series of exercises to crystalize both the limiting and the emerging myth. Then in the third stage, one conceives "a unifying mythic vision." "Mythological development proceeds as a dialectic in which the old myth is the thesis, the countermyth is the antithesis, and a new myth that represents the resolution of the two is the synthesis. As a countermyth develops, it competes with the prevailing myth to dominate perceptions and to guide behavior. Their dialectical struggle may resemble a sort of 'natural selection' within the psyche, a 'survival of the fittest' element of each myth of optimal growth and adjustment." The fourth stage involves moving from "vision to commitment" and the final, and fifth stage, "weaving a renewed mythology into daily life."

The process Feinstein and Krippner describe is also a side product of the journey. The development of the Ego requires us to develop and act out our formative story. When we experience initiation, however, that story begins to fail us. It is simply not adequate to guiding us in the new territory we have entered. For

---

Finding a New Story

1. Examine the myths or stories you have written and determine whether they enliven or interfere with your life.

2. If there are parts of these myths or stories you wish to change, do so. Begin working on a countermyth, remembering that the key to your countermyth will be found in your fantasies.

3. See if you can integrate the best of these two myths or stories.

---

a long time, we feel conflicted, cursed with an inner struggle between two conflicting stories, until there is some resolution. At this point, we may not yet have any conscious knowledge of what the reconciliation is; we may simply feel a void where the struggle used to be. It is often by opening to watch our actions that we discover what the resolution is. Only later do we consciously commit to manifesting this new story in our lives. But when we do, our lives develop a mythic quality.[3]

Entering the Mythic Realm

It is important to distinguish this mythic quality from inflation. Inflation is also a kind of archetypal possession, but unlike a script, in some way we know it. We are not so much oblivious to the archetype's influence in our lives as we are identifying with the archetype itself. This gives our lives a larger-than-life quality, but it ultimately is not good for us. What is happening is that an archetype is possessing us (in positive or negative form—or even in both). The most extreme case of this is in delusion, when someone thinks he or she is Jesus Christ incarnate, for instance.

The difference between living a great story—as inflation—and living your own story is that in the latter, it is genuinely your own story that you are living. This makes you feel deeply satisfied and that there is meaning in your life. It is. not inflation for Jesus Christ to feel like Jesus Christ. It is *not* inflation for me to be me, and you to be you, and it is not inflation to allow an archetype to be expressed *through* you, if you know you are not that archetype.

If you feel grandiose, better than others, or worthless, insignificant or bad, you may be succumbing to some kind of inflation. You are possessed by the positive or negative forms of the archetype. When we are living our own great story, it may be exhilarating in some ways, but there is also always an "of course" quality to it. It is just ourselves that we are being, so it just feels right.

Often the biggest obstacle to finding one's own true story and true work is the fear that the work will be either too big or too insignificant. That is, what if my work is a big work? Maybe I'm not adequate to it. Or what if my work is sweeping floors? I want more success in the world than that. Many times we are blocked from finding our true story because of these "too much, too little" fears. However there is no way to be happy except to live out our own deep, great story. No life, no matter how successful and exciting it might be, will make you happy if it is not really your life. And no life will make you miserable if it is genuinely your own. In a day-to-day way, we live out our story—whether or not we ever write it—as we "follow our bliss," rather than simply doing what is expected or what seems, on the surface, to guarantee success.

The urge to identify our own unique life tasks comes initially from a desire to claim our own individual lives. However, as we embark upon this journey of discovery, we learn that human beings do not really journey alone. Each of our individual journeys is intimately interwoven with the journeys of our friends, our families, our co-workers, our contemporaries, our gender, our culture. Every step we take in becoming more fully ourselves has ripple effects that affect others, just as the steps they take affect us. Finding genuine meaning in our lives, then, contributes to the renewal of the kingdom.

We can succumb to the prevailing "delusion of insignificance" that is the curse of our times, or we can daily claim our own lives and in doing so transform our worlds. The responsibility embedded in this knowledge is our legacy from all the heroes who have come before. The future we face may be a nightmare or a miracle. The choice is ours.

There is no way to be happy except to live out your own deep, great story.

Appendix:
The Heroic Myth Index
(Form E)

The Heroic Myth Index (HMI) is designed to help people better understand themselves and others by identifying the different archetypes active in their lives. Individuals taking the inventory receive a numerical score indicating their degree of identification with the twelve archetypes described in this book. All twelve archetypes are valuable, and each brings with it a special gift. Each has an important contribution to make in our lives. None is better or worse. Hence, there are no right or wrong answers.

Heroic Myth Index (Form E)

Name (optional): _____ Date: _____

Age: _____ Occupation: _____ Gender: _____

Race: _____

Circle your highest completed grade or degree:

11th Grade   12th Grade   High School   A.A.   B.A./B.S.   M.A./M.S.   Ph.D

Directions

A.   Please indicate how often you agree with each statement as descriptive of you by writing in the blank beside the statement number.
  1 = <u>Almost never</u> descriptive of me
  2 = <u>Rarely</u> descriptive of me
  3 = <u>Sometimes</u> descriptive of me
  4 = <u>Usually</u> descriptive of me
  5 = <u>Almost always</u> descriptive of me

B.   Work as quickly as is comfortable; your first reaction is often the best indicator.

C.   Please *do not skip any items,* since doing so might invalidate your results. If you're unsure, just make your best determination and go on.

____ 1.   I collect information without making judgments.

____ 2.   I feel disoriented by so much change in my life.

____ 3.   The process of my own self-healing enables me to help heal others.

____ 4.   I have let others down.

____ 5.   I feel safe.

____ 6.   I put fear aside and do what needs to be done.

____ 7.   I put the needs of others before my own.

| 1 = <u>Almost never</u> descriptive of me | 2 = <u>Rarely</u> descriptive of me | 3 = <u>Sometimes</u> descriptive of me | 4 = <u>Usually</u> descriptive of me | 5 = <u>Almost always</u> descriptive of me |

____ 8. I try to be authentic wherever I am.

____ 9. When life gets dull, I like to shake things up.

___10. I find satisfaction caring for others.

___11. Others see me as fun.

___12. I feel sexy.

___13. I believe that people don't really mean to hurt each other.

___14. As a child, I was neglected or victimized.

___15. Giving makes me happier than receiving.

___16. I agree with the statement, "It is better to have loved and lost than never to have loved at all."

___17. I embrace life fully.

___18. I keep a sense of perspective by taking a long-range view.

___19. I am in the process of creating my own life.

___20. I believe there are many good ways to look at the same thing.

___21. I am no longer the person I thought I was.

___22. Life is one heartache after another.

___23. Spiritual help accounts for my effectiveness.

___24. I find it easier to do for others than to do for myself.

___25. I find fulfillment through relationships.

___26. People look to me for direction.

___27. I fear those in authority.

___28. I don't take rules too seriously.

___29. I like to help people connect with one another.

___30. I feel abandoned.

___31. I have times of high accomplishment that feel effortless to me.

1 = <u>Almost never</u>	2 = <u>Rarely</u>	3 = <u>Sometimes</u>	4 = <u>Usually</u>	5 = <u>Almost always</u>
descriptive of me	descriptive of me	descriptive of me	descriptive of me	descriptive of me

___32. I have leadership qualities.

___33. I am searching for ways to improve myself.

___34. I can count on others to take care of me.

___35. I prefer to be in charge.

___36. I try to find truths behind illusions.

___37. Changing my inner thoughts changes my outer life.

___38. I develop resources, human or natural.

___39. I am willing to take personal risks in order to defend my beliefs.

___40. I can't sit back and let a wrong go by without challenging it.

___41. I strive for objectivity.

___42. My presence is often a catalyst for change.

___43. I enjoy making people laugh.

___44. I use discipline to achieve goals.

___45. I feel loving toward people in general.

___46. I am good at matching people's abilities with tasks to be done.

___47. It is essential for me to maintain my independence.

___48. I believe everyone and everything in the world are interconnected.

___49. The world is a safe place.

___50. People I've trusted have abandoned me.

___51. I feel restless.

___52. I am letting go of things that do not fit for me anymore.

___53. I like to "lighten up" people who are too serious.

___54. A little chaos is good for the soul.

___55. Sacrificing to help others has made me a better person.

___56. I am calm.

| 1 = <u>Almost never</u> | 2 = <u>Rarely</u> | 3 = <u>Sometimes</u> | 4 = <u>Usually</u> | 5 = <u>Almost always</u> |
| descriptive of me | descriptive of me | descriptive of me | descriptive of me | descriptive of me |

___57. I stand up to offensive people.

___58. I like to transform situations.

___59. The key to success in all aspects of life is discipline.

___60. Inspiration comes easily to me.

___61. I do not live up to my expectations for myself.

___62. I have a sense that a better world awaits me somewhere.

___63. I assume that people I meet are trustworthy.

___64. I am experimenting with turning my dreams into realities.

___65. I know my needs will be provided for.

___66. I feel like breaking something.

___67. I try to manage situations with the good of all in mind.

___68. I have a hard time saying no.

___69. I have a lot more great ideas than I have time to act on them.

___70. I am looking for greener pastures.

___71. Important people in my life have let me down.

___72. The act of looking for something is as important to me as finding it.

| 1 = Almost never descriptive of me | 2 = Rarely descriptive of me | 3 = Sometimes descriptive of me | 4 = Usually descriptive of me | 5 = Almost always descriptive of me |

Scoring Directions

Under the name of each archetype are six blanks with numbers corresponding to the questions on the HMI. Transfer your responses (1–5) to the columns below. For example, if your answer to question 17 was 5 ("Almost always"), put a 5 in the blank next to 17, the first number in the column under "Innocent." When you have put a number in each blank, then add up the columns. Your total score for each archetype will be between 6 and 30.

When you have completed scoring the instrument, you may wish to graph your scores on the pie chart on page 23 to get a visual representation of your particular score pattern.

Innocent	Orphan	Warrior	Caregiver	Seeker	Lover
5 _____	14 _____	6 _____	7 _____	33 _____	12 _____
13 _____	22 _____	39 _____	10 _____	47 _____	16 _____
34 _____	27 _____	40 _____	15 _____	51 _____	17 _____
49 _____	30 _____	44 _____	24 _____	62 _____	25 _____
63 _____	50 _____	57 _____	55 _____	70 _____	29 _____
65 _____	71 _____	59 _____	68 _____	72 _____	45 _____
Total _____	_____	_____	_____	_____	_____

Destroyer	Creator	Magician	Ruler	Sage	Fool
2 _____	8 _____	3 _____	26 _____	1 _____	9 _____
4 _____	19 _____	23 _____	32 _____	18 _____	11 _____
21 _____	31 _____	37 _____	35 _____	20 _____	28 _____
52 _____	60 _____	42 _____	38 _____	36 _____	43 _____
61 _____	64 _____	48 _____	46 _____	41 _____	53 _____
66 _____	69 _____	58 _____	67 _____	56 _____	54 _____
Total _____	_____	_____	_____	_____	_____

Understanding Your HMI Results

Remember that no archetype is any "better" or "worse" than any other; each has its own characteristics, gift, and lesson. Notice your highest scores. These indicate archetypes that, based on your HMI scores, would be expected to be very active in your life. Then notice your lowest score or scores (especially those under fifteen). These are archetypes that you are currently choosing to repress or ignore. If the score moves toward the fifteen-and-under range, you may have an aversion to the archetype either because (1) you have overdone it in the past and have developed the equivalent of an "allergy" or (2) you do not approve of it and hence do not allow yourself to express (or notice its expression) in your life.

If the former is the case, you may want to stay away from that archetype; if the latter, the archetype or archetypes that you have not allowed expression may represent alter ego or shadow qualities in you that others may be more aware of than you yourself. Reclaiming these disowned parts of yourself gives you more choices for responding to situations and makes it less likely that you will be blindsided by inadvertent expressions of the less positive attributes of the archetype. If you allow full expression of the archetype, it's likely that its expression will be in a more positive form and that it will provide increased energy and variety in your life.

You may wish to transfer your scores on each archetype to the box provided in each of the archetypal chapters in Parts II to IV. As you read about each archetype, keep in mind your score, and ask yourself if what you are reading fits in with what you know about yourself and the archetype. Throughout the book, boxes are provided that allow you to interpret your HMI scores in different contexts. For example, in "How to Use This Book" (p. 13), you have the opportunity to chart your scores on a pie chart, and in the introduction to Part I (p. 29), you are asked to graph your scores in ways that help you easily see the relative weight of the archetypes related to Ego, Soul, or Self in your life.

No test knows more about you than you do. If you think the archetype is either more or less active in your life than your score on the instrument indicates, adjust the score accordingly.

Notes

Introduction

1. James Hillman's idea is that all our "pathologies" are calls from the gods—including all mental and emotional illness. For more information on this key point, see *Re-Visioning Psychology* (New York: Harper & Row, 1975), 57–112, which is a classic post-Jungian text of archetypal psychology. I have extended the concept to include problems of all kinds, not just pathologies per se.

2. See Joseph Campbell, *The Hero with a Thousand Faces* (Princeton: Princeton Univ. Press, 1949) and Carol S. Pearson and Katherine Pope, *The Female Hero in American and British Literature* (New York: Bowker Book Co., 1981). Campbell's stages are similar: departure, initiation, return.

3. This way of formulating the workings of the archetypes was first articulated by Sharon V. Seivert in our jointly authored publication, *Heroes at Work,* a workbook that is available through Meristem.

Chapter Two: The Ego: Protecting the Inner Child

1. Readers unfamiliar with these terms might consult Sigmund Freud, *The Ego and the Id,* trans. Joan Riviere (New York: W. W. Norton, 1960); Calvin S. Hall, *A Primer of Freudian Psychology* (New York: New American Library, 1954); or Theodore Lidz, *The Person: His Development Throughout the Life Cycle* (New York: Basic Books, 1968). For an excellent discussion of a Jungian perspective on Ego, see Edward F. Edinger, *Ego and Archetype: Individuation and the Religious Function of the Psyche* (New York: Penguin, 1973).

2. Sometimes, as with mental or emotional illness, we are sent on our Soul journeys into the unconscious against our wills and without adequate Ego preparation. Then the journey is too dangerous to do alone. It is essential to have a trained professional as a guide on the path.

Chapter Three: The Soul: Entering the Mysteries

1. See James Hillman, *Re-Visioning Psychology* and *Archetypal Psychology: A Brief Account* (Dallas: Spring Publications, 1985) for a more complete discussion of Soul and the distinction between Soul and Spirit.

2. Esther Harding, *Women's Mysteries: Ancient and Modern* (New York: Harper & Row, 1971), 1.

3. Titus Burckhardt, *Alchemy: Science of the Cosmo, Science of the Soul* (Worcester, England: Element Press, 1987), 11–33.

4. June Singer, in *The Unholy Bible: a Psychological Interpretation of William Blake* (New York: Harper & Row, 1970), 231, has written: "Marriage is a symbol of a union between two separate and distinct entities—a primary purpose of which is to conceive and bring into being the third, an essence individual in itself yet constituted of the characteristics of the first and the second out of which it came. The marriage between a man and a woman—and the bearing of children—is the acting out in a personal and immediate way the fundamental drama of the spheres, the first expression of which was seen in the cosmogonic myths of ancient and primitive peoples. In these myths there was invariably a great 'all' or 'chaos' or 'nothingness' which existed in its oneness until, through some act of desire or thought, a breaking apart took place. Then there were two: sky and earth, light and darkness, male and female, active protagonist god and shadow counterpart—uncountable variations of the representations of duality."

5. June Singer, *Androgyny: Toward A New Theory of Sexuality* (Garden City, N.Y.: Anchor Press/Doubleday, 1976), 183–207.

Chapter Four: The Self: Expressing Ourselves in the World

1. James Hillman, in *Insearch: Psychology and Religion* (New York: Charles Scribner and Sons, 1967), 89, describes the renewal that comes from the tension between the Old King (or, I would add, Old Queen) and the Divine Child: "the Old King's voice . . . and the voice of the Self yet-to-be-born who speaks through the Divine Child are both right. Out of these conflicts a new psychological standpoint can come, which we might also call a new morality. . . . The inner necessity which forces the Old King to alter his views speaks at first with the still small voice of individual conscience."

2. The Fisher King myths tell us that anytime the kingdom becomes a wasteland, it is because the Ruler is wounded. A younger hero is needed to heal the Ruler and renew the kingdom. Various versions of the Fisher King legends ascribe different causes to the wound, but often it is related to the King's sexuality. (The King is typically wounded in the groin or thigh.)

3. Edinger, in *Ego and Archetype,* 228, discusses Christ as a symbol for the Self, and Christ's blood as representing "the life of the Soul." Hence, the significance of drinking the blood of Christ in communion is to take in Soul. Edinger further establishes the link between Christ and Dionysus, seeing both as myths about the Self.

4. Parker Palmer, *The Promise of Paradox: A Celebration of Contradictions in the Christian Life* (Notre Dame, Ind.: Ave Maria Press, 1980), 15–44.

5. Burckhardt, *Alchemy,* 155.

6. See Edinger, *Ego and Archetype,* 231–32. Edinger emphasizes the androgynous aspect of the symbol of the Self, arguing that patriarchal theologians have obscured the androgynous nature of the Christ image.

7. John Matthews and Marian Green, *The Grail Seeker's Companion: A Guide to the Grail Quest in the Aquarian Age* (Wellingborough, Northhamptonshire: The Aquarian Press, 1986), 19.

8. Note that Jacob is also wounded in the thigh, a wound related to the breaking of his relationship to his father and brother, which occurs after he deceives his father to gain his brother's birthright. Yet he receives the wound wrestling with an angel. The wound is both a sign of wounded relatedness and the opening that allows for connection to the numinous.

9. Marion Zimmer Bradley, *The Mists of Avalon* (New York: Alfred A. Knopf, 1983).

10. Emma Jung and Marie-Louise von Franz, *The Grail Legend* (Boston: Sigo Press, 1970), 389.

11. Shunyu Suzuki, *Zen Mind, Beginner's Mind: Informal Talks on Zen Meditation and Practice* (New York: Weatherhill, 1974), 75.

12. Arthur Deikman, in *The Observing Self: Mysticism & Psychotherapy* (Boston: Beacon Press, 1983), 45, asserts that "the observing self is not part of the object world formed by our thoughts and sensory perception because, literally, it has no limits; everything else does. Thus, everyday consciousness contains a transcendent element that we seldom notice because that element is the very ground of our experience. The word *transcendent* is justified because if subjective consciousness—the observing self—cannot itself be observed but remains forever apart from the contents of consciousness, it is likely to be of a different order from everything else. Its fundamentally different nature becomes evident when we realize that the observing self is featureless; it cannot be affected by the world any more than a mirror can be affected by the images it reflects."

13. Barbara Walker, in *The Crone: Woman of Age, Wisdom and Power* (San Francisco: Harper & Row, 1985), 58, associates the cool stare of one who dispassionately observes events with the wise old woman, or crone, embodied in the "huge-eyed Syrian Goddess Mari, who could search men's souls." Walker also notes that in many traditions, wisdom itself is envisioned as female: in India, as Shakti; in the Gnostic tradition, as Sophia; in the Hebrew scriptures, the Shekina. In the Greek pantheon, Metis (or Medusa), "Wisdom," true mother of Athena, also embodied the divine mind.

Chapter Five: Beyond Heroism: The Dance

1. C. G. Jung, "On the Psychology of the Trickster Figure," in Paul Radin, *The Trickster: A Study in American Indian Mythology* (New York: Shocken, 1987), 200.

2. Radin, in *The Trickster,* sums up the myth's key qualities this way: "The overwhelming majority of all so-called trickster myths in North America give an account of the creation of the earth, or at least the transforming of the world, and have a hero who is always wandering, who is always hungry, who is not guided by normal concep-

tions of good or evil, who is either playing tricks on people or having them played on him and who is highly sexed. Almost everywhere he has some divine traits."

3. Hillman, *Re-Visioning Psychology,* 35, 51.

4. Hal Stone, *Embracing Our Selves: The Voice Dialogue Method* (San Rafael, Calif.: New World Library, 1989).

Chapter Six: The Innocent

1. William Irwin Thompson, *The Time Falling Bodies Take to Light: Mythology, Sexuality, and the Origins of Culture* (New York: St. Martin's Press, 1981), 9, 27.

2. Riane Eisler, *The Chalice and the Blade: Our History, Our Future* (San Francisco: Harper and Row, 1987), 186–87.

3. Marion Woodman, *Addiction to Perfection* (Toronto: Inner City, 1982).

Chapter Seven: The Orphan

1. Albert Camus, *The Rebel* (New York: Vintage, 1956), 304, 306.

2. Madonna Kolbenschlag, *Lost in the Land of Oz: The Search for Identity and Community in American Life* (San Francisco: Harper & Row, 1989), 9, 42, 186.

3. James Hillman, "Betrayal," *Loose Ends: Primary Papers in Archetypal Psychology* (Dallas, Texas: Spring Publications, 1975), 63–81.

4. Jean Houston, *The Search for the Beloved: Journeys in Sacred Psychology* (New York: St. Martin's Press, 1987), 104–21.

5. Actually, wounding is related to four different archetypes discussed in this book. First, it is the wounding of the Innocent that awakens the Orphan in us and begins the process of Ego development. Second, the wounding to the established, balanced, and mature Ego by the archetype of the Destroyer and the resulting loss of well-fortified attitudes about who we are, what the world is about, shatters our illusions, making room for us to discover our identities at the level of our Souls. This causes the whole identity structure, which has so carefully been developed, to deconstruct and have to be reconstituted as Ego gives way to allow for the full expression of the Self. Third, the Lover experiences a wounding by Cupid's arrow, when our hard-won autonomy is "invaded" by love for something or someone beyond our selves. After this happens, one can never again act for oneself alone. Finally, we discover the wounding of the Ruler in each of us and how the healing of this wound also restores and transforms the kingdom.

Chapter Eight: The Warrior

1. Eisler, *The Chalice and the Blade,* passim.

2. As Riane Eisler describes in *The Chalice and the Blade,* there once were worldwide gynocentric (female-valuing and goddess-worshiping) cultures that were entirely

peaceable and extremely inventive and prosperous. They discovered fire, invented art, agriculture, the wheel, language, the written word, and many of the other basic human inventions. They had everything one could want except Warriors.

As a result, their peaceable, nurturing societies were destroyed by much more primitive, less inventive patriarchal tribes, which were much less civilized—and indeed moved the world into a regressive period initially—but which were strong and ruthless.

3.   The ways Warriors may come to decisions about the superior and inferior answers or approaches differ, among other ways, by psychological type. Thinking types make fine discriminations between alternative options based on an analytical process, according to which they strive to be objectively fair. Feeling types do so by a subjective process, which tries to be kind, to be true to one's personal values, and to consider the greatest good for the people affected by the decision. Some very highly developed Warriors are eventually able to integrate a feeling with a thinking approach, balancing out the human factors of kindness with more abstract principles of justice.

4. Chogyam Trungpa, *Shambhala: The Sacred Path of the Warrior* (Boston: Shambhala, 1978), 33–34.

Chapter Nine: The Caregiver

1.   Depending upon psychological type, Caregivers appreciate and attend to others' needs and desires by a variety of means. Feeling types, especially intuitive feeling types, may use highly developed empathy to know what others need and want. Sensing thinking types, on the other hand, use their powers of acute observation and reflection to assess the needs of their charges and to find ways to provide them with what they need. But in either case, the Caregivers emphasize helping over criticizing others.

2.   The second Caregiver mode is associated by theorists such as Carol Ochs with patriarchal consciousness, the first with gynocentric (woman-centered) consciousness. For more information about the symbolism of the tree and the goddess and its theological implications, see Carol Ochs, *Behind the Sex of God: Toward a New Consciousness—Transcending Matriarchy and Patriarchy* (Boston: Beacon Press, 1977).

Chapter Ten: The Seeker

1.   Mario A. Jacoby, *Longing for Paradise: Psychological Perspectives on an Archetype*, trans. Myron B. Gubitz (Boston: Sigo Press, 1980), 207.

2.   Pearl Mindell, paper delivered for the Professional Development Program in Depth Psychology, Wainwright House, Rye, New York, September 1989.

3.   Only three knights are pure enough to find the grail—Galahad, Parsifal, and Bors. They travel with it to Sarras, the holy city of the East, where they are initiated into the mysteries of the grail. There Galahad, "expires in an ardor of sanctity. Perceval returns to the Grail Castle to become its new King, and Bors journeys to Camelot to tell of the miracles of the quest," according to John Matthews, *At the Table of the Grail: Magic and the Use of Imagination* (New York: Routledge and Kegan Paul, 1987), 6–7.

4. Brian Cleeve, "The World's Need," from Matthews, *At the Table of the Grail,* 56.

5. Matthews, *At the Table of the Grail,* 6–7.

6. Hillman, *Re-Visioning Psychology,* 55–112.

7. Adrienne Rich, "Fantasia for Elvira Shatayev," *The Dream of a Common Language: Poems 1974–1977* (New York: W. W. Norton & Co., 1978), 4–6.

Chapter Eleven: The Destroyer

1. Both the Orphan and the Destroyer grapple with this existential crisis. For the Orphan, the issue is abandonment, and questioning the existence of a Cosmic Parent caring for us. When the Destroyer strikes, we feel more adult, and are less likely to see God in that parental role. The existential crisis is about meaninglessness, for we still want the universe to make some rational sense!

2. Annie Dillard, *Holy the Firm* (New York: Harper & Row, 1977), 76.

3. John Sanford, *Evil: The Shadow Side of Reality* (New York: Crossroad, 1988), 10.

4. Sylvia Brinton Perera, *Descent to the Goddess: A Way of Initiation for Women* (Toronto: Inner City Books, 1981), 78.

5. Robert Johnson, *Ecstasy: Understanding the Psychology of Joy* (San Francisco: Harper & Row, 1987), 29–30.

Chapter Twelve: The Lover

1. Shirley Gehrke Luthman, *Energy and Personal Power* (San Rafael, Calif.: Mehetabel and Co., 1982), 85.

2. Matthew Fox, *The Coming of the Cosmic Christ* (San Francisco: Harper & Row, 1988), 178.

3. Starhawk, *Truth or Dare* (San Francisco: Harper & Row, 1987), 206.

4. Irene Claremont de Castillejo, *Knowing Woman: A Feminine Psychology* (New York: G. P. Putnam's Sons, 1973).

5. Lex Hixon, *Coming Home: The Experience of Enlightenment in Sacred Traditions* (Los Angeles: Jeremy P. Tarcher, 1978), 120–21.

6. Ntozake Shange, *For Colored Girls who have Considered Suicide When the Rainbow is Enuf* (New York: MacMillan Publishing Co., 1977), 31.

7. Palmer, *The Promise of Paradox,* 37–39.

Chapter Thirteen: The Creator

1. Luthman, *Energy and Personal Power,* 63.

2. Hugh Prather, *A Book of Games: A Course in Spiritual Play* (New York: Doubleday, 1981).

3. Hillman, *Re-Visioning Psychology,* 44

4. James Lovelock, *The Ages of Gaia: A Biography of Our Living Earth* (New York: W. W. Norton & Co., 1988).

5. William Butler Yeats, "Among School Children," in *The Collected Poems of W. B. Yeats* (New York: Macmillan Co., 1956), 214.

Chapter Fourteen: The Ruler

1. Tom Robbins, *Even Cowgirls Get the Blues* (Boston: Houghton Mifflin, 1976), 43.

Chapter Fifteen: The Magician

1. In our own time, most people think of Magicians not as miracle workers, but as Tricksters, using sleight of hand to deceive. Their deceptions may be entertaining, but they are not real magic. Indeed, many and maybe most people in our society do not believe in magic or miracles at all. In fact, not believing in miracles is an important element in Ego development. As children, we all indulge in magical thinking, assuming, for instance, that if something we wished for happens, our thoughts made it happen. Growing up involves letting go of superstitions and also letting go of the belief that problems will magically go away or that we will be rescued.

It is also important that we forego magical thinking until we both experience our journeys and the resulting Soul initiation and take responsibility for being the Rulers of our lives. Because magic can be used as easily for evil as for good, it is best that we not dabble with its conscious manifestations until we have created the Ego container—and have character, strength, discipline, and care for others—and are in touch with our Souls. Our Souls are the part of us in touch with the ultimate in the universe and can help us know how to live in keeping with that flow. Using magic responsibly requires integrity—living in keeping with our own values, but beyond even that, being true to our own Soul purpose. Otherwise we can do harm. This is why the Magician is an archetype of the Self—because in its positive form it is only seen in people who have deepened and grown and become real so that their Egos have expanded to let in their Souls.

2. What we have come to think of as witches were really members of the Wiccan faith, which venerated the Goddess immanent in nature and in people. The negative associations most of us have with the term *witch* has resulted from the Christian church's persecution of native religions because they associated nature/the flesh/sexuality/women with the devil. Our images of the Christian devil, for instance, are very related to the impish nature god, Pan, who also had horns and cloven feet. Pan, however, was not evil. He served as a link between the human and the natural world, being half human, half beast. As Joseph Campbell explains, one people's gods become the next religion's embodiment of evil. Indeed, under a strong patriarchal authority, all power in women came to be associated with this forbidden nature, goddess power. So women's magical power has gone underground. We have few positive images (beyond the fairy godmother or comic characters such as the genie in the TV series "I Dream of Jeannie") for female magicians. Generally, female magicians are assumed to be evil magicians.

3. Claremont de Castillejo, *Knowing Woman,* 178.

4. Serge King, "The Way of the Adventurer," in Shirley Nicholson, *Shamanism: An Expanded View of Reality* (Wheaton, Ill.: Theosophical Publishing House, 1987), 193.

5. Of course, we may also have obstacles to awakening the Warrior in us. Sometimes it is not time to be a Magician, no matter how much we might wish it were. We may simply need to work on asserting ourselves or fighting for our values.

6. Michael Harner, in *The Way of the Shaman* (San Francisco: Harper & Row, 1980) and in workshops on the subject, teaches people how to enter an altered state of consciousness through rhythmic drumming at a certain tempo. Such drumming changes one's brain wave patterns and allows consciousness to enter another space.

Don Juan, the shamanic guide in the works of Carlos Castaneda, helps Castaneda move into altered states with the use of drugs. He later acknowledges that drugs are not at all necessary to reaching those states. They were just a means of getting Castaneda's attention. Indeed, drugs were used widely in the 1960s and 1970s to help people access other planes until it became clear that it is too dangerous for most people to use such methods. Drug addiction is too pressing a modern problem to in any way perpetuate drug use.

7. This is also a good approach to take with worries. When a worry comes into mind, imagine the feared event happening and imagine a constructive way of dealing with it. This changes it from a potential catastrophe to one of many possible events in one's life that are manageable. One can use this for as simple a worry as will the airline lose my luggage ("I'll take a carry-on case so I won't be entirely stuck") or what would happen if I get cancer (I'll have medical insurance and I will investigate all current traditional and alternative cures. Maybe my horizons would be expanded).

8. It is important not to sentimentalize this idea or to confuse choosing our lives with being to blame for them. For instance, to use a very extreme example (the most extreme I can imagine), if I were in a concentration camp and assumed that I chose this at some level, it would not take away the immense pain of being in such a situation, nor would it mean that I was to blame nor that I chose it out of some masochistic need to suffer. But if I see this as an opportunity I chose for growth, then I can open up to see what kind of growth this means.

For some, it might mean a chance to get past our attachments to happiness and ease (as the Buddha said we must if we are to transcend desire). It might be a choice for initiation by the Destroyer and greater resulting spiritual depth. For another, it might be an opportunity to test one's courage and to know that one will stay faithful to one's values and convictions under great threat and duress. For another, it might be experiencing love and care with other concentration camp survivors and the pride of knowing that whatever was done to them, they did not become like their victimizers. They retained their own Souls. For another, it might be a way of learning about power and powerlessness.

For someone else, naming a concentration camp experience, or any other oppressive or painful experience, as something they chose would feel like an assault—like at some level they chose something unhealthy. To suggest to them that they created their own reality would also be a kind of cruel, unkind "unnaming."

It is best, therefore, that Magicians think complexly and never assume that the "naming" that is good for one person is necessarily good for another.

9. This example is from the process work developed by Anne Wilson Schaef, the author of *Women's Reality* (Minneapolis: Winston Press, 1981) and *When Society Becomes an Addict* (San Francisco: Harper & Row, 1987).

10. Many healers specialize in one aspect alone. Our medical doctors specialize in healing the body and until recently tended to deny the viability of healing on any other level (except in cases of psychosomatic illness). Psychologists focus on the life of the emotions, helping us to be free of the effects of emotional trauma and to learn to express our feelings in a healthy way. Counselors and educators specialize in teaching people healthy ideas, to develop and in many cases heal their minds; shamans and other spiritual healers or teachers focus on effecting a cure on the spiritual level.

To a degree, this specialization makes sense, but not if it is extreme and exclusionary so that practitioners become so devoted to one means of healing that they become one-sided, to the detriment of themselves and their client group. We have all known physicians who are totally out of touch with their feelings and their Souls—and often, as a result, do not even care well for their own bodies. Conversely, people who focus on healing at the spiritual level often have bodies that are neglected and out of shape. The most powerful healers—although they still often specialize—integrate all four elements in healing. Sometimes they do so by referring. Sometimes (as with the doctor with the great "bedside manner") they integrate them by who they are. Their own wholeness has a ripple effect. In practice, in the modern world, we often have to piece together our healing, finding one healer to work on one area of our woundedness, and another on another area.

11. See Shirley Nicholson, ed., *Shamanism: An Expanded View of Reality* (Wheaton, Ill.: Theosophical Publishing House, 1987), and Harner, *The Way of the Shaman*.

12. Ursula Le Guin, *A Wizard of Earthsea* (New York: Bantam Books, 1968), 180.

Chapter Sixteen: The Sage

1. Lee Knefelkamp, "Faculty and Student Development in the 80s: Renewing the Community of Scholars," in *Integrating Adult Development Theory with Higher Education Practice,* Current Issues in Higher Education, No. 5, American Association for Higher Education, 1980, 13–25. See also William Perry, Jr., *Forms of Intellectual and Ethical Development in the College Years: A Scheme* (New York: Holt, Rinehart and Winston, 1970).

2. Idries Shah, *The Sufis* (New York: Anchor Books, 1971), 351.

3. Luthman, *Energy and Personal Power*, 62.

Chapter Seventeen: The Fool

1. William Willeford, *The Fool and His Scepter: A Study in Clowns and Jesters and Their Audience* (Evanston, Ill.: Northwestern Univ. Press, 1969), 155.

2. Willeford, *The Fool and His Scepter.*

3. Enid Welsford, *The Fool: His Social and Literary History* (Garden City, N.Y.: Doubleday, 1961), 326–27.

4. Suzuki, *Zen Mind, Beginner's Mind,* 62.

5. Hixon, *Coming Home,* 123.

6. Jane Wagner, *The Search for Signs of Intelligent Life in the Universe* (New York: Harper & Row, 1985), 18.

7. Annie Dillard, *Pilgrim at Tinker Creek* (New York: Harper & Row, 1974), 278.

Chapter Eighteen: From Duality to Wholeness: A Life Stage Model

1. The most similar developmental model to this one that I have found is Erik Erikson's, even though his model—like those of most other developmental theorists—focuses more attention on development within childhood than in the adult years. See Erik Erikson, *The Life Cycle Completed* (New York: W. W. Norton, 1982).

I am also aware that my thinking in developing this model was very likely influenced by my early reading of Erikson and, of course, my ongoing study of Jung, whose theories provide the fundamental framework for even thinking about an archetypal progression through the life span.

Erikson's first four stages focus on the childhood years, the years in the model encapsulated in the Innocent/Orphan duality. Erikson's four stages, then, shed additional light on aspects of the Innocent/Orphan/Divine Child dialectic. Erikson observed that the basic issue in infancy is this conflict between basic trust and mistrust. The virtue to be gained through resolving this dilemma (which focused upon the child's relationship with the mother) is hope.

In early childhood (2–3), a child's growth task involves autonomy versus shame and doubt. The virtue to be gained through resolving this dilemma (which is worked out in the relationship with the father) is will. At the play age (3–5), the basic tension is initiative versus guilt. The virtue to be gained (which is worked out in the basic family context) is purpose. Finally in school age (6–12), the child wrestles industry and feelings of inferiority. The virtue to be gained (worked out in the neighborhood and in school) is competence.

Perhaps because I observe so many people who have not worked out the infant's issue of basic trust versus mistrust, this model emphasizes this dilemma throughout the childhood years—and indeed, for all but those with the most ideal childhoods, into early adulthood. The next three of Erikson's childhood stages help us resolve the Innocent/Orphan duality by gradually increasing our sense of autonomy and self-esteem so that we are not as dependent upon and conflated with our surroundings. They also provide detail on the gradual progression of our dependence from the mother (or other initial nurturers and Caregivers) to the father (or other person who models greater autonomy in relationships) to the family unit, to the school, community, and larger social context.

Erikson's stages 2–4 evidence childhood contributions to developing the Warrior archetype. Overcoming shame, doubt and guilt, and feelings of inferiority to become autonomous and to show initiative and industry and in the process to develop will, purpose, and competence are all aspects of Ego formulation, aided by the archetype of the Warrior.

The final four of Erikson's stages trace our development past the childhood years. For Erikson (12–18), the key issue of adolescence is identity versus identity confusion (leading to the virtue of fidelity), and in young adulthood (19–35), intimacy versus isolation (leading to the virtue of love). The first stage parallels the challenge of the Seeker and the second, the Lover.

To Erikson, the challenge of the adult years (35–65) is that of generativity versus stagnation (leading to the virtue of care). This corresponds to the archetypes of the Caregiver, Ruler, and Magician, as we not only create our realities but choose to care for what we have created. Finally, to Erikson, the challenge of old age is integrity versus despair, leading to the virtue of wisdom. One needs to come to terms with one's life by making meaning of it (Sage). The overcoming of despair also involves an opening to joy (Fool).

Chapter Nineteen: Gender and Human Development over the Life Span

1. Sigmund Freud argued that boys and girls feared punishment from desiring union with the parent of the opposite sex. Boys, in particular, feared castration, believing that girls were essentially punished, castrated boys. Girls, too, he observed felt that something had been taken away from them, experienced "penis envy," and found vicarious fulfillment through finding their identity in relationship to someone possessing a penis. Others, such as Karen Horney, have also argued persuasively for male "womb envy," as at least an equally powerful psychological motivation, which may, in fact, motivate male denigration of women. Perhaps this means that we envy what we do not have until we discover that although our bodies differ, men and women have access, psychologically, to the full range of human feelings and behaviors (i.e., the "masculine" and the "feminine," animus and anima, within).

2. See Mara Donalson, "Woman as Hero" in Margaret Atwood's *Surfacing* and Maxine Hong Kingston's *The Woman Warrior* in *The Hero in Popular Culture,* ed. Pat Brown (Bowling Green, Ohio: Bowling Green State Univ. Press, 1989), 101–13.

3. At present, this pattern is being strongly challenged as both men and women are encouraged to be competitive and aggressive to achieve their ambitions. This may result in early dominance of "masculine" energy in many women. When this happens, a woman often will experience a crisis in her early thirties to midthirties around the need to experience the "feminine." Frequently, this crisis takes the form of wishing either to have a child or to be home more to care for her children. Or it may take the form of a yearning for romance.

4. See Carol Gilligan, *In a Different Voice: Pychological Theory and Women's Development* (Cambridge, Mass.: Harvard Univ. Press, 1982), for a very useful and enlightening discussion of male and female differences in moral development, one which has greatly influenced this model.

5. Indeed, the typical traditional relationship could easily be diagnosed as dependent or even addictive in today's world. The challenge in the contemporary world is for us all to develop a reasonable amount of androgynous potential even in the adult years—expressed by the ability to successfully do what was traditionally defined as "male" tasks and "female" tasks. Not to do so stresses the organism because of how repressive and limiting the traditional roles seem in the modern world. But becoming more androgynous creates its own strain. Doing so without retreating to an adolescent kind of unisex identity requires great psychological stretching for most people.

To be truly masculine or feminine but not outwardly limited by that inner gender certainly helps us and the species evolve, but it is not that easy to do!

Finding your true gender identification does not require (or preclude) a sexual preference for the other sex. You may be gay or lesbian. If you are, the issue is to express your unique masculinity, femininity, or mix thereof. The same is true whether one is heterosexual or bisexual. Whatever our sexual orientation, loving our *own* sex—whether or not we act this out by sexual love—is as important a part of the journey as loving the opposite sex.

6. See Joanna Russ, *The Female Man* (New York: Bantam, 1975), 119.

7. Wagner, *The Search for Signs of Intelligent Life in the Universe,* 18. This one-woman play, starring Lily Tomlin, is particularly apt social commentary for the generation that came to adulthood in the 1970s, and are now experiencing their mid-life crisis. Indeed, for all of us affected by the massive changes of the 1970s—the feminist movement, the human potential movement, the New Age movement—it is a must-see or must-read touching and humane comedy.

8. Judith Duerk, *A Circle of Stones: Woman's Journey to Herself* (San Diego: Lura Media, 1989), 26–27, 66.

9. John Rowan, *The Horned God: Feminism and Men as Wounding and Healing* (London and New York: Routledge and Kegan Paul, 1987), 7. In the passage described, Rowan quotes Starhawk's *The Spiral Dance* (San Francisco; Harper & Row, 1979) extensively, so the ideas included here are hers as well as his.

10. Any experience of one's genuine sexuality links up the erotic, sexual element of life and its spiritual Soul dimension. While the experience of transcendence—moving out of the Self—is often associated with the Sky Gods and Goddesses, the discovery of the God or Goddess Within, which links one with instinctive, sexual life, is generally associated with more earthy, pagan, primitive gods and goddesses. Individuals may find their authentic gender identity anywhere on this continuum. Although there are great cultural prohibitions (especially in organized religion) against welcoming the most instinctual eroticism related to both male and female sexuality, the experience itself of connecting with one's deep masculine or feminine nature tends to explode these categories, and flesh and spirit can be experienced as one.

11. Singer, *Androgyny,* 333.

Chapter Twenty: Gender, Diversity, and the Transformation of Culture

1. There are now any number of fine books that trace the change from goddess-worshiping cultures to patriarchy and its impact on culture and its functioning. Such early works include Merlin Stone's *When God Was a Woman* or Carol Ochs's *Behind the Sex of God* and William Irwin Thompson's *The Time It Takes Falling Bodies to Light.* More recent must-read books on relating to gender and culture include Marija Gimbutas's *The Language of the Goddess* (San Francisco: Harper & Row, 1989), Elinor W. Gadon's *The Once and Future Goddess* (San Francisco: Harper & Row, 1989), and John Rowan's *The Horned God.*

2. In a Christian tradition, witches—or the goddess worshipers—were lumped with devil worshipers, even though the practitioners of wicca were not initially evil at all.

They practiced a fertility religion that, like native American and African religions, had a strong emphasis on magic.

3. You can explore the role of Goddess spirituality; you can respect the wisdom of many traditions; you can explore the many layers of Christ's teachings. If you look around, you may find many professed Christians who would share these beliefs—many of whom are clergy.

Chapter Twenty-One: Claiming Your Life Myth

1. Houston, *The Search for the Beloved*, 112.

2. I am indebted both to Transactional Analysis therapist Marcia Rosen for introducing me to the fundamental ideas of T.A. and to Eric Berne's books, such as *Games People Play* and *What to Do After You Say Hello*.

3. David Feinstein and Stanley Krippner, *Personal Mythology: The Psychology of Your Evolving Self* (Los Angeles: Jeremy P. Tarcher, 1988), passim.